INSTRUCTOR'S MANUAL

FOR
LUTHER'S SMALL CATECHISM

By
H. J. BOETTCHER

CONCORDIA PUBLISHING HOUSE

Saint Louis - 1964 - Missouri

Copyright by
Concordia Publishing House
Saint Louis, Missouri
Revised Edition 1964

Printed in the U. S. A.

FOREWORD

The publication of an instructor's manual for Luther's Small Catechism was authorized at the Fort Wayne convention of The Lutheran Church — Missouri Synod in 1941 (*Proceedings,* 1941, page 334). A three-man committee, Rev. Erwin Kurth, Mr. John Runge, and Prof. O. C. Rupprecht, were placed in charge of the project. After careful consideration, they chose Dr. H. J. Boettcher, then Director of Christian Education in the Minnesota District, to carry out the assignment. Dr. Boettcher not only brought outstanding professional competence to the task, but also a great deal of consecration and unusual resourcefulness.

Dr. Boettcher went to work swiftly and methodically, and in 1946, just three years after the appearance of the 1943 edition of *Luther's Small Catechism,* the *Instructor's Manual* was published.

Dr. Boettcher was well aware of the trend much religious education had taken in that day: the trend toward a weak moral and ethical emphasis. He was also aware of the fact that, while Biblical truth could be retained, instruction might become lifeless, mechanical, and even artificial.

The author believed Christian education to be a vital living thing, intimately related to the other subjects in the school curriculum. With this clearly in mind, he dedicated his efforts in the manual to prevent cold, formal teaching. He sought to explode the idea that would restrict religion to a tight little compartment, separated from the rest of life. Every page of the *Instructor's Manual* testified to the fact that Christianity is comprehensive and all-inclusive.

The Instructor's Manual for Luther's Small Catechism served Lutheran teachers for more than a decade before it went out of print. In 1963 Synod's Board of Parish Education urged that the *Instructor's Manual* be revised and reprinted. This volume is the result of that urging and again fills an expressed need — a resource book for teachers of Lutheran doctrine. Like the earlier edition, this handbook seeks to stimulate creative teachers to present Christian education in all its vitality. No teacher should be dismayed by the wealth of material this volume contains. The very purpose of the book is to provide a variety of suggestions. Successful teaching does not depend on using all the suggestions, but on the judicious and conscientious use of some of them.

A special word of recognition needs to be given to Dr. H. J. Boettcher for his fine work in revising the manual, and to Mr. Robert Hinz of Concordia Audio-Visual Aids Service for his painstaking efforts in verifying the audio-visuals listed in each unit.

May the Lord of the church grant His gracious blessings that this new edition of the *Instructor's Manual* glorify His name and serve His redemptive purposes.

FREDERICK A. MEYER
Board of Parish Education
The Lutheran Church — Missouri Synod

PREFACE

*God's People
and Religious Education*

Proper religious training of the young has been the serious concern of God's people since the day of the patriarchs (Deut. 6:6-7). At the threshold of the New Testament era the Great Teacher Himself said: "Suffer the little children to come unto Me and forbid them not, for of such is the Kingdom of God" (Mark 10:13-15). "Go ye therefore and teach all nations, baptizing them in the name of the Father and of the Son and of the Holy Ghost; teaching them to observe all things whatsoever I have commanded you: and, lo, I am with you alway, even unto the end of the world" (Matt. 28:19-20). The early Christian church instructed and critically observed its catechumens usually for several years prior to accepting them into membership. The church of the Reformation has an enviable reputation for emphasizing elementary Christian education. In America, the Lutheran church laid its foundations with the help of Christian schools. About one hundred years ago the state began to provide free, compulsory, and tax-supported schools in America, and these, of necessity, had to be nonreligious. Church-supported elementary schools have since then declined rapidly. Lutheran, Roman Catholic, and Dutch Reformed churches, however, have continued to maintain parochial schools. Under the blessing of God, Lutheran schools have achieved a splendid record. While their work in secular branches has been recognized by educational authorities and business, they have above all served the cause of true religion by developing church members with depth and strength of conviction. Since the common schools of America have as a whole discontinued religious instruction, many Christian churches, as well as other religious groups, have attempted to provide a modicum of religious education through so-called part-time agencies, such as the Sunday school, the Saturday school, vacation Bible schools, and released time religious education classes. Some churches have fostered religious knowledge through confirmation instruction, Bible classes, and auxiliary study and service groups such as young people's societies, ladies' organizations, and men's clubs.

Textbooks

Among Lutherans the foundation of religious teaching is the Bible, and the principal textbook for religious instruction has been Luther's Small Catechism. Most of the synods have supplemented this basic text with an exposition of Luther's Catecism. In The Lutheran Church — Missouri Synod, expositions by Dietrich, and more especially by Schwan, have been used almost to the exclusion of all others during the past one hundred years. Because of recent trends in elementary education, a growing need for additional and improved instructional materials has been noted. Privately initiated materials of instruction have therefore appeared on the market. To meet the growing demand for an improved Catechism exposition, Synod, in convention at Fort Wayne in 1941, resolved to publish a new text. This had been in a state of preparation for a number of years and was principally prepared by Professor Richard C. Neitzel, D. D. It was published in 1943. To meet the requests of those who desired also instructional aids which would reflect present trends in the organization of textbook materials, with study helps, vocabulary, and collateral readings, Synod in 1941 also resolved to prepare and publish an instructor's manual for the new Catechism, as well as pupil workbooks, and an elementary Catechism. The present volume is the *Instructor's Manual*.

PREFACE

INSTRUCTOR'S MANUAL

Why a manual? How will it help the instructor? What are the essential features of the manual? How can the instructor use it for his particular class?

Units of Instruction

A brief perusal of the manual will show that it is based on the 1943 Exposition of Luther's Small Catechism. These materials have been organized into *units of instruction*. The organization of *thirty-four* units is based on the assumption that all six chief parts will be taught and learned each year. Religious teaching and learning will thus come to be a matter of gradual, year to year, maturation in the basic concepts of the Christian religion. The nature and amount of materials from each unit taken up for study will depend on the age of maturity level and the frequency of class periods per week of each class. Since there are about thirty-four full teaching weeks during the common school year, it is suggested that one week be devoted to each unit. This unit organization is, therefore, usable whether there be one, two, three, or five periods of instruction per week.

The units may be taught in the order in which they appear here. This follows the basic text. The order may, however, also be adjusted to the church year and to the local parish program for worship and work. Some of such possible adjustments to the church year have been indicated. The allocation of collects, under Prayers, will indicate other possible adjustments to the church year. Particular community or national occasions may also guide in the selection of a particular unit for a particular week. Meaningful and purposeful teaching and learning will be greatly enhanced by such adjustments to place and time. The unit organization of the material thus makes for flexibility in the curriculum. It also calls for teacher alertness, resourcefulness, and consciousness of aims.

Furthermore, a handbook with numerous suggestions for enrichment (audio-visual aids, group activities, supplementary reading, and correlations with other subjects) would be impossible without the unit organization of materials. The names of the units can readily be adjusted to the age level of the class. At the primary school level it would not be difficult for a resourceful instructor to bring the name of JESUS into the name of each unit. That would, throughout the year, stress the fact that our teaching and learning are Jesus-centered, and that our school is really a JESUS SCHOOL.

Some educators prefer to think in terms of fewer and larger units. Where this seems desirable, we suggest that they think in terms of six sections:

Section One: *God's Word and God's Will*
(Units Introductory—10)
Section Two: *God and Nature* (Units 11–14)
Section Three: *God in Christ* (Units 15–20)
Section Four: *God and His Church* (Units 21–24)
Section Five: *Speaking with God* (Units 25–28)
Section Six: *God's Means of Grace* (Units 29–33)

In public education the trend toward unit organization of the curriculum has grown with the emergence of the Gestalt psychology, which tends to emphasize that education is the gradual growth, adjustment, and maturation of the individual whole child in his whole environment during his whole life from crib to college and from the cradle to the grave. It stresses the importance of interested, purposeful participation of the learner in the teaching-learning processes. It focuses attention upon problem-solving activities of observing, thinking, evaluating, and acting on the part of learners. Discovery and retention of truths which seem important to the learner at this time, rather than mere identification and memorization of words in which he is not particularly interested, receives priority rating. Thus the teacher's role comes to be one of an understanding guide and shepherd.

Lutheran educators have always, at least in principle, protested against learning in isolation. They have contended for the education of the whole child (body, mind, and soul), for his whole life, meaning childhood, adolescence, maturity, and old age, as well as for his life beyond the grave. They have always regarded

PREFACE

walking with God, sanctified living, and well-developed, well-integrated, socially well-adjusted, God-centered characters and personalities as the end product of a good education. As Luther clearly states it: "Christ has redeemed me, a lost and condemned creature — that I may be His own and live under Him in His kingdom, and serve Him in everlasting righteousness, innocence, and blessedness." The unifying objective of Lutheran educators has been to make the Gospel effective in men's lives, and thus to bring Christ, God, salvation, happiness, and true nobility to them. This manual hopes to contribute its mite toward making these accepted principles more effective in practice in Lutheran parish education. It is intended to call attention to correlation possibilities and audio-visual-tactual aids to instruction that are available today for the more effective assimilation of the curriculum.

The manual suggests procedures and helpful materials for each of the thirty-four units, always under five major headings: Scope and Importance, Aim, Curriculum Materials, Instructional Methods and Materials, and Correlations. We comment briefly on the nature, purpose, and use of each.

I. SCOPE AND IMPORTANCE

Some preliminary prayerful meditation as well as firsthand observation on the real scope and present-day importance of the topic seems indispensable for effective leadership in the classroom discussions. This meditation will tend to eliminate teaching which limits itself too exclusively to textbook phraseology and which as a consequence suffers from bookishness. To believe in the importance of a central truth for the class is to be enthusiastic about the subject matter and to be able and eager to pray warmly over it. Such belief makes it possible to converse naturally, easily, intimately, directly, and sincerely in connection with the topic.

Luther's Large Catechism has been extensively quoted here. The reasons for including these quotations from Luther in a handbook for Lutheran instructors in religion seem to be obvious.

II. AIM

Visualizing the aim and outcome of each week's and each year's efforts is very important. Every conscientious teacher will want to be clear in his own mind as to what he hopes to accomplish in each unit. To have no definite aim is to teach aimlessly. Lack of specific aims and anticipated outcomes accounts for bookish, stereotyped, mechanical, uninteresting, and relatively ineffectual attempts at religious training. If we do not set out to get somewhere in particular, we will probably get nowhere in particular. The trend in education today is to re-emphasize the importance of aims, objectives, and outcomes. The aims for each unit have been stated in terms of knowledge, attitude, and habits.

A. Knowledge

One important objective of Christian education is knowledge, understanding, insight. The suggested approaches, the concrete and semi-concrete instructional materials, visits in the community, firsthand observation at home and on the way to and from school, the enriched vocabulary, symbols, graphs, charts, the chalkboard — all, provided they are Bible-centered, will help foster observation and thinking which will lead to clear, vivid, and correct information and knowledge. Thorough memorization for use of a limited amount of memory material is still a very important part of our catechism learning. Bible instructors must constantly pray, however, that their pupils will be not only knowers but also doers of the Word.

B. Attitude

Religion has much to do with the heart. Therefore a special word of encouragement needs to be said in behalf of appealing to the heart of the learners. Truths understood must be used to stir the sentiments — either pro or con. Pupils must be encouraged to take a stand, to make a decision! "How long halt ye between two opinions?" asked the prophet Elijah indignantly. (1 Kings 18:21.) Facts of the Law and sin must be presented so as to lead to shame, humility, penitence. The Gospel needs to be applied to comfort, console, encourage, cheer, bring joy and new strength to the soul. "It should be the teacher's aim to proclaim the Gospel to his hearers till their hearts are melted, till they give up their resistance and confess that the Lord has been too strong for them and henceforth they wish to abide with Jesus" (Walther). "The minister wants to rouse his people and warn them against self-deception. That, however, cannot be his ultimate aim. His ultimate aim must be to lead his hearers to the assurance that they have forgiveness of sins with God, the hope of the future blessed life, and confidence to meet death cheerfully. Anyone who does not make these things his ultimate aim is not an evangelical minister" (Walther, *The Proper Distinction Between Law and Gospel*, p. 308). Christ-centered teachers in Christ-centered classrooms should always be mindful of the fact that they have a glorious and joyful task, as St. Paul indicates in 2 Cor. 1:24: "Not for that we have dominion over your faith, but are helpers of your joy."

The admonition to Christian educators in 2 Tim. 2:15 is very important: "Study to show thyself approved unto God, a workman that needeth not to be ashamed, rightly dividing the Word of truth." Law and Gospel must be rightly divided and rightly applied. It is one thing, for instance, to develop clearly the concept of stealing. It is another thing to stir the emotions so that the pupil will feel a deep shame for, a righteous indignation over against, every form of dishonesty, and a desire, out of gratitude to Jesus, to be scrupulously honest about everything. The knowledge of the Law which some people have tends to make them "smugly sophisticated Pharisees." It leads them to self-sufficiency and satiety. A superficial knowledge of the Law may lead away from the Cross, and yet the Law should be a "schoolmaster unto Christ." Values, emotions, desires, will, moods, sentiments — these are the areas of living into which effective religious teaching must reach. The discovery of facts must therefore be followed by repeated strong emotional appeals, particularly by an appeal to the pupil's gratitude to his Savior.

We believe that especially the Christian arts (pictures, music, poetry) as well as participation in actual group activities, such as dramatizations and service projects, will prove helpful in fostering desirable attitudes, moods, and sentiments. The facts of Christ's resurrection, for instance, will assuredly become emotionally colored with exultant joy when supplemented by such audio aids as "Christ Is Arisen" or "I Know That My Redeemer Lives" from Handel's *Messiah*. A purposeful study of "The Angelus" or "The Gleaners" by Millet will certainly aid in creating right attitudes and moods in connection with the Honest Life (Unit Seven). Grateful and affectionate attachment to Jesus in faith — that sums up the anticipated outcomes of a Christ-centered education. Religion has always and everywhere had to do with the selection, appreciation, and preservation of the highest values. Attitudes express values. Christ is the Christian's highest good and highest joy.

C. Habits — Skills — Behavior Patterns

Justification is the core of the Bible. The doctrine that we are saved alone by grace through faith without the deeds of the Law gives all glory to God and provides an unfailing source of comfort for penitent sinners. In the light of this central Bible truth none dare boast and none need despair. Let Catechism teachers keep this truth always in the foreground. The Bible makes it important. There are numerous texts, however, which associate redemption and sanctified living in such a way as to leave no room for doubt that knowing, believing, and doing, or justification and sanctification, while clearly distinguished, must be kept closely associated in the teaching-learning processes of the Christian classroom. The very purpose of Christ's redemptive work is often stated in terms of a sanctified life, for example: "He died for all *that* they which live should not henceforth live unto themselves, but unto Him which died for them and rose again" (2 Cor. 5:15). "*That* we, being delivered out of the hand of our enemies, might serve Him without fear, in holiness and righteousness before Him, all the days of our life" (Luke 1: 74, 75). Question 157 in the Catechism focuses attention on the importance of this end-product of Christ's redemptive work.

D. Sanctification

The relative importance of justification and sanctification has been the subject of many discussions. Faith in Christ, justification, joy in Jesus, comes first in time and first in importance. Concerning justification and sanctification the Scriptural fact is, however, that even as works which do not flow from faith are dead works, so also faith without works is dead. Intellectually it is necessary to separate the two. In life it seems impossible to separate one from the other. They belong together as roots and fruits belong together. While on guard against pietism, we should not be afraid to foster true piety. We pray for a pious spouse, pious children, pious servants, pious rulers. The Lutheran church has been calling for a faith in action. There seems to be a growing feeling among Lutheran educators that the positive should receive more emphasis. Our classrooms should indeed serve as conversion centers for those who are yet unbaptized and for those baptized who may have fallen from grace. But in general we may assume that the members of our Catechism classes are truly born again by water and the Spirit; that they are therefore new creatures, God's children, members of His family. The new man should therefore be gently and kindly coached, nurtured, and encouraged to seek and find expression. Seeing that our pupils have been "buried with Christ by Baptism into death," it is our task to encourage and guide them "to walk in newness of life" (Romans 6).

While we are opposed to the "social gospel," we ought not to be unmindful that the Gospel has important social implications. And that calls for practical Christianity and for a program of group action in every parish. The Christian educator, above all other educators, should try not only to make impressions but to elicit expressions. "Ye are our epistles written in our hearts, known and read of all men" (2 Cor. 3:2). "Be ye doers of the Word and not hearers only, deceiving your own selves. For if any be a hearer of the Word and not a doer, he is like unto a man beholding his natural face in a glass; for he beholdeth himself, and goeth his way and straightway forgetteth what manner of man he was" (James 1:22-24). "Not every man that saith unto Me, Lord, Lord, shall enter into the kingdom of heaven; but he that doeth the will of My Father which is in heaven" (Matt. 7:21). "This is the will of God, even your sanctification." (1 Thess. 4:3)

To be trained in an agency of Christian education in knowing but not doing is nothing short of tragedy. The instructor who uses this handbook will find emphasis on "doing something about it." The claim that "we learn by doing" has at times been misapplied. But it is true that learning tends to become more interesting, more meaningful, and more fruitful if it is preceded by, accompanied by, and followed up with individual and group action. Learning to walk in the footsteps of Jesus requires constant practice and frequent revision, checking, and modification of the learner's habitual way of living. Our pupils must learn by practice to witness for Christ, to win souls for Christ. A good church member is one who is trained in personal evangelism.

III. CURRICULUM MATERIALS

A. Bible

The Curriculum Materials are essentially those texts, Bible stories, Catechism questions and answers which are found in the 1943 Exposition of Luther's Small Catechism. Anyone using another kind of Lutheran Catechism will not find it difficult to change the question numbers to fit in with these units. The Bible stories which are found in the Catechism are marked with an asterisk. The popular titles for each story will help to make these interesting and more easily remembered by the pupils. All stories found in the *Advanced Bible History* (CPH) are included. The Bible church will want its youth to be familiar with the Bible itself. Hence the importance of much actual Bible reading.

B. Catechism

The suggested materials for memorization contain texts, appropriate sections from Luther's Small Catechism, appropriate hymn stanzas for each unit, and prayers. It is not expected,

PREFACE

however, that the prayers will be literally memorized. The Catechism contains 703 Bible texts. The *Memory Book for Lutheran Schools* suggests about 350 of these for literal memorization. A serious attempt has been made to adjust the memory materials of this manual to the *Memory Book*. It has not been possible to make this a 100 percent coordination, since some units have no corresponding memory verses in the memory course for each grade. The same applies to the hymn stanzas.

C. Hymns and Singing

The hymns were selected on the basis of their content, and they should contribute substantially toward the thorough assimilation of the basic truths of the unit, particularly if they are memorized and sung frequently, day after day and year after year. The hymn stanzas and their tunes should thus become permanently enjoyable possessions. Truths thus learned and used will probably be remembered and used much longer than Catechism texts, which lack rhyme and rhythm and which cannot be sung. All but two stanzas are taken from *The Lutheran Hymnal* (CPH). If the suggested plan is carried through, the children will have learned to sing 136 hymn stanzas and almost as many tunes from our hymnal. For the creation and expression of desirable feelings, sentiments, attitudes, and moods, few things give more promise of success than the spirited singing of well-selected classic hymns and chorales. Singing, both listening and actual singing, provides an excellent period of relaxation during the school day, and gives pupils and teachers a refreshed feeling. In schools where future soldiers and officers in the army of the Lord receive their basic training there should be much singing. Singing builds morale.

Prayer

To have diligently prayed over a matter is to have half succeeded in that matter. Once the instructor is saturated with the central truths of a unit, it will be possible for him to pray extempore over this matter with the class, in easy conversational language. The prayers reprinted here are mostly classic collects found in *The Lutheran Hymnal* and in *The Lutheran Liturgy*. The practice of having pupils make and use their own prayers in the classroom is fairly general practice. "Oh, that our knowledge might be transformed into worship," we heard a pastor say recently. As our learning becomes emotionally colored, we will begin to wish, to yearn, and to pray in connection with this knowledge. One way of making our Christian day schools increasingly Christ-centered schools throughout the day and to establish correlations is to pray frequently. The general atmosphere and school morale will be lifted through prayer before and after lesson presentations.

D. Summary Outline

A summary outline has been prepared for each unit. The teacher may write this outline on the chalkboard and have his pupils copy it for their own notebooks. Or, he may have it duplicated and distribute copies to them. The outline should serve to summarize important learnings in the unit. It may also help teacher and pupils review the unit topic in a more systematic way.

IV. INSTRUCTIONAL METHODS AND MATERIALS

Verbalism

Words are symbols. One purpose of the educative process is to have the pupil discover content and meaning of symbols. This requires considerable understanding of the laws of learning on the part of the teacher. Attempts to have a child repeat, use, or memorize meaningless words are the marks of a poor teacher. That practice leads to verbalism. Anyone in doubt about the seriousness of this matter should once again read Bacon's *Novum Organum*. Meaningless memorizations result in recitations which are wordy, jerky, soon forgotten. It has been statistically shown that non-meaningful materials are forgotten ten times faster than meaningful materials.

Concrete and semiconcrete instructional materials will help

to counteract verbalism in education. Learning through the senses of sight, hearing, touch, and even of taste and smell, helps to provide sensory experiences and to make words meaningful.

A. Approach

The main purpose of the approach is to arouse the interest and to make sure that the process of apperception will take place. A word becomes meaningful in terms of what the learner already understands. The importance of proceeding from the known to the unknown, from the experienced to what is to be experienced, from the concrete to the abstract, has been referred to. A human interest story, a picture, an object, a significant problem situation are good ways of starting a period of instruction.

The suggested approach for each of the units in this handbook sets a problem for solution. Teacher and pupils should discuss the problem briefly, arriving at tentative solutions. These solutions will be modified, broadened, or discarded as the unit topic is studied in detail.

B. Content

Section III listed many curriculum materials that the teacher might use in teaching the unit. This section, however, selects from, extends, and rearranges those materials to form an outline for a teaching unit. The selected materials are listed under five headings: devotions, Bible story, memory passages, Catechism selections, and liturgy. It remains the task of the classroom teacher to adapt the selected materials to the needs of his class, and to organize them for most efficient use.

C. Aids to Learning

A variety of learning aids are suggested to help the pupils gain a more thorough understanding of the unit topic. These aids include filmstrips and recordings, suggestions for bulletin boards, workbook references, and others. These are by no means an exhaustive listing. The alert and creative teacher will be able to add many more to the list. The teacher should feel free to select, adapt, or enlarge this list to meet the needs of the class.

D. Evaluation

One or two questions are included merely to remind the teacher that no unit is ever complete without an evaluation of what has been accomplished by way of learnings. The teacher may prepare his own materials for evaluation, or he may use the unit tests that accompany several of the workbooks suggested. He may also elect to use the Unit Tests in Luther's Small Catechism available from Concordia Publishing House.

V. CORRELATIONS WITH OTHER SUBJECTS
Possible and Desirable

This section of the handbook will be of interest mainly to Christian day school teachers. For them it will be important. "We have religious education during six hours of the school day." We say this of our Christian day schools. This is, in a measure, true even when few or no correlations with other subjects occur. But usually this is not as true as it could and should be. Teaching all subjects from the Christian viewpoint could and should mean much more than correcting some unbiblical ideas found in textbooks on science, geography, and history. We see no reason why the basic skills in arithmetic, in reading, in oral and written language could not be taught quite as effectively with materials taken from areas of living that are of special interest and importance to the Christian.

Since man, according to the Christian view of life, does not live by bread alone, why should not the Christian's values and interests be integrated with his arithmetic teaching and learning? Good arithmetic teaching today calls for the development of desirable interests, attitudes, and ways of living. This applies to an even greater extent to the teaching of reading, speaking, and writing.

The project method is closely related to this discussion. In this method the class undertakes to plan and to carry through a definite undertaking, such as planning a trip, putting on a school program, engaging in a service project. There will be letters, interviews, reference reading, visits in the community, oral and written reports. There will also be discussion, thinking, evaluation, decisions. Incidentally, the pupils will learn to read, to speak, to write, to think, to figure, to participate in group action. These outcomes are, after all, among the fundamental school objectives. Pupils will thus learn by practice to participate in democratic group processes. And the Lutheran church is a democratic institution. We know of no other schoolroom method which lends itself so well toward making our schools really God-centered. We know of no other method which allows the underlying philosophy of a school to penetrate and permeate the entire school day to the same extent. Provided the teacher is resourceful and familiar with this method, he will find it very interesting and fruitful, fruitful particularly in those outcomes in which we as religious educators are particularly interested.

It must be said, however, that correlation merely for the sake of correlation leads to absurdities. This must be avoided. Any correlation should be meaningful or not made at all. For this reason the reader will find gaps in the suggestions for correlations. If reasonable correlations were not found, none were suggested.

Reading

Reading skills may be developed in connection with the Bible and Biblical reading materials. Suggestions include correlations with silent, oral, and choral reading.

English

The art of saying and writing may be developed in connection with witnessing for Christ. Suggestions include oral and written English, vocabulary and spelling and handwriting.

Social and Physical Sciences

The Christian sees the footprints of the Creator in his physical environment. He sees the hand and influence of God in his social environment of yesterday and of today. It is hoped that the practical suggestions in connection with each unit will aid in developing God-centered familiarity with current events, history, geography, science, and health.

Arithmetic

Even the "life hidden with Christ in God" has quantitative aspects. And even so, Christ should have a place in our counting, adding, dividing, and other types of computation.

Fine Arts

The possibilities of teaching Christ through the fine arts can hardly be overstated. "Christ in the Fine Arts" is more than a fine book title. Time spent in the classroom on cultivating an appreciation of good pictures, good musical compositions, always selected in relation to the unit of instruction, will be time well spent. Christian education aims also at refinement in taste and conduct.

Work of the Holy Spirit

By this time some good reader has raised the question, But does not the Holy Spirit make words meaningful in the teaching of the Christian religion? True, but the Holy Spirit chooses human agencies, not angels, to teach the Word. And a teacher can effectively stand in the way of the effective working of the Holy Spirit. Two adjoining farms, with practically the same kind of soil, the same temperatures, the same amount of rainfall, the same amount of sunshine, and the same seed, may present two contrasting fields when harvesttime comes. Why? One farmer may have been less diligent, less intelligent. The soil may not have been well worked and the weeds not well exterminated on one of the farms. Methods of growing a harvest differ as between neighboring farms and as between yesterday and today. The man with a hoe and a one-horse plow cannot expect to do what modern mechanized farming can do. Harvest hazards, as we know, are still great. So in education. Methods do make a difference. But we know that His Word will never return void. When it does bear fruit, all glory goes to God. Soli Deo gloria.

May the Lord of the church use this manual to make our parish education and more especially our Catechism teaching and learning as efficient as possible.

H. J. BOETTCHER

TABLE OF CONTENTS

	PAGE
Introductory Unit: The Bible	1
(Catechism, Prayer Book, Hymnal)	

UNITS

1. The True Worship of the True God — 13
   (First Commandment)
2. The Reverent Life — 25
   (Second Commandment)
3. The Devotional Life — 36
   (Third Commandment)
4. The Obedient Life — 47
   (Fourth Commandment)
5. The Kind and Helpful Life — 57
   (Fifth Commandment)
6. The Chaste and Decent Life — 67
   (Sixth Commandment)
7. The Honest Life — 77
   (Seventh Commandment)
8. The Charitable Life — 87
   (Eighth Commandment)
9. The Contented Life — 97
   (Ninth and Tenth Commandments)
10. The Penitent Life — 107
    (Close of Commandments)
11. God and Creation — 118
    (First Article)
12. Angels — 128
    (First Article)

UNITS	PAGE
13. Man .... (First Article)	136
14. God's Government and Preservation .... (First Article) Thanksgiving or New Year	144
15. Jesus Christ, God and Man (1) .... (Second Article) Christmas or Advent	153
16. Jesus Christ, God and Man (2) .... (Second Article) Christmas or Epiphany	163
17. Christ Our Prophet, Priest, King .... (Second Article) Pre-Palm Sunday, Epiphany	173
18. The Story of Redemption .... (Second Article) A Lenten Unit	184
19. The Exalted Jesus (1) .... (Second Article) Descent, Resurrection, Ascension	195
20. The Exalted Jesus (2) .... (Second Article) Session, Judgment	204
21. The Holy Ghost and His Work .... (Third Article) Pentecost Unit	214
22. The Church .... (Third Article) Church Anniversary	226
23. The Forgiveness of Sins .... (Third Article) Pre-Reformation	238
24. Eternity .... (Third Article) Judgment, Resurrection, Hell, Heaven	248
25. Prayer .... (The Lord's Prayer) Rogate Sunday	259
26. Prayers for the Kingdom .... (Petitions 1, 2, 3) Pre-Mission Day	270
27. Prayer for Daily Bread .... (Earthly Blessings) Seedtime or Harvesttime	281
28. Necessities on Our Pilgrimage .... (Petitions 5, 6, 7) Faith, Grace, Charity, Fortitude, Deliverance	291

UNITS	PAGE
29. Baptism - - - - - - - - - - - 303 (Fourth Chief Part) What It Is	
30. Baptism - - - - - - - - - - - 312 (Fourth Chief Part) Its Blessings and Implications	
31. Office of the Keys and Confession - - - - - 321 (Fifth Chief Part)	
32. The Sacrament of the Altar - - - - - - 332 (Sixth Chief Part) History and Nature	
33. The Sacrament of the Altar - - - - - - 341 (Sixth Chief Part) Blessings, Power, Salutary Use, Implications	

TO THE USER

In the interest of saving space and avoiding monotonous repetition, the following shortcuts were employed:

LLC Luther's Large Catechism
LSC Luther's Small Catechism
LH   *The Lutheran Hymnal*
CGS *Child's Garden of Song*

* All publications indicated by an asterisk (*) are published by Concordia Publishing House, 3558 S. Jefferson Ave., St. Louis 18, Mo. Those from other publishers are furnished with the publisher's name in parenthesis.

All audio-visuals are available from Concordia Publishing House. Recordings are also available from local distributors.

LUTHER'S SMALL CATECHISM WITH EXPOSITION

Organized into 34 Units of Instruction

	QUESTIONS
Introductory Unit: The Bible and the Catechism	1-23

UNITS

1.	The Worship of the True God First Commandment	24-33
2.	The Reverent Life — Second Commandment	34-44
3.	The Devotional Life — Third Commandment	45-51
4.	The Obedient Life — Fourth Commandment	52-58
5.	The Kind and Helpful Life — Fifth Commandment	59-60
6.	The Chaste and Decent Life — Sixth Commandment	61-65
7.	The Honest Life — Seventh Commandment	66-67
8.	The Charitable Life — Eighth Commandment	68-69
9.	The Contented Life Ninth and Tenth Commandments	70-78
10.	The Penitent Life — Sin: Nature, origin, kinds, punishment, confession, and cure	79-99
11.	God and Creation	100-107
12.	Angels	108-111
13.	Man	112-115
14.	God's Government and Preservation (Thanksgiving)	116-120
15.	Jesus: True God and True Man (I) (A Christmas Unit)	121-124; 128; 135-137

UNITS	QUESTIONS
16. Jesus: True God and True Man (II) (An Epiphany Unit)	125-127; 129-131
17. Jesus: Prophet, Priest, and King	132-134
18. The Story of Redemption (A Lenten Unit)	138-147
19. The Exalted Jesus (I) (An Easter or Ascension Unit)	148-153
20. The Exalted Jesus (II) (End of Church Year)	154-159
21. The Holy Ghost and His Work (A Pentecost Unit)	160-174
22. The Church (A Church Anniversary Unit)	175-186
23. Justification (A Reformation Week Unit)	187-194
24. Eternity, Hell, Judgment	195-200
25. Prayer (Rogate Sunday)	201-218
26. Prayers for the Kingdom (Petitions 1—3) (Mission Day)	219-227
27. A Prayer for Earthly Blessings (Thanksgiving)	228-230
28. Prayers for Deliverance (Petitions 5—7)	231-241
29. Baptism — Nature	242-252
30. Baptism — Blessings (An Introductory Unit)	253-266
31. Office of the Keys and Confession	267-295
32. Holy Communion — Nature (A Holy Week Unit)	296-312
33. Holy Communion — Blessings (A Pre-Communion Week Unit)	313-331

UNIT PLAN

The organization of the 34 resource units generally follows the outline below:

I. SCOPE AND IMPORTANCE

II. AIM
- A. KNOWLEDGE
- B. ATTITUDE
- C. HABITS, SKILLS
- D. ANTICIPATED OUTCOME

III. CURRICULUM MATERIAL
- A. BIBLE STORIES
- B. LUTHER'S SMALL CATECHISM
- C. MEMORY MATERIALS
    1. Bible Texts
    2. Luther's Small Catechism
    3. Hymns
    4. Prayers
- D. SUMMARY OUTLINE FOR THE CHALKBOARD

IV. INSTRUCTIONAL METHODS AND MATERIALS
- A. PROBLEM AND APPROACH
- B. SUGGESTED TEACHING UNIT
    1. Devotion
    2. Bible Story
    3. Memory Passages
    4. Luther's Small Catechism
    5. Liturgy
- C. AIDS TO LEARNING
    1. Visual
    2. Audio
    3. Objects
    4. Workbooks
    5. Bulletin Board
    6. Chalkboard
    7. Group Activity
    8. Music
    9. Art
    10. Library
- D. EVALUATION

V. SUGGESTIONS FOR CORRELATIONS WITH OTHER SUBJECTS

    A. READING
        1. Silent
        2. Oral
        3. Choral

    B. ENGLISH
        1. Oral
        2. Written
        3. Vocabulary and Spelling
        4. Handwriting

    C. SOCIAL SCIENCES
        1. Home and Family Life
        2. Community and Nation
        3. History

    D. PHYSICAL SCIENCES
        1. Nature Study
        2. Geography
        3. Health
        4. General Science

    E. ARITHMETIC

    F. ART

    G. MUSIC

SAMPLE

Series of DAILY LESSON PLANS: (*ONE* Period per Week)

Unit 7: THE HONEST LIFE

Week: _____

Topic: _____

Aim:
  General: _____
  Particular: _____

Approach: _____

_____

Opening Devotion:
  Hymn: _____
  Reading: _____
  Prayer: _____

Bible Story: _____

_____

Bible Texts: _____
Catechism Qus.: _____
Hymn Stanza: _____
Things to Do: _____

_____

Personal Appeal: _____

Closing Devotion:
  Hymn: _____
  Reading: _____
  Prayer: _____

SAMPLE LESSON PLANS

SAMPLE

Series of DAILY LESSON PLANS: (*ONE* Period per Week)

Unit 7: THE HONEST LIFE

Week: ─────────

Topic: The Honest Life

Aim:
 General: See MANUAL.
 Particular: What does God say about honesty and dishonesty?

Approach: As in MANUAL: What do you really own? How did you get it? etc.

Opening Devotion:
 Hymn: *LH* 287:1-8.
 Reading: Matt. 25:14-30.
 Prayer: * *Teen-Agers Pray*, p. 42.

SAMPLE LESSON PLANS XXXI

Bible Story:	Joshua 7:16-26. God hates thievery. Achan is stoned to death.
Bible Texts:	160–172.
Catechism Qus.:	66–67 – Take *after* texts have been presented. The Seventh Commandment.
Hymn Stanza:	LH 287:8 Appreciate. Memorize. Sing.
Things to Do:	Discuss worksheet. Assign memory work. Suggest readings. Discuss scrapbook, gathering of pictures and clippings. Suggest what to observe in community, at home, around school and parish grounds, re property condition. Focus attention on next week's topic: The Charitable Life.
Personal Appeal:	Are YOU guilty? Alas! Confess. Flee to Christ. Accept grace. Consecrate self. Promise obedience.
Closing Devotion:	
Hymn:	LH 400:1-4.
Reading:	Luke 10:25-37.
Prayer:	Summary, extempore.

SAMPLE

Series of DAILY LESSON PLANS: (*TWO* Periods per week)   Grades 4–8

Unit 7: THE HONEST LIFE

Week: ....

Periods:	First	Second
Topics:	Dishonesty.	Honesty.
Aim:		
General:	See MANUAL.	
Particular:	Knowledge and attitude re dishonesty in all forms.	Knowledge, attitude, and action re honest living.
Approach:	As in MANUAL.	A pertinent news item.
Opening Devotion:		
Hymn:	*LH* 287:1-8.	*LH* 395:1, 5.
Reading:	Matt. 25:14-30.	James 2:14-17.
Prayer:	* *Teen-Agers Pray*, p. 42.	*LH* 438:1-5.

SAMPLE LESSON PLANS XXXIII

Bible Story:	Joshua 7:16-26. God hates thievery. Thief Achan is stoned.	Luke 10:25-36. Shame on the robbers. Shame on priest and Levite. God bless the Samaritan.
Bible Texts:	Nos. 160–166.	Nos. 167–172.
Catechism Qus.:	No. 66. The Seventh Commandment.	No. 67. The Seventh Commandment.
Hymn Stanza:	LH 287:8: "Steal not, all usury abhor."	LH 395:5: "No goods unjustly got." Review LH 287:8: "Steal not, all usury abhor."
Things to Do:	Assign memory work. Discuss worksheet and scrapbook. Sing. Observe property owned personally by parish, family, community.	As in first period. Hear memory work. Sing. Report on observations. Service project. Improve school or church grounds.
Personal Appeal:	Are YOU guilty? Alas! Confess. Flee to Christ. Accept grace.	As in first period. Pledge honest effort.
Closing Devotion:		
Hymn:	LH 395:1, 5.	LH 287:1, 8.
Reading:	John 12:1-9.	2 Kings 5:20-24.
Prayer:	Summary, extempore	Summary, extempore

SAMPLE

Series of DAILY LESSON PLANS: (*THREE* Periods per Week)

Unit 7: THE HONEST LIFE

Week: _____

	Monday	Wednesday	Friday
Periods:			
Topic:	Dishonesty.	Honesty.	Stewardship.
Aim:			
General:	See MANUAL.	To foster the honest life.	
Particular:	Know sin. Feel shame. Appreciate Jesus.	Know sins of omission. As on Monday.	Know sin of selfishness. As on Monday.
Approach:	MANUAL.	News item.	Human interest story.
Opening Devotion:			
Hymn:	*LH* 287:1-8.	*LH* 395:1, 5.	400:1-4.
Reading:	Matt. 25:14-30.	Joshua 7:16-26.	James 2:14-17.
Prayer:	* *Teen-Agers Pray*, p. 42.	Extempore, on Seventh Commandment.	Extempore.

SAMPLE LESSON PLANS   XXXV

Bible Story:	Joshua 7:16-26. God hates thievery. Thief Aachan is stoned.	Luke 10:25-27. Shame on the robbers. Shame on those who pass by on other side.	Ex. 36:1-8. True liberality.
Bible Texts:	160—166.	167—168.	169—172.
Catechism Qus.:	66. Seventh Commandment	67 A. Seventh Commandment.	67 B-C. Seventh Commandment.
Hymn Stanza:	LH 287:8	LH 355:5. LH 287:8. — Review.	LH 395:5. LH 287:8.
Things to Do:	Assign memory work. Workbook. Scrapbook. Sing. Encourage observing.	As on Monday. Hear memory work. Check progress. Encourage home contact.	As on Wednesday. Service project. Improve parish property.
Personal Appeal:	Are YOU guilty? Be honest. Confess. Accept Christ.	As on Monday. Ask for God's Spirit. Pledge improvement.	As on Wednesday. Offer cooperation.
Closing Devotion:			
Hymn:	LH 395:1, 5.	LH 287:1. 8.	LH 348:1-3.
Reading:	John 12:1-9.	2 Kings 5:20-24.	1 Cor. 16:1-2.
Prayer:	MANUAL.	Extempore.	Summary, extempore.

XXXVI SAMPLE LESSON PLANS

SAMPLE
Series of DAILY LESSON PLANS: (*FIVE* Periods per week) (As in parish school)

Unit 7: THE HONEST LIFE

Week: ———

	Monday	Tuesday	Wednesday	Thursday	Friday
Periods:					
Topics:	Dishonesty.	Honesty.	Stewardship.	Restitution.	Industry.
Aim:					
General:	See MANUAL.				
Particular:	Know sin. Feel shame. Appreciate Christ.	Cf. Monday.	Do. Motivate good stewardship.	Do. Inaugurate corrective action.	Do. Inaugurate and motivate a new life pattern.
Approach:	MANUAL.	News item.	Observed instance of stewardship.	Observed instance of dishonesty.	Observed instance of laziness.
Opening Devotion:					
Hymn:	*LH* 287:1-8.	*LH* 395:1, 5.	*LH* 400:1-4.	*LH* 395:1, 5.	*LH* 395:1, 2, 5.
Reading:	Matt. 25:14-30.	Joshua 7:16-26.	Mal. 3:8-12.	James 2:14-17.	Prov. 13:1-11.
Prayer:	* *Teen-Agers Pray,* p. 42.	Extempore.	*LH,* p. 107—48.	Extempore.	*LH,* p. 108—68.

SAMPLE LESSON PLANS

	Monday	Tuesday	Wednesday	Thursday	Friday
Bible Story:	Joshua 7:16-26.	Luke 10:25-37.	Ex. 36:1-8.	Luke 19:1-10.	Matt. 25:14-30.
Bible Texts:	160-166.	167-168.	169-172.	160, 164, 168.	163, 160.
Catechism Qus.:	66. 7th Comm.	67 A. 7th Comm.	67 B-C. 7th Comm. 4th Petition.	67 A. 7th Comm.	7th Comm.
Hymn Stanza:	LH 287:8	LH 287:8. — Review 395:5.	As on Tues. 400:4.	As on Wed. 348:1.	As on Thursday.
Things to Do:	Memorize: Assign memory work. Workbook. Scrapbook. Correlate. Sing.	As on Monday. Service project: Improve parish property.	As on Monday. Show filmstrip: "The 7th Commandment."	As on Monday. Chalkboard outline.	As on Monday. Recording:
Personal Appeal:	Guilty? Be honest. Confess. Accept Christ.	As on Monday. Cling to Christ.	As on Monday. Perfect? Attained?	As on Monday. Look at Christ.	As on Monday. Keep eyes on Christ.
Closing Devotion:					
Hymn:	LH 395:1, 5.	LH 287:1, 8.	LH 348:1.	LH 395:1, 5.	LH 400:1-5.
Reading:	John 12:1-9.	2 Kg. 5:20-24.	1 Cor. 6:1-2.	Mal. 3:8-12.	Matt. 25:14-30.
Prayer:	Extempore.	MANUAL.	Extempore.	LH, p. 108-62.	LH, p. 108-63.

INTRODUCTORY UNIT

THE BIBLE

(Catechism, Prayer Book, Hymnal)

•

I. Scope and Importance

The Bible is our Jesus Book. "And they said one to another, Did not our heart burn within us while He talked with us by the way and while He opened to us the Scriptures?" Luke 24:32.

"And this is the record, that God hath given to us eternal life, and this life is in His Son. He that hath the Son hath life; and he that hath not the Son of God hath not life." 1 John 5:11, 12.

"To wit, that God was in Christ, reconciling the world unto Himself, not imputing their trespasses unto them; and hath committed unto us the word of reconciliation." 2 Cor. 5:19.

"But these are written that ye might believe that Jesus is the Christ, the Son of God; and that believing ye might have life through His name." John 20:31.

"Nothing is so effectual against the world, the flesh, and the devil, and all evil thoughts as to be occupied with **God's Word,** in conversation and meditation. The first Psalm, in the second verse, calls those blessed who meditate upon the Law of the Lord day and night. No smoke of incense or other savor will be so offensive to

Satan as your occupying yourself with God's Commandments and words, speaking, singing, and thinking concerning them. This is the truly consecrated water, the sign which Satan avoids and which puts him to flight." (Luther's Large Catechism.)

"Let the Word of Christ dwell in you richly in all wisdom; **teaching and admonishing** one another in psalms and hymns and spiritual songs, singing with grace in your hearts to the Lord." Col. 3:16.

The Word is the Living Seed; the Bread of Life; Manna from Heaven.

II. Aim

A. KNOWLEDGE

Clear, vivid, and correct ideas concerning the Bible. Very important for all Christians today. Vivid ideas on the origin, nature, purpose, and makeup of the Bible; its relation to the Catechism and the Exposition, *The Lutheran Hymnal,* prayer books. Present the Bible as essentially the Jesus Book. John 20:31; Luke 24:27. Foster familiarity with related vocabulary.

B. ATTITUDE

Aim to cultivate a "trembling" attitude over against the Bible and all Biblical books. Stress necessity of faith in the Word and a personal faith in, and attachment to, Him who is the very heart of the Word, Jesus. Foster appreciation of the Bible as the story of our redemption. Is. 53; Heb. 4:1, 2; 1 John 5:13: "That ye may believe." Create desire to own, and to become better acquainted with, these books; strengthen the will and determination to make these desires effective. Foster love of God's Word. Ps. 119:103, 167. Motivate Bible learning. Create favorable group sentiment and a sustained interest in Biblical books.

C. HABITS, SKILLS, WAYS OF LIFE

Develop, through practice, functional familiarity with the Bible, the Catechism, and the Hymnal. Train pupils to read the Bible, to study the Catechism, and to use the Hymnal regularly,

THE BIBLE – Introductory Unit

habitually, preferably at a certain place and time. Develop skill in use of concordance, locating Bible reference. Accustom children to sing Bible songs frequently, at home and in social groups. Train in the ability to pray over this matter.

D. ANTICIPATED OUTCOME IN TERMS OF CHRIST-CENTERED PERSONALITIES

Men and women who know and love and use their Bible, Catechism, Hymnal, and Prayer Book; who have acquired the habit of reading Christian books and Lutheran periodicals; who appreciate Biblical pictures and who appreciate chorales and other church music.

III. Curriculum Material

A. BIBLE STUDIES

DATE USED

- _____ The One Thing Needful. *Luke 10:38-42.*
- _____ The Sower. *Matt. 13:1-23.*
- _____ Christ Crucified – the Heart of the Bible. *1 Cor. 1:18-24.*
- _____ His Delight Is in the Law. *Psalm 1.*
- _____ Harvest Hazards. *Mark 4:1-10.*
- _____ Praise of the Law. *Ps. 119:9-16.*
- _____ The Great Commandment. *Matt. 22:34-40.*
- _____ The Law Came from God. *Ex. 19:20.*
- _____ Written That You May Believe. *John 20:30, 31.*
- _____ The Bible Is Complete. *Rev. 22:12-21.*
- _____ The Bible Is the Jesus Book. *Luke 24:25-27.*
- _____ The Word Endureth Forever. *1 Peter 1:22-25.*
- _____ The Seed Is the Word of God. *Luke 8:4-18.*
- _____ The Father's Witness of His Son. *1 John 5:9-13.*
- _____ These Words Shall Be in Thine Heart. *Deut. 6:1-15.*
- _____ We Follow Not Cunningly Devised Fables. *2 Peter 1:16-21.*
- _____ The Central and Saving Truth. *2 Cor. 5:14-21.*

B. LUTHER'S SMALL CATECHISM

Questions 1–23.

C. MEMORY MATERIAL

1. Bible Texts

GRADE

1   Thou shalt love thy neighbor as thyself. *Matt. 22:39.* (1)
    Blessed are they that hear the Word of God and keep it. *Luke 11:28.* (1)

2   Love is the fulfilling of the Law. *Rom. 13:10.* (2)
    Thou shalt love the Lord, thy God, with all thy heart and with all thy soul and with all thy mind. *Matt. 22:37.* (2)

3   All Scripture is given by inspiration of God. *2 Tim. 3:16.* (3)
    God so loved the world that He gave His only-begotten Son, that whosoever believeth in Him should not perish, but have everlasting life. *John 3:16.* (2)

4   Search the Scriptures; for in them ye think ye have eternal life; and they are they which testify of Me. *John 5:39.* (5)
    If a man love Me, he will keep My words. *John 14:23.* (2)

5   Mary kept all these things and pondered them in her heart. *Luke 2:19.*
    Thy Word is truth. *John 17:17.*
    Thy Word is a lamp unto my feet and a light unto my path. *Ps. 119:105.* (2)

6   Holy men of God spake as they were moved by the Holy Ghost. *2 Peter 1:21.* (5)
    These words which I command thee this day shall be in thine heart; and thou shalt teach them diligently unto thy children. *Deut. 6:6, 7.* (5)
    The Scripture cannot be broken. *John 10:35.* (2)

7   I am not ashamed of the Gospel of Christ; for it is the power of God unto salvation. *Rom. 1:16.* (7)
    We speak, not in the words which man's wisdom teacheth, but which the Holy Ghost teacheth. *1 Cor. 2:13.*
    In this was manifested the love of God toward us, because that God sent His only-begotten Son into the world that we might live through Him. *1 John 4:9.* (7)

8   From a child thou hast known the Holy Scriptures, which are able to make thee wise unto salvation through faith which is in Christ Jesus. All Scripture is given by inspiration of God and is profitable for doctrine, for reproof, for correction, for instruction in righteousness, that the man of God may be perfect, thoroughly furnished unto all good works. *2 Tim. 3:15-17.* (8)
    Ye shall be holy; for I, the Lord, your God, am holy. *Lev. 19:2.* (2)

THE BIBLE — Introductory Unit

GRADE

When the Gentiles, which have not the Law, do by nature the things contained in the Law, these, having not the Law, are a law unto themselves: which show the work of the Law written in their hearts, their conscience also bearing witness, and their thoughts the meanwhile accusing or else excusing one another. *Rom. 2:14, 15.*

2. Luther's Small Catechism

6–8 The Table of Duties: To All in Common. (P. 30.)

4–8 The Books of the Bible. (P. 209.)

6–8 Creeds and Confessions. (Catechism, p. 210.)

3. Hymns

1–2 How precious is the Book Divine,
    By inspiration given!
Bright as a lamp its doctrines shine
    To guide our soul to heaven.   *LH 285:1*

3–4 Abide, O dear Redeemer,
    Among us with Thy Word,
And thus now and hereafter
    True peace and joy afford.   *LH 53:2*

5–6 We have a sure prophetic Word
By inspiration of the Lord;
And though assailed on every hand,
Jehovah's Word shall ever stand.   *LH 290:1*

7–8 The Gospel shows the Father's grace,
Who sent His Son to save our race,
Proclaims how Jesus lived and died
That man might thus be justified.   *LH 297:1*

4. Prayers

Grant us, we beseech Thee, Almighty God, steadfast faith in Jesus Christ, cheerful trust in Thy mercy, and sincere love to Thee and to all our fellowmen; through Jesus Christ, Thy Son, our Lord. Amen.

Bring to naught, O Christ, the schisms of heresy which seek to subvert Thy truth, that, as Thou art acknowledged in heaven and in earth as one and the same Lord, so Thy people, gathered from all nations, may obey Thy Word and serve Thee in unity of faith. Amen.

Heavenly Father, grant us Thy Holy Spirit, so that by Thy grace we may believe Thy Holy Word and lead a godly life, here in time and hereafter in eternity. We ask it in Jesus' name. Amen.

The Collect for the Word. *LH,* p. 14.

D. SUMMARY OUTLINE FOR THE CHALKBOARD

The Bible
1) is our Jesus Book
2) is verbally inspired
3) is therefore altogether true — no mistakes
4) is the story of our redemption
5) makes wise unto salvation
6) is the highest court of appeal in faith and conduct
7) is the sword of the Spirit (manna, seed)
8) is a collection of 66 books (39 and 27)
9) contains Law and Gospel, demands and promises.

   Let us as God's people therefore eagerly read, study, search, quote, believe, live the Bible.

The Catechism
1) contains the "milk" of the Word
2) was published by Luther (1483—1546) in 1529
3) is a handbook of religion for parents and instructors (Read Preface)
4) contains Six Chief Parts, prayers, Table of Duties, Christian Questions
5) is one of the nine Lutheran Confessions.

The Lutheran Hymnal
An inherited treasury of Christian doctrine and sentiments, in
   a) Meter and rhyme, with tunes, some sources distinctively Lutheran, some the appreciated possession of all Christians, for use in home, school, church.
   b) Liturgical forms for group worship.
   c) Prayers.

IV. Instructional Methods and Materials

A. PROBLEM AND APPROACH
How does God speak to ME? Through nature? Through conscience? Through the Scriptures?

B. SUGGESTED TEACHING UNIT

1. Devotion
Hymn: How Precious Is the Book Divine. *LH* 285.
Scripture Reading: 2 Tim. 3:15-17.
Prayer: Extempore.

2. Bible Story
Luke 10:38-42.

THE BIBLE – Introductory Unit

3. **Memory Passages**

   John 14:23: If a man love Me.
   Psalm 119:105: Thy Word is a lamp.
   2 Tim. 3:15-17: From a child.
   That Man a Godly Life Might Live. *LH* 287:1-12.

4. **Luther's Small Catechism**

   Questions 7—13.

5. **Liturgy**

   The Magnificat. *LH*, p. 43.

C. AIDS TO LEARNING

1. **Visual:** Introductory filmstrip from *The Ten Commandments* visualized — 79-101 — 10 filmstrips.
   The Land of the Bible series — 7 films.
   How Our Bible Came to Us — 79-5345 — 4 sound filmstrips (a set of 16, 9×12 color posters, 29-1050, correlate with these filmstrips). For additional suggestions see the Bible-Backgrounds section of the AVAS Catalog.

2. **Audio:** "Abide, O Dearest Jesus" — *LH* 53 — (Let the Earth Rejoice) KFUO, HA 61.
   "Lord, Keep Us Steadfast in Thy Word" — *LH* 261 — (Sing Unto The Lord) KFUO, HA 60.
   "O Come, Everyone That Thirsteth" — Mendelssohn: *Elijah* — Angel 3558-C.

3. **Objects:** Exhibit old Bible, catechisms, hymnals.

4. **Workbook:** * *The New Life,* Introductory unit.
   * *Learning About God,* Unit X.
   * *Growing in Faith,* Unit VIII.
   * *Building for Eternity,* Unit X.

5. **Bulletin Board:** Clippings and pictures from Sunday School lessons.

6. **Chalkboard:** Summary outline.

7. **Group Activity:** Visit a Bible House or religious book store.

8. **Music:** The Venite. *LH*, p. 33.

9. **Art:** "Christ Among the Doctors" — Hofmann.

10. **Library:** * *The Church Through the Ages.*
    * *Treasury of Christian Literature,* Unit V.
    Bible maps and charts.
    Bernard R. Youngman, *Lands and Peoples of the Living Bible* (Hawthorn).
    Alan Honour, *Cave of Riches: The Story of the Dead Sea Scrolls* (McGraw-Hill).

D. EVALUATION

Did we reach the objectives stated? Which topic needs further development?

V. Suggestions for Correlations with Other Subjects

A. READING
1. **Silent:** For content — "The Book Goes Forth," from * *Treasury of Christian Literature*, p. 262.
2. **Oral:** Psalm 1.
3. **Choral:** "Great Men on the Greatest Book," from * *Treasury of Christian Literature*, p. 265.

B. ENGLISH
1. **Oral:** Why and How I Use My Bible.
2. **Written:** The Book of the Bible I Like Best and Why.
3. **Vocabulary and Spelling:** Biblical, inspiration, orthodox, theology.
4. **Handwriting:** b — book, B — Bible.

C. SOCIAL SCIENCES
1. **Home and Family Life:** Using the Bible in family devotions. The family Bible.
2. **Community and Nation:** Are there Bibles in the public library?
3. **History:** Has the Bible helped make history? When? Where?

D. PHYSICAL SCIENCES
1. **Nature Study:** Do nature and the Bible both tell us about God? How?
2. **Geography:** Where is the Bible known and used? Where are other sacred books used?
3. **Health:** The Bible is good medicine for the soul. See Mal. 4:2.
4. **General Science:** Why can there be no real conflict between true science and the Bible?

E. ARITHMETIC
Use the * *Statistical Yearbook* to develop problems using the fundamentals in arithmetic. Develop line, bar, and circle graphs.

F. ART
"Christ Among the Doctors" — Hofmann.

G. MUSIC
The Venite. *LH*, p. 33.

UNIT
1

THE TRUE WORSHIP OF THE TRUE GOD

First Commandment

•

I. Scope and Importance

"The simple meaning of this commandment is, you shall worship Me alone as your God. What do these words mean and how are they to be understood? What is it to have a god, or what is God? Answer: A god is that to which we look for all good and where we resort for help in every time of need. To have a god is simply to trust and believe in one with our whole heart. As I have often said, the confidence and faith of the heart alone make both God and an idol. If your faith and confidence are right, then likewise your God is the true God. On the other hand, if your confidence is false, if it is wrong, then you have not the true God. For the two, faith and God, have inevitable connection. Now, I say, whatever your heart clings to and confides in, that is really your God." (LLC)

To have a god means to worship, to believe in, to love above everything else; to value most highly; to expect help from; to make sacrifices for; to be ready to die for.

"No people has ever been so godless as not to establish and maintain some divine service. Everyone sets up a god of his own, to whom he looks for blessings, help, and comfort. For example, the heathen who placed their hope in power and dominion exalted Jupiter as their supreme god; they who sought riches, happiness, or pleasure, and a life of ease, venerated Hercules, Mercury, Venus, or others; women with child worshiped Diana or Lucina; and so on, each making that his god to which his heart inclined." (LLC)

"We should fear and love God." Motivation is all-important in Christian ethics, and determines the quality of every moral or ethical act.

II. Aim

A. KNOWLEDGE

Stimulate thinking about God. Lead to a knowledge of God in Christ. Develop clear, vivid, and correct ideas about idols, idolatry, the Triune God, and true worship. Aid in recognition of personal guilt. Develop familiarity with related vocabulary. Encourage thorough memorization of pertinent memory material.

B. ATTITUDE

Induce attitude of awe, reverence, and love toward God. Lead individual members of class to confess humbly and penitently: Lord, have mercy upon me, an idolater. Foster loyalty to Jesus. Create desire to know more about God; arouse feeling of pity for those who still worship idols; create desire to bring knowledge of true God to idol-worshipers. Kindle desire to become a missionary. Foster desirable group spirit.

C. HABITS, SKILLS

Help pupils to break with idolatrous habits; form good habits of prayer; joyful participation in public worship; churchgoing; giving liberally and regularly for church and mission. Some schools have mission coin holders always available in school.

THE TRUE WORSHIP OF THE TRUE GOD – Unit 1

D. ANTICIPATED OUTCOME IN TERMS OF CHRIST-CENTERED PERSONALITIES

Children who are God-conscious at all times. Graduates who are truly converted and who will put first things first and live Christ-centered lives.

III. Curriculum Material

A. BIBLE STUDIES

DATE USED

- _____ °About the God Who Protects Against Fire. *Dan. 3.*
- _____ °Can a Camel Go Through a Needle's Eye? *Matt. 19:16-26.*
- _____ °Eat, Drink, and Be Merry? What of the Poor? What of Eternity? *Luke 16:9-31.*
- _____ A Strange Baptismal Service (Jesus). *Matt. 3:13-17.*
- _____ God Revealed in Jesus Christ. *2 Cor. 4:3-6.*
- _____ °A Case of Gross Idolatry (Golden Calf). *Ex. 32:1-6.*
- _____ °Let None of Them Escape. Why Not? (Prophets of Baal.) *1 Kings 18:17-40.*
- _____ °When All Worshipers Rejoiced Too Soon (Samson). *Judges 16:21-31.*
- _____ God is a Spirit (Samaritan Woman). *John 4:1-26.*
- _____ °Implicit Obedience (Isaac's Offering). *Gen. 22.*
- _____ °Even a Slingshot May Be Mighty. *1 Sam. 17:37-50.*
- _____ The Express Image of His Person. *Hebrews 1.*
- _____ God is Glorified in Jesus. *John 13:31-35.*
- _____ Graven Image or the Redeemer? Choose! *Is. 44.*
- _____ Is Jesus the Shepherd and Bishop of Your Soul? *1 Peter 2:21-25.*
- _____ The Folly of Idolatry. *Psalm 115.*
- _____ Happy is the Man That Findeth Wisdom. *Prov. 3:13-20.*
- _____ Have You Put Your Trust in the Lord? *Psalm 73.*
- _____ Two Men Who Feared God More Than Man (Peter and John). *Acts 4:13-22.*
- _____ My Glory Will I Not Give to Another. *Is. 42:5-9.*
- _____ Ye Shall Not Turn Aside. *Deut. 5:29-33.*
- _____ A Faithful Confessor. *Daniel 1 and 2.*

DATE USED

---------------- Abraham and the True God. *Gen. 12–14.*
---------------- The Father of Believers. *Gen. 15–18.*
---------------- The Golden Calf. *Ex. 32–34.*
---------------- *The Triune God Is Revealed. *Matt. 3:16, 17.*
---------------- *About the Unknown God. *Acts 17:22-31.*
---------------- God Comes First. *Matt. 10:28-39.*
---------------- Warning Against Worldliness. *1 John 2:15-17.*
---------------- He Was Not Afraid of Ten Thousand Men. *Ps. 3.*
---------------- The Source of True Manliness. *Ps. 37:1-9.*

B. LUTHER'S SMALL CATECHISM

Questions 24–33.

C. MEMORY MATERIAL

1. Bible Texts

GRADE

1   God is Love. *1 John 4:8.* (1)
    Thou shalt worship the Lord, thy God, and Him only shalt thou serve. *Matt. 4:10.* (1)

2   Trust in the Lord with all thine heart, and lean not unto thine own understanding. *Prov. 3:5.* (2)
    With God nothing shall be impossible. *Luke 1:37.* (2)

3   I am the almighty God. *Gen. 17:1.* (1)
    Go ye therefore and teach all nations, baptizing them in the name of the Father and of the Son and of the Holy Ghost. *Matt. 28:19.* (2)
    The Lord is good to all, and His tender mercies are over all His works. *Ps. 145:9.* (3)
    How, then, can I do this great wickedness and sin against God? *Gen. 39:9.* (3)

4   The fear of the Lord is to hate evil. *Prov. 8:13.* (3)
    It is better to trust in the Lord than to put confidence in man. *Ps. 118:8.* (3)
    Hear, O Israel: The Lord, our God, is one Lord. *Deut. 6:4.* (4)
    All men should honor the Son even as they honor the Father. He that honoreth not the Son honoreth not the Father, which hath sent Him. *John 5:23.* (4)

5   Thou art the same, and Thy years shall have no end. *Ps. 102:27.* (4)
    Every house is builded by some man; but He that built all things is God. *Heb. 3:4.* (3)

THE TRUE WORSHIP OF THE TRUE GOD – Unit 1

GRADE

    The Lord is the true God, He is the living God and an everlasting King. *Jer. 10:10.* (4)

    I am the Lord; that is My name. *Is. 42:8.* (5)

6 Let all the earth fear the Lord; let all the inhabitants of the world stand in awe of Him. *Ps. 33:8.* (5)

    The heavens declare the glory of God, and the firmament showeth His handiwork. *Ps. 19:1.* (6)

    He that loveth father or mother more than Me is not worthy of Me; and he that loveth son or daughter more than Me is not worthy of Me. *Matt. 10:37.* (6)

    Fear not them which kill the body, but are not able to kill the soul; but rather fear Him which is able to destroy both soul and body in hell. *Matt. 10:28.* (6)

7 Our God is in the heavens; He hath done whatsoever He hath pleased. Their idols are silver and gold, the work of men's hands. *Ps. 115:3, 4.* (6)

    This is life eternal, that they might know Thee the only true God, and Jesus Christ, whom Thou hast sent. *John 17:3.* (6)

    Lord, Thou hast been our Dwelling Place in all generations. Before the mountains were brought forth or ever Thou hadst formed the earth and the world, even from everlasting to everlasting, Thou art, God. *Ps. 90:1, 2.* (7)

    How hard is it for them that trust in riches to enter into the kingdom of God! *Mark 10:24.* (7)

8 Trust in the Lord with all thine heart, and lean not unto thine own understanding. *Prov. 3:5.* (7)

    Whom have I in heaven but Thee? And there is none upon earth that I desire beside Thee. My flesh and my heart faileth; but God is the Strength of my heart and my Portion forever. *Ps. 73:25, 26.* (6)

    Whose god is their belly and whose glory is in their shame, who mind earthly things. *Phil. 3:19* (7)

    O Lord, Thou hast searched me and known me, Thou knowest my downsitting and mine uprising, Thou understandest my thought afar off. Thou compassest my path and my lying down and art acquainted with all my ways. For there is not a word in my tongue but, lo, O Lord, Thou knowest it altogether. *Ps. 139:1-4.* (8)

    The fool hath said in his heart, There is no God. They are corrupt, they have done abominable works. *Ps. 14:1.* (8)

2. Luther's Small Catechism

1–2 The First Commandment. Expl. 3–8.
7–8 Table of Duties: To the Young in General.

GRADE

4–8 Introduction to the Lord's Prayer.

4–8 The Apostles' Creed.

3. Hymns

1–2 Holy, holy, holy! Lord God Almighty!
    Early in the morning our song shall rise to Thee;
Holy, holy, holy, merciful and mighty!
    God in Three Persons, blessed Trinity!   LH 246:1

3–4 Now thank we all our God
    With heart and hands and voices,
Who wondrous things hath done,
    In whom His world rejoices;
Who from our mother's arms
    Hath blessed us on our way
With countless gifts of love,
    And still is ours today.   LH 36:1

5–6 A mighty Fortress is our God,
    A trusty Shield and Weapon;
He helps us free from every need
    That hath us now o'ertaken.
The old evil Foe
Now means deadly woe;
Deep guile and great might
Are his dread arms in fight;
    On earth is not his equal.   LH 262:1

7–8 Jehovah, let me now adore Thee,
    For where is there a God such, Lord, as Thou?
With songs I fain would come before Thee;
    Oh, let Thy Holy Spirit teach me now
To praise Thee in His name through whom alone
Our songs can please Thee, through Thy blessed Son!   LH 21:1

4. Prayers

O Lord, our heavenly Father, almighty and everlasting God, who hast safely brought us to the beginning of this day, defend us in the same with Thy mighty power and grant that this day we fall into no sin, neither run into any kind of danger, but that all our doing, being ordered by Thy governance, may be righteous in Thy sight; through Jesus Christ, Thy Son, our Lord, who liveth and reigneth with Thee and the Holy Ghost, ever one God, world without end. Amen. (*LH*, p. 40, The Collect for Grace.)

O God, from whom all holy desires, all good counsels, and all just works do proceed, give unto Thy servants that peace which the world cannot give, that our hearts may be set to obey Thy commandments, and also that by Thee, we, being defended from the fear of our enemies, may pass our time in rest and quietness; through the merits of Jesus Christ, our

THE TRUE WORSHIP OF THE TRUE GOD – Unit 1

Savior, who liveth and reigneth with Thee and the Holy Ghost, ever one God, world without end. Amen. (*LH*, p. 45, The Collect for Peace.)

Collects for Trinity Sunday. *The Lutheran Liturgy*, p. 133.

Prayer for the Heathen (No. 24 – *LH*, p. 104); General Prayers Nos. 62, 63, 64, 76, 77 (*LH*, p. 108).

D. SUMMARY OUTLINE FOR THE CHALKBOARD

1) The Living God is known from
   nature
   conscience
   Bible

2) The Living God is

eternal	omniscient	benevolent
changeless	holy	merciful
omnipotent	just	gracious
omnipresent	faithful	

3) Therefore, let us as His people
   shun all other gods
   have the living God as truly our God
   urge others to believe in Him.

IV. Instructional Methods and Materials

A. PROBLEM AND APPROACH

Is there a God? Are there many Gods? Who is the true God? Where is He?

B. SUGGESTED TEACHING UNIT

1. Devotion
Hymn: Holy, Holy, Holy. *LH* 246.
Scripture Reading: John 4:1-24.
Prayer: Extempore, or * *Teen-Agers Pray*, p. 2.

2. Bible Story
1 Kings 18:17-41.

3. Memory Passages
Psalm 73:25-26: Whom have I in heaven?
Matt. 4:10: Thou shalt worship the Lord.
Prov. 3:5: Trust in the Lord.
I am thy God and Lord alone. *LH* 287:2.
The First Commandment.
The Introduction to The Lord's Prayer.

4. Luther's Small Catechism
Questions 24-33.

5. Liturgy
The Venite. *LH*, p. 33.

C. AIDS TO LEARNING

1. **Visual:** *The First Commandment* from *The Ten Commandments* visualized — 79-101 — 10 filmstrips.
   The Fiery Furnace — film.
   The Rich Fool — film.
2. **Audio:** "Now Thank We All Our God" — *LH* 36 — (The Lutheran Hour) RCA, LPM-1863 (Stereo — LSP-1863); also RCA, LM-2199 and KFUO, HA 61.
   "A Mighty Fortress Is Our God" — *LH* 262 — *(Album titled the same)* RCA, LM-2199; also Word, W-4017 (Stereo, WST-9003).
   Mendelssohn: *Reformation Symphony*, Columbia ML-4864.
   "Holy, Holy, Holy Is God the Lord" — Mendelssohn: *Elijah* — Angel 3558-C.
3. **Objects:** Pagan and American idols.
4. **Workbook:** * *The New Life*, Unit I.
   * *Living for God*, Unit I.
   * *Building for Eternity*, Unit I.
5. **Bulletin Board:** Pictures and clippings.
6. **Chalkboard:** Summary outline.
7. **Group Activity:** Speaker from foreign mission field.
8. **Music:** The Sanctus. *LH*, p. 26.
9. **Art:** Symbols for the Triune God — cloverleaf, etc.
10. **Library:** Wm. Arndt, * *Bible Difficulties.*
    A. Koehler, * *Light from Above.*
    T. Graebner, * *Story of the Catechism.*
    Liturgy for Family Study (Augsburg).

D. EVALUATION
What questions need further clarification?

V. Suggestions for Correlations with Other Subjects

A. READING
1. **Silent:** Acts 4:13-22.
2. **Oral:** Psalm 115, to be read to the class or at family worship.
3. **Choral:** Psalm 2.

THE TRUE WORSHIP OF THE TRUE GOD — Unit 1

B. ENGLISH
1. **Oral:** Report on Acts 4:13-22.
2. **Written:** report on atheism; gods of the American Indian, etc.
3. **Vocabulary and Spelling:** atheism, idolatry, polytheism, secularism, materialism.
4. **Handwriting:** G — God, g — good.

C. SOCIAL SCIENCES
1. **Home and Family Life:** Table prayers. One thing needful in home life.
2. **Community and Nation:** The public schools and God.
3. **History:** God and Godlessness in the world; select the area under study.

D. PHYSICAL SCIENCES
1. **Nature Study:** Discuss Bible animals; nature reveals God.
2. **Geography:** God as various world peoples see Him.
3. **Health:** Discuss Ps. 4:11; relate this to life.
4. **General Science:** Orderliness in nature. Who controls nature?

E. ARITHMETIC
Prepare problems comparing Christians to non-Christians, atheists; use fractions, percentages, decimals; prepare graphs.

F. ART
"Adoration of Kings" — Gerard.

G. MUSIC
The Gloria in Excelsis. *LH* p. 17.

UNIT 2

THE REVERENT LIFE

Second Commandment

•

I. Scope and Importance

On the use and abuse of God's name and all holy things. Cursing is an American vice. "Fortunetellers collect $125,000,000 annually from gullible Americans." *(The Lutheran Witness)* "Strong delusions" flourish in our land.

"As the First Commandment instructed the heart and taught faith, so this Commandment leads us into the outer sphere and trains our lips and tongue Godward. For words are the first issue and revelation of the heart." (LLC)

"This is the universal way of the world. Like a great deluge, the practice has flooded all lands; therefore we have our reward, which we seek and merit: pestilence, wars, famines, fires, floods, faithless wives, spoiled children, worthless servants, and all kinds of evil. From what other source should such dire misery spring? It is a great mercy that the earth still bears and nourishes us." (LLC)

In this Commandment God condemns vehemently all

THE REVERENT LIFE — Unit 2

irreverence, sham, pretense, hypocrisy, parading under false colors in matters of doctrine and life. God wants us to pray and strive so that His name will be hallowed.

II. Aim

A. KNOWLEDGE

Foster observation and thinking which will lead to clear and correct ideas about the sacredness of holy things; reverence; awe. Make sincerity meaningful. Make hypocrisy, superstition detestable. Enable pupils to recognize not only "fine idolatry" but also "fine profanity." Familiarize them with related vocabulary. Memorize thoroughly for use selected memory materials.

B. ATTITUDE

Foster reverent attitude toward God's name and all holy things. Strive to create feeling of shame for sin of not using God's name rightly, and so show need of grace. Let the Commandment thus become "a schoolmaster unto Christ." Foster feeling of abhorrence for cursing, sham, hypocrisy. Break up idea that it is "big" and "smart" to use cuss words. Foster right group sentiment.

C. HABITS, SKILLS

Aid pupils in actually breaking with bad habits in language as "damn," "darn," "My God!" "By Heaven!" "Hell, no!" Train to think of beauty, majesty, comfort in God's names. Train in proper posture during worship, prayer, and singing of sacred songs. Folded hands, not hands in pocket. (Luther, I:1547 f., 200 f.) Facial expression; train in habit of fifteen seconds of quietness after a prayer. Train in kneeling at appropriate occasions. Bowed head. Fervent facial expression in singing sacred songs. Train in habits adjusted to Matthew 23.

D. ANTICIPATED OUTCOME IN TERMS OF SANCTIFIED PERSONALITIES

Visualize your pupils as young people and adults who guard their language, are in earnest, and are sincere in all religious matters. Visualize boys and girls who impress the observer as being truly reverent in church and on all sacred occasions. Graduates who know and exercise the power of prayer and who will be a salt in their social group. Adults who engage in familiar, easy, and conversational use of the names of God, whose very presence in group will silence profanity.

III. Curriculum Material

A. BIBLE STUDIES

DATE USED

- *Jesus, Have Mercy on Us! *Luke 17:11-19.*
- *A Woman Who Frequently Used the Name of God. *1 Sam. 1—2.*
- *A Curse with a Long History. *Matt. 27:24, 25.*
- *You Can't Fool God. *Acts 5:1-11.*
- Guard Your Language. *Eph. 4:25, 29.*
- Profane Language Forbidden! *Matt. 5:33-37.*
- Death for the Blasphemer. *Lev. 24:10-23.*
- The Precious Name of Jesus Dare Be Used. *John 14:12-14.*
- *Paul Makes an Oath. *2 Cor. 1:18-23*
- Beware of Pretenders. *Matt. 7:15-20.*
- *Woe to the Make-Believe Church Members! *Matt. 23:13-28.*
- A Sad Mother Makes a Solemn Vow. *1 Sam. 1:9-18.*
- The Magnificat. *Luke 1:46-56.*
- An Oath in Uncertain Things. *Mark 6:23-29.*
- A Notable Bonfire. *Acts 19:13-20.*
- *Cursing Didn't Win This Fight. *1 Sam. 17:43-51.*
- Woe to the Impenitent Sinner! *Deut. 28:58-63.*
- *First He Cursed. Then He Cried. *Matt. 26:69-75.*
- *Matters of Real Moment Deserve an Oath. *Gen. 24:1-6.*
- *Ridiculing God's Holy One. *Matt. 27:39-43.*
- *Blasphemous Boasting. *2 Kings 18:28-35.*
- *A Conspiracy to Murder. *Acts 23:12-16.*
- *Frivolous Swearing. *Matt. 14:6-9.*
- *The Same and Yet Different. *Ex. 7, 8.*
- *Beware of False Prophets. *1 Kings 13:11-32.*
- Not Blasphemy but a Court Oath. *Matt. 26:59-68.*
- Right for Moses. Wrong for the Magicians. Why? *Ex. 1—8.*

THE REVERENT LIFE — Unit 2

DATE USED
- _____ A Strange Interview with a Witch. *1 Sam. 28:7-14*.
- _____ Mixing Truth with Error. *Numbers 22—24*.
- _____ A Hypocritical King. *1 Kings 12:14*.

B. LUTHER'S SMALL CATECHISM
Questions 34—44.

C. MEMORY MATERIAL
1. Bible Texts

GRADE

1   I am the Lord; that is My name. *Is. 42:8*.

2   Bless the Lord, O my soul, and all that is within me, bless His holy name. *Ps. 103:1*. (2)

3   This people draweth nigh unto Me with their mouth and honoreth Me with their lips; but their heart is far from Me. *Matt. 15:8*. (6)

   Call upon Me in the day of trouble. I will deliver thee, and thou shalt glorify Me. *Ps. 50:15*. (2)

4   Not everyone that saith unto Me, Lord, Lord, shall enter into the kingdom of heaven; but he that doeth the will of My Father which is in heaven. *Matt. 7:21*. (4)

   Oh, give thanks unto the Lord, for He is good; because His mercy endureth forever. *Ps. 118:1*. (2)

5   This is His name whereby He shall be called, The Lord Our Righteousness. *Jer. 23:6*. (4)

   The Lord will not hold him guiltless that taketh His name in vain. *Ex. 20:7*. (5)

   Be not deceived; God is not mocked: for whatsoever a man soweth, that shall he also reap. *Gal. 6:7*.

   Behold, I am against the prophets, saith the Lord, that use their tongues and say, He saith. *Jer. 23:31*. (6)

6   Thou shalt fear the Lord, thy God, and serve Him and shalt swear by His name. *Deut. 6:13*. (5)

   Ask, and it shall be given you; seek, and ye shall find; knock, and it shall be opened unto you. *Matt. 7:7*. (3)

   Ye shall not swear by My name falsely. *Lev. 19:12*. (4)

   In vain they do worship Me, teaching for doctrines the commandments of men. *Matt. 15:8*.

7   Whosoever curseth his God shall bear his sin. *Lev. 24:15*. (4)

   In all places where I record My name I will come unto thee, and I will bless thee. *Ex. 20:24*.

   (With the tongue) bless we God, even the Father, and therewith

GRADE

curse we men, which are made after the similitude of God. Out of the same mouth proceedeth blessing and cursing. My brethren, these things ought not so to be. *James 3:9, 10.* (7)

Ye have heard that it hath been said by them of old time, Thou shalt not forswear thyself, but shalt perform unto the Lord thine oaths. But I say unto you, Swear not at all: neither by heaven, for it is God's throne; nor by the earth, for it is His footstool; neither by Jerusalem, for it is the city of the great King. Neither shalt thou swear by thy head, because thou canst not make one hair white or black. But let your communication be, Yea, yea; Nay, nay; for whatsoever is more than these cometh of evil. *Matt. 5:33-37.* (5)

8   I call God for a record upon my soul. *2 Cor. 1:23.*

Let every soul be subject unto the higher powers. *Rom. 13:1.* (5)

Men verily swear by the greater; and an oath for confirmation is to them an end of all strife. *Heb. 6:16.*

There shall not be found among you anyone that maketh his son or his daughter to pass through the fire or that useth divination, or an observer of times, or an enchanter, or a witch, or a charmer, or a consulter with familiar spirits, or a wizard, or a necromancer. For all that do these things are an abomination unto the Lord; and because of these abominations the Lord, thy God, doth drive them out from before thee. *Deut. 18:10-12.*

Regard not them that have familiar spirits, neither seek after wizards, to be defiled by them. I am the Lord, your God. *Lev. 19:31.*

What thing soever I command you, observe to do it; thou shalt not add thereto nor diminish from it. *Deut. 12:32.* (7)

2. *Luther's Small Catechism*

1-2   The Second Commandment. Expl. 3—8.

4-8   The First Petition.

3. *Hymns*

1-2   How sweet the name of Jesus sounds
        In a believer's ear!
    It soothes his sorrows, heals his wounds,
        And drives away his fear.   LH 364:1

3-4   By idle word and speech profane
    Take not My holy name in vain
    And praise but that as good and true
    Which I Myself say and do.
        Have mercy, Lord!   LH 287:3

THE REVERENT LIFE — Unit 2

GRADE

5–6 From all that dwell below the skies
     Let the Creator's praise arise:
       Alleluia! Alleluia!
     Let the Redeemer's name be sung
     Through ev'ry land, by ev'ry tongue.
       Alleluia! Alleluia!
       Alleluia! Alleluia! Alleluia!   LH 15:1

7–8 Oh, let me never speak
      What bounds of truth exceedeth;
     Grant that no idle word
      From out my mouth proceedeth;
     And then, when in my place
      I must and ought to speak,
     My words grant power and grace
      Lest I offend the weak.   LH 395:3

4. Prayers

Almighty God, unto whom all hearts are open, all desires known, and from whom no secrets are hid, cleanse the thoughts of our hearts by the inspiration of Thy Holy Spirit, that we may perfectly love Thee and worthily magnify Thy holy name; through Jesus Christ, Thy Son, our Lord.
(*LH*, p. 108, For Purity)

Dear Father in Heaven, forgive where we have professed to believe Thy Word and yet have failed to live according to Thy Word. Grant, O God, that at all times Thy Word may be taught and received in its truth and purity, and that we, as Thy children, may lead a holy life according to it and that thus Thy name be hallowed among us. We ask it in Jesus' name. Amen.

Teachers and pupils make and use their own prayers.

D. SUMMARY OUTLINE FOR THE CHALKBOARD

God's names: Jesus, Christ, Almighty, God, Lord — and all sacred and serious things, as heaven, hell, devil.

It is a *sin* to use God's name:
    to curse
    to swear falsely
    to swear frivolously
    to swear in uncertain things
    to swear to commit an evil act
    to perform supernatural feats by an unwarranted use of God's Word
    to adorn false doctrine
    to hide a sinful life.
      Have mercy, Lord.

Let us as sanctified and enlightened members of God's family use God's name:
> to call for help; pray, praise, give thanks
> to propagate pure, Biblical doctrine
> to honor it with a Christian life
> to take an oath, if necessary, in court.
> All for Jesus' sake.

IV. Instructional Methods and Materials

A. PROBLEM AND APPROACH

Many people do not use, some misuse, and others use and misuse God's name. How about you?

B. SUGGESTED TEACHING UNIT

1. Devotion
Hymn: How Sweet the Name of Jesus Sounds. *LH* 364:1.
Scripture Reading: Acts 5:1-11.
Prayer: Extempore.

2. Bible Story
1 Samuel 17:43-51.

3. Memory Passages
Matt. 15:8: This people draweth nigh unto Me.
Psalm 50:15: Call upon Me.
Psalm 103:1: Bless the Lord, O my soul.
By idle word and speech profane. *LH* 287:3.
The Second Commandment.
The Second Petition.

4. Luther's Small Catechism
Questions 34—44.

5. Liturgy
The Magnificat. *LH*, p. 43.

C. AIDS TO LEARNING

1. **Visual:** *The Second Commandment* from *The Ten Commandments* visualized — 79-101 — 10 filmstrips.
2. **Audio:** "Praise to the Lord, the Almighty" — *LH* 39 — (Let The Earth Rejoice) KFUO, HA 61. Also RCA, LM-2199.
   "Now Thank We All Our God" — *LH* 36 — (The Lutheran Hour) RCA, LPM-1863 (Stereo LSP-1863). Also RCA, LM-2199, and KFUO, HA 61.
   "A Mighty Fortress Is Our God." See Listing under Unit I.

THE REVERENT LIFE — Unit 2

"Lord, How Excellent Thy Name Is" — Mendelssohn: *Elijah* — Angel 3558-C.
3. **Objects:** Horseshoe, rabbit's foot.
4. **Workbook:** ° *The New Life,* Unit II.
   ° *Living for God,* Unit I.
5. **Bulletin Board:** Clippings and pictures of related items.
6. **Chalkboard:** Summary outline.
7. **Group Activity:** Visit a courtroom while a trial is in session.
8. **Music:** Mendelssohn's *Elijah* — "How Excellent" (Columbia).
9. **Art:** "Saying Grace" — Chardin.
10. **Library:** Luther D. Reed, *Worship: A Study of Corporate Devotion* (Muhlenberg).
    Robbie Trent, *To Church We Go* (Follett). (For 5—7 yr. olds)
    Marie Olander, *My Church Book* (Augustana). (For 6—8 yr. olds)

D. EVALUATION

How well did we reach our goals? What topic or idea might we have given more emphasis?

V. Suggestions for Correlations with Other Subjects

A. READING
1. **Silent:** "Hymns Through the Ages," from ° *Treasury of Christian Literature,* p. 100.
2. **Oral:** Luke 17:11-19, to be read to the class.
3. **Choral:** Psalm 32.

B. ENGLISH
1. **Oral:** Report on silent reading above.
2. **Written:** Guarding my tongue; or Why Jesus' name is sweet to me.
3. **Vocabulary and Spelling:** Jehovah, Jesus, Christ, blaspheme, cursing, swearing.
4. **Handwriting:** c — curse; C — Christ.

C. SOCIAL SCIENCES
1. **Home and Family Life:** Discuss the topic "No cursing, ladies present." Table prayers.
2. **Community and Nation:** Using an oath in court; Superstitions, such as the number 13.
3. **History:** In the area or period in history studied, did the people use God's name? Which name?

D. PHYSICAL SCIENCES
1. **Nature Study:** Is there such a thing as magic?
2. **Geography:** Do the people in the area studied use God's name?
3. **Health:** Can "medicine men" cure disease? Discuss and evaluate.
4. **General Science:** Can science and religion agree?

E. ARITHMETIC
Prepare graphs and tables showing number of persons at worship services for a given period.

F. ART
"The Angelus" — Millet.

G. MUSIC
The Introit for Rogate Sunday. *LH*, p. 71.

UNIT
3

THE DEVOTIONAL LIFE

Third Commandment

•

I. Scope and Importance

Christ is everything. Faith in Christ is indispensable. Faith comes and is sustained through the use of the means of grace. Hence the importance of using the means of grace regularly, humbly, believingly, at all times and on special days and occasions. Hence the importance of sanctifying the holy day.

We keep holy days that people may have time and opportunity to worship with the congregation, which otherwise they could not do. Also, that they may assemble in meetings to hear and discuss God's Word and appropriately praise Him with song and prayer.

"Just that is the sin which hitherto has been reckoned among mortal sins and which is called *akedia*, that is indolence and disgust; a malignant, dangerous plague, with which Satan charms and deceives many hearts that he may get them into his power and once more deprive them of the Word by stealth." (LLC)

"To sanctify the rest day means nothing more than to be occupied with holy words, holy works and life." (LLC)

II. Aim

A. KNOWLEDGE

Foster thinking which will lead to clear, vivid, and correct ideas about "holy days" and "sanctifying"; on the function of "the means of grace" and of assembling for group worship. Develop familiarity with the Liturgy as used in public worship, the ceremonies and customs observed in public worship; the Christian Church Year; church architecture, use of art in fostering the devotional life. Familiarize pupils with related vocabulary. Memorize thoroughly, for use, appreciated and quotable memory gems.

B. ATTITUDE

Aim to foster a feeling of shame for having failed to appreciate rightly the preaching and teaching of the Word; lead to repentance and confession; a felt need for the cleansing blood of Christ; new appreciation of the Cross; foster a group sentiment which expresses itself sincerely in the words: "I was *glad* when they said unto me, Let us go into the house of the Lord." Motivate learning and living by centering it in Jesus. Create right group morale. Sensitize the conscience with regard to "hearing the Word."

C. HABITS, SKILLS

Train in regular and devout participation in the devotional life, privately, at home, in school, at church. Use records, graphs, and checkups to train in the churchgoing habit; have study of the Catechism, reading of the Bible at home and in school; daily private and family prayer. Reporting on pastor's and on radio sermons. Train in proper postures during worship: folded hands, bowed head, kneeling, making of cross.

Develop, by practice, skill in winning others for Christ and His church; canvassing, inviting to church; various forms of social service, visiting the sick, the poor, the delinquent.

THE DEVOTIONAL LIFE — Unit 3   29

D. ANTICIPATED OUTCOMES IN TERMS OF
CHRIST-CENTERED PERSONALITIES

Boys and girls who enjoy regular spirited participation in various forms of the devotional life; young people who enjoy and would rather participate in this than in anything else; church worship, private devotions, Sunday morning and weekday Bible classes; parish and community enterprises aimed at aiding the congregation to fulfill its purpose of soul winning and soul keeping.

III. Curriculum Material

A. BIBLE STUDIES

DATE USED

_____   *None Like Jesus — Being About Father's Business. *Luke 2:41-52.*

_____   *One Thing is Needful. *Luke 10:38-42.*

_____   *Keeping and Pondering Each Word. *Luke 2:15-20.*

_____   Mary Couldn't Get Over It. *Luke 2:8-19.*

_____   *Can Our Minister and Teachers Get Along on Their Salaries? *1 Cor. 9:7-14.*

_____   Woe to Those Who Despise Preaching and His Word! *Luke 10:10-16.*

_____   How Foolish to Neglect Church Attendance for Earthly Gain! *Ex. 16:23-30.*

_____   Some Persons Will Never See Death. Who Are They? *John 11:1-26.*

_____   About the Hired Girl Who Brought Others to Church. *2 Kings 5:1-14.*

_____   Word of Men or Word of God? *1 Thess. 2:9-13.*

_____   Do You Keep Silence Before Him? *Hab. 2:18-20.*

_____   Man for the Sabbath or the Sabbath for Man? Which? *Mark 2:23-28.*

_____   A Man Who Enjoyed Churchgoing. *Ps. 26:1-8.*

_____   Doctrines of Devils. *1 Tim. 4:1-5.*

_____   Turn Not Back to Bondage. *Gal. 4:8-11.*

_____   The Tabernacle and Its Ceremonials. *Ex. 35—40.*

_____   The Story of Samuel. *.1 Sam. 1—7.*

_____   Jesus Makes a Point About the Sabbath. *Luke 14:1-11.*

_____   *Of Some People Who "Rejected the Counsel of God." *Luke 7:24-30.*

_____   *On Rejecting and Being Rejected (Saul). *1 Sam. 15:10-23.*

_____   *A Whole City Goes to Church. *Acts 13:44-52.*

DATE USED

---------------- *Bereans as Model Bible Students. *Acts 17:10-13.*
---------------- *The Offering Is Important (Widow's Mite). *Mark 12:41-44.*
---------------- Now, Concerning the Collection. *1 Cor. 16:1-4.*

B. LUTHER'S SMALL CATECHISM

Questions 45-51.

C. MEMORY MATERIAL

1. Bible Texts

GRADE

1 Blessed are they that hear the Word of God and keep it. *Luke 11:28.*

2 The Son of Man is Lord even of the Sabbath day. *Matt. 12:8.* (4)

3 Let the Word of Christ dwell in you richly. *Col. 3:16.* (3)
   He that is of God heareth God's words; ye therefore hear them not because ye are not of God. *John 8:47.* (3)

4 He that heareth you heareth Me; and he that despiseth you despiseth Me; and he that despiseth Me despiseth Him that sent Me. *Luke 10:16.* (5)

   Keep thy foot when thou goest to the house of God, and be more ready to hear than to give the sacrifice of fools; for they consider not that they do evil. *Eccl. 5:1.* (8)

5 Not forsaking the assembling of ourselves together, as the manner of some is. *Heb. 10:25.* (5)

   To this man will I look, even to him that is poor and of a contrite spirit and trembleth at My Word. *Is. 66:2.* (7)

   Go ye into all the world and preach the Gospel to every creature. *Mark 16:15.* (3)

6 They continued steadfastly in the Apostles' doctrine and fellowship and in breaking of bread and in prayers. *Acts 2:42.* (5)

   Let him that is taught in the Word communicate unto him that teacheth in all good things. Be not deceived; God is not mocked; for whatsoever a man soweth, that shall he also reap. *Gal. 6:6, 7.* (7)

   When ye received the Word of God which ye heard of us, ye received it not as the word of men, but, as it is in truth, the Word of God. *1 Thess. 2:13.* (6)

7 This Book of the Law shall not depart out of thy mouth; but thou shalt meditate therein day and night. *Joshua 1:8.* (7)

   Ye observe days and months and times and years. I am afraid of you lest I have bestowed upon you labor in vain. *Gal. 4:10, 11.*

THE DEVOTIONAL LIFE – Unit 3

GRADE

Let no man therefore judge you in meat or in drink or in respect of an holy day or of the new moon or of the Sabbath days; which are a shadow of things to come; but the body is of Christ. *Col. 2:16, 17.*

8   Lord, I have loved the habitation of Thy house and the place where Thine honor dwelleth. *Ps. 26:8.* (8)

Obey them that have the rule over you, and submit yourselves; for they watch for your souls as they that must give account, that they may do it with joy and not with grief; for that is unprofitable for you. *Heb. 13:17.* (8)

One man esteemeth one day above another; another esteemeth every day alike. Let every man be fully persuaded in his own mind. He that regardeth the day regardeth it unto the Lord; and he that regardeth not the day, to the Lord he doth not regard it. *Rom. 14:5, 6.*

2. Luther's Small Catechism

1–2   The Third Commandment. Expl. 3–8.
4–6   Table of Duties: To the Hearers 1, 2, 3.
7–8   Table of Duties: To Pastors; To the Hearers 4, 5, 6.

3. Hymns

1–2   This is the day the Lord hath made;
    He calls the hours His own;
Let heav'n rejoice, let earth be glad
    And praise surround the throne.   *LH 10:1*

3–4   Open now thy gates of beauty,
    Zion, let me enter there,
Where my soul in joyful duty
    Waits for Him who answers prayer.
Oh, how blessed is this place,
Filled with solace, light, and grace!   *LH 1:1*

5–6   Hallow the day which God hath blest
That thou and all thy house may rest;
Keep hand and heart from labor free
That God may so work in thee.
    Have mercy, Lord!   *LH 287:4*

7–8   Hark! the voice of Jesus crying,
    "Who will go and work today?
Fields are white and harvests waiting,
    Who will bear the sheaves away?"
Loud and long the Master calleth,
    Rich reward He offers thee;
Who will answer, gladly saying,
    "Here am I, send me, send me?"   *LH 496:1*

4. Prayers

Blessed Lord, who hast caused all Holy Scriptures to be written for our learning, grant that we may in such wise hear them, read, mark, learn, and inwardly digest them that by patience and comfort of Thy holy Word we may embrace, and ever hold fast, the blessed hope of everlasting life which Thou hast given us in our Savior Jesus Christ. Amen.

(*LH*, p. 107, No. 49)

(*LH*, p. 102, No. 4; p. 103, No. 16; p. 108, No. 62; pp. 120, 122.)
Collects for 17th Sunday after Trinity.

D. SUMMARY OUTLINE FOR THE CHALKBOARD

Sanctify the holy day. Use the means of grace reverently and regularly. It is a *sin*

- to neglect the written or spoken Word
- to neglect the Sacrament
- to be inattentive or unbelieving when the Word of God is in use.

Have mercy, Lord!

Let us as Christian boys and girls

- attend services every Sunday
- be reverent before, during, and after the church service
- attend a Christian school and Bible classes if at all possible
- gladly read and memorize the Word
- sing Christian hymns
- discuss, quote, and apply God's Word to current problems and events
- have private and home devotions
- work and sacrifice time and money to beautify public services and to win others.

All for Jesus' sake and in His name.

A Good Slogan

On God's day, in God's house, with God's people, to hear God's Word, to be imbued with God's Spirit, to share in God's work, and to enjoy God's peace.

IV. Instructional Methods and Materials

A. PROBLEM AND APPROACH

Many people never go to church. Do you? Why? Do you enjoy attending worship services?

B. SUGGESTED TEACHING UNIT

1. Devotion

Hymn: Open Now Thy Gates of Beauty. *LH* 1.

THE DEVOTIONAL LIFE – Unit 3

    Scripture Reading: Psalm 26.
    Prayer: Extempore.

2. **Bible Story**
   Luke 10:38-42.

3. **Memory Passages**
   Eccl. 5:1: Keep thy foot.
   Col. 2:16: Let no man therefore judge you.
   Joshua 1:18: This Book of the Law.
   Hallow the day which God hath blest. *LH* 287:4.
   The Third Commandment.

4. **Luther's Small Catechism**
   Questions 45—51.

5. **Liturgy**
   The Order of Service with Communion. *LH,* p. 15.

C. AIDS TO LEARNING

1. **Visual:** *The Third Commandment* from *The Ten Commandments visualized* — 79-101 — 10 filmstrips.
   The Lord's Day — 79-648 — from the *Christian Living* series, 79-0080.
2. **Audio:** "Open Now Thy Gates of Beauty" — *LH* 1 — (The Lutheran Hour) LPM-1863 (Stereo LSP-1863).
   "Lord, Keep Us Steadfast in Thy Word" — *LH* 261 — (Sing Unto The Lord) KFUO, HA 60.
   "How Blest Are They Who Hear God's Word" — *LH* 48 — (Praise the Almighty) Word, W-4019.
3. **Objects:** Church art objects.
4. **Workbook:** * *The New Life,* Unit III.
     * *Learning About God,* Unit IX.
     * *Living for God,* Unit VI.
     * *Building for Eternity,* Unit VI.
5. **Bulletin Board:** Pictures and clippings on worship, church art, and architecture.
6. **Chalkboard:** Summary outline.
7. **Group Activity:** Visit and study your church building.
8. **Music:** Jubilate Deo. *LH* 666.
9. **Art:** "Pilgrims Going to Church."
10. **Library:** V. C. Frank, * *The Rainbow in My Church.*
    * *Collects.*
    Marie Olander, *My Church Book* (Augustana). (For 6—8 yr. olds)

D. EVALUATION

Have we gained a clearer understanding of worship and its purposes? What areas are still unclear?

V. Suggestions for Correlations with Other Subjects

A. READING
1. **Silent:** "The Months," from * *Treasury of Christian Literature*, p. 72.
2. **Oral:** "Sabbath Morning," from * *Treasury of Christian Literature*, p. 53.
3. **Choral:** Psalm 33.

B. ENGLISH
1. **Oral:** Report on silent reading above.
2. **Written:** 3-paragraph composition on the topic "My Church."
3. **Vocabulary and Spelling:** sermon, nave, devotion, liturgy, chancel, narthex.
4. **Handwriting:** w — worship.

C. SOCIAL SCIENCES
1. **Home and Family Life:** Discuss family worship. Prepare a devotion for use in family worship.
2. **Community and Nation:** Good manners in church; freedom to worship.
3. **History:** The image of God in world history.

D. PHYSICAL SCIENCES
1. **Nature Study:** God in nature; Can we worship God by going fishing? Discuss these and similar topics.
2. **Geography:** Types of temples in various countries and cultures.
3. **Health:** Discuss private confession as a means toward mental and emotional health.
4. **General Science:** God and our scientific world.

E. Arithmetic

Develop problems using the fundamentals: church attendance, parish membership.

F. ART

Christian symbolism.

G. MUSIC

Learn an anthem to sing in church.

UNIT

4

THE OBEDIENT LIFE

Fourth Commandment

•

I. Scope and Importance

Ideal child-parent, employee-employer, citizen-government relationships.

"Eli-parents" are too common. Brutal and negligent parents have not disappeared; delinquency is on the increase. Proper child training is greatly wanting. The concept of democracy makes for desirable freedom and self-determination but opens the door to license and a self-determination for which the immature are not ready. It is therefore very important also in America that we provide training which will teach us properly to fuse authority, obedience, and democratic cooperation. Civic efficiency demands strict discipline and intelligent obedience in all areas, even in a democracy.

The idea that parents, employers, governors, kings, are God's representatives is being questioned very widely. Divine right of kings must be rightly understood.

"The young must be taught to reverence their parents in God's stead, and to remember that even though they be lowly, poor, frail, and peculiar, they are still father and mother, given by God. Their way of living and their failings cannot rob them of their honor. Therefore, we are not to regard the manner of their persons, but God's will that appointed and ordained them to be our parents." (LLC)

"In conversation with them, we measure our words, lest our language be discourteous, domineering, quarrelsome, yielding to them in silence, even if they do go too far. And thirdly, that we honor them by our actions, both in our bearing and the extension of aid, serving, helping, and caring for them when they are old or sick, frail or poor; and that we not only do it cheerfully, but with humility and reverence, as if unto God." (LLC)

"All authority has its roots and warrant in parental authority." (LLC)

II. Aim

A. KNOWLEDGE

Develop clear, vivid, and correct concept of "superiors"; nature of sin against law and order; nature and blessings of obedience, even in free America; limits of obedience; familiarize with related vocabulary. Memorize quotable memory gems. Better to learn a few thoroughly than many superficially.

B. ATTITUDE

Aim to foster respect for authority, willingness to obey even when no tangible reason for obedience is evident; foster a felt need for confessing sins and shortcomings to God, mother, father, teacher, pastor, employers, and others in authority and asking for pardon. Create atmosphere of cheerful service and cooperation in school and at home. "For Jesus' sake!" Let this be the basis of your appeal. Create right group morale.

C. HABITS, SKILLS

Train in habits of respect for elders and prompt, cheerful obedience to superiors; remove hat, offer chair, help aged cross

THE OBEDIENT LIFE — Unit 4

street, salute flag respectfully and properly. Break habit of pouting, grumbling, making long face when told to do something; habituate to worthwhile mores and customs.

D. ANTICIPATED OUTCOMES IN TERMS OF CHRISTLIKE CHARACTERS

Children who are like Jesus: "He was subject unto them." Young people who still consult father and mother and regard their wishes; employees whom the employer hates to lose; citizens who are loyal, patriotic, dependable, actively participating in the solution of community problems by voting and holding office.

III. Curriculum Material

A. BIBLE STUDIES

DATE USED

_____ °And He Was Subject Unto Them. *Luke 2:51, 52.*
_____ °Righteous Indignation (Jonathan). *1 Sam. 20:30-34.*
_____ °The Model Son Provides for His Heartbroken Mother. *John 19:25-27.*
_____ °A King Honors His Mother. *1 Kings 2:19.*
_____ °God Takes a Hand Where a Father Failed. *1 Sam. 2:12-15; 4:12-18.*
_____ °A Spiritual Son Honors His Spiritual Father (Elisha). *2 Kings 2:12-15.*
_____ God Loves and Blesses Obedience. *Jer. 35:1-19.*
_____ Respect Your Superiors. This Is About You and Your Father. *Eph. 6:1-9.*
_____ Death for the Rebellious Son. *Deut. 21:18-21.*
_____ "Speak, for Thy Servant Heareth." *1 Sam. 3:1-18.*
_____ The Sermon on the Mount. *Matt. 5–7.*
_____ A Lesson on Authority and Obedience. *Matt. 8:1-13.*
_____ God and Caesar! *Matt. 22:15-22.*
_____ About Spies and Rebellion. *Num. 13:17–14:5.*
_____ A Famous Father (Isaac). *Gen. 25–27.*
_____ Envy in a Family Circle (Joseph). *Gen. 37.*
_____ A Family of Boys. *Gen. 42.*
_____ Consult Your Parents! (Choosing a spouse.) *Gen. 28:1-5.*
_____ °Affectionate Father-Son Relationship. *Gen. 46:28-34 (v. 29).*
_____ Ruth's Great Affection for Her Mother-in-law. *Ruth 1:6-18.*

DATE USED

.... This Means Christian Education. *Deut. 6:1-9.*

.... *So Big, But Not Ashamed of His Father. *Gen. 47:1-12.*

.... The Successful Young Man Who Didn't Forget His Father. *Gen. 45:1-15.*

.... *The Prince Who Stole Hearts from His Father. *2 Sam. 15:1-6.*

.... A Handsome Young Man Buried Under a Heap of Stones. *2 Sam. 18:9-17.*

.... Stripes Are for the Backs of Fools. *Prov. 19:18-29.*

B. LUTHER'S SMALL CATECHISM
   Questions 52—58.

C. MEMORY MATERIAL
   1. Bible Texts
GRADE
1 Children, obey your parents in all things; for this is well-pleasing unto the Lord. *Col. 3:20.* (1)

2 Love your enemies. *Matt. 5:44.* (1)

3 We ought to obey God rather than men. *Acts 5:29.* (2)

4 Hearken unto thy father that begat thee, and despise not thy mother when she is old. *Prov. 23:22.*

5 Honor thy father and mother; which is the first commandment with promise: that it may be well with thee and thou mayest live long on the earth. *Eph. 6:2, 3.* (5)

   Thou shalt rise up before the hoary head and honor the face of the old man. *Lev. 19:32.* (5)

6 All things whatsoever ye would that men should do to you, do ye even so to them; for this is the Law and the Prophets. *Matt. 7:12.* (5)

   The eye that mocketh at his father and despiseth to obey his mother, the ravens of the valley shall pick it out, and the young eagles shall eat it. *Prov. 30:17.* (6)

7 As we have therefore opportunity, let us do good unto all men, especially unto them who are of the household of faith. *Gal. 6:10.* (6)

   Servants, be subject to your masters with all fear; not only to the good and gentle, but also to the froward. *1 Peter 2:18.*

8 Whosoever therefore resisteth the power resisteth the ordinance of God; and they that resist shall receive to themselves damnation. *Rom. 13:2.* (7)

   Let them learn first to show piety at home and to requite their parents; for that is good and acceptable before God. *1 Tim. 5:4.* (6)

THE OBEDIENT LIFE — Unit 4

GRADE
2. Luther's Small Catechism
1–2 Fourth Commandment. Expl. 3—8.
4–8 Table of Duties: To Children.
6–8 Table of Duties: Of Civil Government; to Parents
7–8 Table of Duties: To Employers; Of Subjects; To Servants.

3. Hymns

1–2 Dear Father in Heaven,
    Look down from above;
Bless Father and Mother
    And those whom I love.   CGS 35

3–4 Give to thy parents honor due,
Be dutiful, and loving, too,
And help them when their strength decays;
So shalt thou have length of days.
    Have mercy, Lord!   LH 287:5

5–6 Oh, blest the house, whate'er befall,
Where Jesus Christ is all in all!
Yea, if He were not dwelling there,
How dark and poor and void it were!   LH 625:1

7–8 God bless our native land!
Firm may she ever stand
    Through storm and night!
When the wild tempests rave,
Ruler of wind and wave,
Do Thou our country save
    By Thy great might.   LH 577:1

4. Prayers
For Civil Authorities — *LH,* p. 104, No. 25.
For Mothers — *LH,* p. 105, No. 38.
For Humility — *LH,* p. 109, No. 70.
Collects for 23d Sunday after Trinity.

D. SUMMARY OUTLINE FOR THE CHALKBOARD

Superiors: Parents (grandparents), employers, teachers, government officers.

It is a sin
    to despise or to rebel against superiors, *e. g.,* by talking back to them
    to provoke them to anger by noncooperation, *e. g.,* "stalling," slow on assembly line
    to fail to carry out the positive command.
        Have mercy, Lord!
Let us as God's children

honor our parents and other superiors as God's gifts and representatives
obey them promptly and cheerfully
make life pleasant for them.
For Jesus' sake! In imitation of Jesus!

IV. Instructional Methods and Materials

A. PROBLEM AND APPROACH

Do your parents ever scold you? Why? How do you feel when they scold you?

B. SUGGESTED TEACHING UNIT

1. **Devotion**

   Hymn: That Man a Godly Life Might Live. *LH* 287:1-5.
   Scripture Reading: Luke 2:40-52.
   Prayer: Extempore, or * *Teen-Agers Pray*, page 38.

2. **Bible Story**

   John 19:25-27.

3. **Memory Passages**

   Eph. 6:2-3: Honor thy father and mother.
   Proverbs 30:17: The eye that mocketh.
   1 Tim. 5:4: Let them learn first to show piety.
   Give to thy parents honor due. *LH* 287:5.
   The 4th Commandment.
   Tables of Duties: To Children; To the Young.

4. **Luther's Small Catechism**

   Questions 52—58.

5. **Liturgy**

   The magnificat. *LH*, p. 43.

C. AIDS TO LEARNING

1. **Visual:** *The Fourth Commandment* from *The Ten Commandments* visualized — 79-101 — 10 filmstrips.
   Tokens of Love — film.
2. **Audio:** "Star Spangled Banner" and "America" — (This Is My Country) RCA, LM-2662 (Stereo LSC-2662).
3. **Objects:** Family pictures of class members.
4. **Workbook:** * *The New Life*, Unit IV.
   * *Learning About God*, Unit VII.

THE OBEDIENT LIFE — Unit 4   41

* *Growing in Faith*, Unit VII.
* *Growing in Grace*, Unit VII.
5. **Bulletin Board:** Clippings and pictures of family life.
6. **Chalkboard:** Summary outline.
7. **Group Activity:** Prepare a special class program for parents.
8. **Music:** Learn the hymn "Oh, Blest the House, Whate'er Befall" for the class program.
9. **Art:** "Christ Taking Leave of His Mother" — Plockhorst.
10. **Library:** "What Is Family Life Education?" from * *Ministry to Families*, by O. Feucht (for teachers).
    O. Feucht, * *Helping Families Through the Church* (for teachers). Elizabeth B. Jones, *God Plans for Happy Families* (Warner). (Gr. 1—4)

D. EVALUATION

Have we made progress in knowledge, attitude, and conduct?

V. Suggestions for Correlations with Other Subjects

A. READING

1. **Silent:** Jer. 35:1-19; Gen. 47:1-12.
2. **Oral:** Prov. 3:1-12; "My Mother," from * *Treasury of Christian Literature*, p. 48.
3. **Choral:** Prov. 15:1-10; "A Prisoner Meets God," from * *Treasury of Christian Literature*, p. 450.

B. ENGLISH

1. **Oral:** Report on one of the silent readings above; or "Why Mothers Grow Gray."
2. **Written:** Original proverbs or riddles.
3. **Vocabulary and Spelling:** paternal, traitor, maternal, obedient, delinquent, dictator.
4. **Handwriting:** a — angry, A — Absalom.

C. SOCIAL SCIENCES

1. **Home and Family Life:** Tract — * *Let Us Show Love*.
2. **Community and Nation:** List community laws; discuss delinquency; decide what the class can do.
3. **History:** Discuss how national problems may have roots in the home.

D. PHYSICAL SCIENCES

1. **Nature Study:** Parents and offspring in the animal world.
2. **Geography:** Parent-child relationships in area being studied.

3. **Health:** Is long life good or bad? How does the 4th Commandment relate to it?
   4. **General Science:** The laws of nature as God's laws; list laws and give examples.

E. ARITHMETIC

Prepare charts and graphs showing how tax money is used. Compare cost of education with costs of crime prevention and damage by vandals.

F. ART

"Whistler's Mother" — James McNeill Whistler.

UNIT
5

THE KIND AND HELPFUL LIFE

Fifth Commandment

•

I. Scope and Importance

Human life is sacred. Humans are the foremost visible creatures. Human individuals are an end, not a means to an end.

"People Come First." Human welfare must have priority rating, even among peoples who are bent on making profits.

Institutions and professions intended to prolong and sweeten human life are on the increase (doctors, nurses, hospitals, welfare agencies, insurance, old age pensions, social security, hospitalization). Many thought war and brutality and cruelty had been entirely and forever eliminated. Unfortunately war and rumors of war persist. Aggressor nations are still much in evidence. Murder and manslaughter statistics are disturbing. Hatred and the war spirit are artificially enflamed. Jealousy and the spirit of revenge are deeply rooted in the human heart. The Good Samaritan spirit requires long and persistent cultivation. What shall we think and say about race suicide?

"Briefly, God's purpose here is to have all persons protected, set free, and enabled to live peaceable lives in the presence of the injustice and violence of all men. This commandment is likewise a wall, a fortress of defense, about our neighbor to protect him in his liberty and to guard him from bodily harm and suffering." (LLC)

II. Aim

A. KNOWLEDGE

Insight, understanding: Foster thinking which leads to clear, correct, vivid ideas on our duty to preserve, lengthen, and sweeten human life by thoughts, desires, words, and programs of action. Develop Biblical concept of "killing." Provide guidance in selection of a calling or profession which is in conformity with this commandment. Familiarize with related vocabulary. Memorize thoroughly quotable memory materials.

B. ATTITUDE

Foster feeling of high regard for human life, its safety and well-being. Develop feeling of sympathy for sick, weak, helpless, crippled, handicapped. Create desire to do something about it.

Aim to develop feeling of remorse and shame for failure to be more active in neighborly enterprises; for cherishing hatred and revenge against playmates. Show need of Jesus. Strengthen desire to do something that helps to eliminate human suffering (nurse, doctor). Foster desire to be helpful, kind, neighborly, Christlike, peace-loving. Sensitize the conscience in matters of others' feelings. Create right group morale.

C. HABITS, SKILLS

Train in observance of health rules and first aid skills; provide practice in "making up" after a quarrel. Train in the technique of a group service project aimed at making life more bearable and pleasant for invalids, shut-ins, aged, hospital patients, etc. Habituate in clean, healthy outdoor sports and leisure-time recreational activities.

THE KIND AND HELPFUL LIFE – Unit 5

D. ANTICIPATED OUTCOMES IN TERMS OF "GOOD-SAMARITAN" CHARACTERS

Boys and girls who are actively kind, helpful, sympathetic, for Jesus' sake. Young people who have time and money to do good to all men especially to those who are of the household of faith. Adult men and women who will not callously pass by on the other side but welcome opportunities to show neighborliness in their community for Jesus' sake. Adults who are known as peacemakers.

III. Curriculum Material

A. BIBLE STUDIES

DATE USED

    *Jesus Befriends Those Whom the Doctor Gave Up. *Luke 17:11-16.*

    *Jesus a Friend to Employers and Employees. *Matt. 8:5-13.*

    *A Little Brother – But Big Enough to Forgive. *Gen. 45:1-15.*

    *Shame! They Gnashed Their Teeth on Him. *Acts 7:54-60.*

    *Why Is Thy Countenance Fallen? *Gen. 4:1-8.*

    *An Uncle Comes to the Rescue of His Nephew. *Gen. 14:12-16.*

    *The Life of an Enemy Is Spared. *1 Sam. 11:12-15.*

    Agree with Thine Adversary Quickly. *Matt. 5:21-26.*

    Capital Punishment Demanded by God. *Num. 35:30-34.*

    *A Case of Indirect Murder. *2 Sam. 11:14-17.*

    *Penalty Fits the Crime. *Ex. 21:18-21.*

    Safety First. *Deut. 22:8.*

    *Remorse and Suicide. *Matt. 27:1-5.*

    Too Ready with the Sword. *Matt. 26:47-56.*

    *They Made Their Lives Bitter. *(Ex. 1–2) Ex. 1:7-14.*

    *A Father Grieved Nigh Unto Death. *Gen. 37:29-36.*

    *The Kind and Helpful Foreigner. *Luke 10:25-37.*

    *Show Kindness to Bird and Beast. *Deut. 22:6-8.*

B. LUTHER'S SMALL CATECHISM

Questions 59, 60.

C. MEMORY MATERIAL
1. Bible Texts

GRADE

1   Be ye kind one to another, tenderhearted, forgiving one another, even as God for Christ's sake hath forgiven you. *Eph. 4:32.*

2   All they that take the sword shall perish with the sword. *Matt. 26:52.* (2)

3   Be ye angry, and sin not; let not the sun go down upon your wrath. *Eph. 4:26.*

4   If ye forgive not men their trespasses, neither will your Father forgive your trespasses. *Matt. 6:15.* (3)

       Whosoever hateth his brother is a murderer; and ye know that no murderer hath eternal life abiding in him. *1 John 3:15.* (4)

5   Whoso sheddeth man's blood, by man shall his blood be shed; for in the image of God made He man. *Gen. 9:6.* (5)

       Blessed are the meek; for they shall inherit the earth. Blessed are the merciful; for they shall obtain mercy. Blessed are the peacemakers; for they shall be called the children of God. *Matt. 5:5, 7, 9.* (5)

6   Agree with thine adversary quickly, whiles thou art in the way with him, lest at any time the adversary deliver thee to the judge, and the judge deliver thee to the officer, and thou be cast into prison. *Matt. 5:25.*

       Out of the heart proceed evil thoughts, murders, adulteries, fornications, thefts, false witness, blasphemies. *Matt. 15:19.* (6)

7   Dearly beloved, avenge not yourselves, but rather give place unto wrath; for it is written, Vengeance is Mine; I will repay, saith the Lord. *Rom. 12:19.* (7)

       I say unto you, That whosoever is angry with his brother without a cause shall be in danger of the judgment. *Matt. 5:22.*

8   If thine enemy hunger, feed him; if he thirst, give him drink; for in so doing, thou shalt heap coals of fire on his head. *Rom. 12:20.* (4)

       He (the government) beareth not the sword in vain; for he is the minister of God, a revenger to execute wrath upon him that doeth evil. *Rom. 13:4.*

2. Luther's Small Catechism

1–2   The Fifth Commandment. Expl. 3–8.

6–8   The Fifth Petition.

7–8   Table of Duties: To All in Common.

THE KIND AND HELPFUL LIFE — Unit 5

3. Hymns

GRADE

1–2 Jesus, Savior, wash away
All that has been wrong today;
Help me every day to be
Good and gentle, more like Thee.   LH 653:2

3–4 In sinful wrath thou shalt not kill
Nor hate nor render ill for ill;
Be patient and of gentle mood,
And to thy foe do thou good.
Have mercy, Lord!   LH 287:6

5–6 Give me a faithful heart,
   Likeness to Thee,
That each departing day
   Henceforth may see
Some work of love begun,
Some deed of kindness done,
Some wanderer sought and won,
   Something for Thee.   LH 403:3

7–8 Order my footsteps by Thy Word
   And make my heart sincere;
Let sin have no dominion, Lord,
   But keep my conscience clear.   LH 416:2

4. Prayers

Forgive, we beseech Thee, O Lord, our enemies and them that despitefully use us, and so change their hearts that they may walk with us in meekness and peace; through Jesus Christ, Thy Son, our Lord. Amen. (*LH*, p. 104, For Our Enemies)

Collects for 13th Sunday after Trinity; *LH*, p. 104, No. 27; p. 105, No. 31; p. 105, No. 36; p. 109, No. 69; The Morning Prayer; The Evening Prayer; The Litany (*LH*, p. 110).

Teacher and pupils make and use their own original prayers.

D. SUMMARY OUTLINE FOR THE CHALKBOARD

Human life is sacred.

It is a *sin*
   to destroy, shorten, or embitter human life
   to take, or plan to take, revenge
   to bear a grudge against anyone
   to hate anyone
   to fail to help and befriend anyone in need.
     Have mercy, Lord!

Let us as children of our heavenly Father cheerfully
   help and befriend the needy
   be always ready to make up

be kind even to the unkind
cooperate actively to protect, lengthen, and sweeten human life
seek peace at home and abroad.
All for Jesus' sake! And in imitation of Jesus!

IV. Instructional Methods and Materials

A. PROBLEM AND APPROACH
Have you ever seen a fatal car accident? Whose fault was it?

B. SUGGESTED TEACHING UNIT

1. **Devotion**

    Hymn: That Man a Godly Life Might Live. *LH* 287:1-6.
    Scripture Reading: James 4.
    Prayer: Savior, Thy Dying Love. *LH* 403:1-3.

2. **Bible Story**

    Luke 10:25-37.

3. **Memory Passages**

    Eph. 4:32: Be ye kind one to another.
    Romans 12:10-21: Dearly beloved, avenge not yourselves.
    Matt. 5:5-9: Blessed are the meek.
    In sinful wrath thou shalt not kill. *LH* 287:6.
    The 5th Commandment.
    The 5th Petition.

4. **Luther's Small Catechism**

    Questions 59—60.

5. **Liturgy**

    The Litany. *LH* p. 110.

C. AIDS TO LEARNING

1. **Visual:** *The Fifth Commandment* from *The Ten Commandments* visualized — 79-101 — 10 filmstrips.
    Overture — film.
    Problems of Living with Others — 79-693 — filmstrip.
    The Good Samaritan — 79-614 — filmstrip.
    Act of Faith — film.
2. **Audio:** "Battle Hymn of the Republic" — (This Is My Country) RCA, LM-2662.
3. **Objects:** Red Cross symbol; basket of food.
4. **Workbook:** * *The New Life,* Unit V.
    * *Learning About God,* Unit VII.

THE KIND AND HELPFUL LIFE – Unit 5

* *Growing in Faith,* Unit VII.
* *Growing in Grace,* Unit VII.
* *Growing in Christ,* Unit 5.

5. **Bulletin Board:** Pictures and clippings related to personal injury and/or death.
6. **Chalkboard:** Summary outline.
7. **Group Activity:** Visit police station to learn about traffic laws, safety, law enforcement; visit auto junk yard to view car damaged in accident.
8. **Music:** The Order of Morning Worship. *LH,* p. 5.
9. **Art:** Safety posters; accident prevention charts; pictures and posters relating to the positive side of the 5th Commandment.
10. **Library:** *The Cross and the Caduceus* (Lutheran Medical Mission Association).
    Maud Petersham, *Joseph and His Brothers* (Macmillan). (Gr. 3—5)
    Gladys Stump, Six Dreams and a Golden Collar (Pacific). (Gr. 4—6)

D. EVALUATION

Are we more concerned about the welfare of others? Have we become more careful in thought, word, and deed?

V. Suggestions for Correlations with Other Subjects

A. READING

1. **Silent:** 2 Sam. 11:12-17; Deut. 22:6-8; Rom. 12:1-5.
2. **Oral:** Luke 10:25-37.
3. **Choral:** "Duty Mine," from * *Treasury of Christian Literature,* p. 420; dramatize.

B. ENGLISH

1. **Oral:** Report on silent readings above; recitation — "Duty Mine," from * *Treasury of Christian Literature,* p. 425.
2. **Written:** Original story about a helpful person.
3. **Vocabulary and Spelling:** philanthropy, precaution, sanitary, injurious.
4. **Handwriting:** D — David.

C. SOCIAL SCIENCES

1. **Home and Family Life:** Show love at home; observe the family, evaluate its actions, improve.
2. **Community and Nation:** The Red Cross; Community Fund; Walther League "Inasmuch" program.
3. **History:** the Red Cross Story; Blue Cross, Blue Shield.

D. PHYSICAL SCIENCES

1. **Nature Study:** Discuss nature as a community of living things (plant and animal ecology).
2. **Geography:** Providing for orphans, aged.
3. **Health:** Physical fitness program; first aid; hygiene in home and community.
4. **General Science:** Recent advances in medical science; increasing the life expectancy through science.

E. ARITHMETIC

Develop problems on kinds and frequency of accidents.

F. ART

"A Helping Hand" — Renouf.

G. MUSIC

Alas, and Did My Savior Bleed. *LH* 154.
Beati Pauperes. *LH* 660.

UNIT
6

THE CHASTE AND DECENT LIFE

Sixth Commandment

•

I. Scope and Importance

One out of every six marriages is prematurely dissolved in America. The home shows marks of disintegration. Our industrial, mechanized, urbanized civilization threatens the very existence of the home life. The strength of state and of church lie in the home.

An alarming increase of juvenile delinquency in the United States was noted by J. Edgar Hoover as long ago as 1943, when he cited statistics listing increases of arrests among girls alone which on various counts rose by as much as 124 percent within a year. This increase in girl delinquency may be due at various times to economic and social conditions, but it may also reflect an emphasis in public education on self-expression rather than self-discipline.

"Significantly He established it (marriage) as the first of all institutions, and with it in view He did not create man and woman alike. God's purpose, as is plain, was not that they should live a life of wickedness, but that they might be true to each other, beget children, and nourish and rear them to His glory.

"Since there is among us such a shameful and vile mixture of all forms of vice and lewdness, this commandment is directed against every form of unchastity, under any name. Not only the actual deed is forbidden, but also every prompting and incentive to it. Heart, lips, and the whole body must be chaste and give no occasion, no help or suggestion to unchastity." (LLC)

II. Aim

A. KNOWLEDGE

Develop thinking that leads to clear, vivid, and correct ideas about marriage, decency, chastity, adultery. Answer clearly the question: Am I a sinner and do I need Jesus? Develop correct ideas on proper boy-girl, husband-wife relationships. Identify "worldly" and permissible amusements. Familiarize with related vocabulary. Memorize selections as given in memory materials.

B. ATTITUDE

Sharpen the conscience on matters of boy-girl relationships; on personal purity; foster humble penitent attitude. Create felt need: Jesus, I need Thee every hour. Foster taste for clean fun. Strengthen will and determination to say NO under certain circumstances. Create ideals for young womanhood, manhood, and ideal home life. Stimulate the desire of youths for ideal youth companionships. Foster right group morale.

C. HABITS, SKILLS

Train children in the habit of being respectful to the other sex. Chaste, clean, gentlemanly and ladylike language and conduct. Break crude, coarse, boorish habits of behavior and speech. Provide training in planning and carrying out clean Christian fun and sociability. Accustom children to parties, games, and entertainments in which mother, father, and the pastor may joyfully participate. Train in refined manners.

D. ANTICIPATED OUTCOMES IN TERMS OF CLEAN, STRONG, CHRISTIAN CHARACTERS

Boys who are boys and full of fun, but who know what is proper and behave accordingly. Girls who are clean and healthy

THE CHASTE AND DECENT LIFE — Unit 6

in mind and body, who have a taste for innocent fun. Young people who avoid the typical pleasures of the world and who can have a good time without hurting their conscience. Eventually, brides who are entitled to a white veil and grooms who are happy in their first love. Husbands and wives who can happily and gratefully celebrate their 25th, 50th, and if it please God, their 60th wedding anniversary.

III. Curriculum Material

A. BIBLE STUDIES

DATE USED

....	*It Is Not Good that Man Should Be Alone. *Gen. 2:18-24.*
....	*How Can I Do This Great Wickedness? *Gen. 39:1-13.*
....	Blessed Are the Pure in Heart. *Matt. 5:1-9.*
....	*The Holy Family: Mary, Joseph, and Jesus. *Matt. 1:18-25.*
....	Let Jesus Attend the Whole Wedding Celebration. *John 2:1-11.*
....	*The Tragedy of the Triangle (Uriah). *2 Sam. 11:1-21.*
....	Irreconcilable Opposites: Unclean Hands and Pure Hearts. *Psalm 24:3-6.*
....	Tears of Repentance. *Ps. 51.*
....	*Dancing, Dining, Adultery, and Murder. *Mark 6:17-28.*
....	Mixed Marriages Are Disapproved (Isaac). *Gen. 24:1-9*
....	Woe to Those Who Forget *Gen. 16:13! Is. 29:15.*
....	Jesus Makes a Happy Home (Cana). *John 2:1-11.*
....	An Engagement Is Binding (Joseph). *Matt. 1:18-20.*
....	Against Foul and Coarse Language. *Eph. 4:22-32.*
....	A Study in Contrasts. *Gal. 5:16-25.*
....	Mutual Love of Husband and Wife. *Eph. 5:22-33.*
....	Obtain Parental Consent Before Engagement! *Gen. 24:49-59.*
....	Believers Should Marry Believers. *Gen. 27:46—28:9.*

B. LUTHER'S SMALL CATECHISM

Questions 61—65.

C. MEMORY MATERIAL

1. Bible Texts

GRADE

1   Create in me a clean heart, O God. *Ps. 51:10.*

GRADE
2   How, then, can I do this great wickedness and sin against God? *Gen. 39:9.*

3   My son, if sinners entice thee, consent thou not. *Prov. 1:10.* (3)

4   Whatsoever things are pure ... whatsoever things are of good report; if there be any virtue, and if there be any praise, think on these things. *Phil. 4:8.*

5   They are no more twain, but one flesh. What therefore God hath joined together, let not man put asunder. *Matt. 19:6.*
    Whoremongers and adulterers God will judge. *Heb. 13:4.*
    It is a shame even to speak of those things which are done of them in secret. *Eph. 5:12.* (5)

6   Let no corrupt communication proceed out of your mouth, but that which is good to the use of edifying, that it may minister grace unto the hearers. *Eph. 4:29.* (6)
    Flee also youthful lusts. *2 Tim. 2:22.* (7)

7   Know ye not that your body is the temple of the Holy Ghost, which is in you, which ye have of God, and ye are not your own? *1 Cor. 6:19.* (7)
    Whosoever shall put away his wife, except it be for fornication, and shall marry another, committeth adultery. *Matt. 19:9.* (7)
    Out of the heart proceed evil thoughts, murders, adulteries, fornications, thefts, false witness, blasphemies. *Matt. 15:19.*
    As the church is subject unto Christ, so let the wives be to their own husbands in everything. Husbands, love your wives, even as Christ also loved the church and gave Himself for it. *Eph. 5:24, 25.*

8   Fornication and all uncleanness or covetousness, let it not be once named among you, as becometh saints; neither filthiness nor foolish talking nor jesting, which are not convenient, but rather giving of thanks. *Eph. 5:3, 4.* (8)
    Flee fornication. *1 Cor. 6:18.* (8)
    Abstain from fleshly lusts, which war against the soul. *1 Peter 2:11.*

2. *Luther's Small Catechism*
1–2   The Sixth Commandment. Expl. 3—8.
5–8   The Sixth Petition.
7–8   Table of Duties: To Wives — To Husbands.

3. *Hymns*
1–2   Oh, blest that house where faith ye find,
      And all within have set their mind
      To trust their God and serve Him still
      And do in all His holy will!   LH 625:2

THE CHASTE AND DECENT LIFE – Unit 6

GRADE

3–4   Destroy in me the lust of sin,
From all impureness make me clean.
Oh, grant me power and strength, my God,
To strive against my flesh and blood!   LH 398:2

5–6   Be faithful to thy marriage vows,
Thy heart give only to thy spouse;
Thy life keep pure, and lest thou sin,
Use temperance and discipline.
Have mercy, Lord!   LH 287:7

7–8   Let us ever walk with Jesus,
  Follow His example pure,
Flee the world, which would deceive us
  And to sin our souls allure.
Ever in His footsteps treading,
  Body here, yet soul above,
  Full of faith and hope and love,
Let us do the Father's bidding.
Faithful Lord, abide with me;
Savior, lead, I follow Thee.   LH 409:1

4. *Prayers*

Forgive, O holy Lord, my impure thoughts, my unchaste words. Grant, O gracious God, that I may, in Thy strength, lead a chaste and decent life in word and deed, for Jesus' sake. Amen.

D. SUMMARY OUTLINE FOR THE CHALKBOARD

Boy-girl; young man-young woman; husband-wife relationships.

It is *sinful*
    to have impure thoughts and desires
    to use indecent language
    to act or dress suggestively
    to break an engagement or marriage vow
    to fail to do what this Commandment calls for.

    Have mercy, Lord!

Let us as redeemed followers of Jesus strive to lead a chaste and decent life and therefore
    use God's Word regularly and purposefully
    pray fervently and frequently
    work industriously
    be temperate
    avoid bad company, indecent pictures, filthy books, indecent amusements
    create a taste for Christian fellowship, good pictures, good literature
    remember that our body is a temple of the Holy Spirit.
        All for Jesus' sake.

IV. Instructional Methods and Materials

A. PROBLEM AND APPROACH

Have you read or heard about "juvenile delinquency"? What is it? What causes it? Can a well-mannered boy or girl be a delinquent?

B. SUGGESTED TEACHING UNIT

1. **Devotion**

    Hymn: That Man a Godly Life Might Live. *LH* 287:1-7.
    Scripture Reading: Matt. 1:18-25.
    Prayer: Extempore; or * *Teen-Agers Pray*, p. 41.

2. **Bible Story**

    John 2:1-11.

3. **Memory Passages**

    Eph. 5:3-4: Fornication and all uncleanness.
    1 Cor. 6:19: Know ye not that your body.
    Eph. 4:29: Let no corrupt communication.
    Be faithful to thy marriage vows. *LH* 287:7.
    The 6th Commandment.
    Table of Duties: To Wives; To Husbands.

4. **Luther's Small Catechism**

    Questions 61—65.

5. **Liturgy**

    The Offertory. *LH*, p. 12.

C. AIDS TO LEARNING

1. **Visual:** *The Sixth Commandment* from *The Ten Commandments* visualized — 79-101 — 10 filmstrips.
    The Prodigal Son — 79-214 — filmstrip.
    Preparation for Marriage series — 79-009 — five filmstrips on dating and sex.

2. **Audio:** "Come, Holy Spirit, God and Lord" — *LH* 224 — (Great Lutheran Hymns) LR, RF-6903.
    "Jesu, Joy of Man's Desiring" — (Inspiration — Great Music for Chorus and Orchestra) RCA, LM-2593. Also Columbia ML-5364.
    "Jesus, Priceless Treasure" — *LH* 347 — (Let the Earth Rejoice) KFUO, HA 61.

3. **Objects:** Exhibit engagement and wedding rings.

4. **Workbook:** * *The New Life,* Unit VI
    * *Learning About God,* Unit VII.
    * *Growing in Faith,* Unit VII.

THE CHASTE AND DECENT LIFE – Unit 6

* *Growing in Grace,* Unit VII.
* *Growing in Christ,* Unit 6.

5. **Bulletin Board:** Parents' wedding picture; pictures and clippings about weddings.
6. **Chalkboard:** Summary outline.
7. **Group Activity:** Attend a church wedding.
8. **Music:** Hymns appropriate for a wedding.
9. **Art:** "Marriage at Cana" — Hofmann.
10. **Library:** A. Schmieding. * *Sex in Childhood and Youth,* for teachers. Hugh C. Warner. * *Sex Education Booklets.*

D. EVALUATION

How well did we reach our goals? What still needs improvement? What topics need further development?

V. Suggestions for Correlations with Other Subjects

A. READING

1. **Silent:** Eph. 5; Gen. 2:18-25; Eph. 4:17-32.
2. **Oral:** "Wedding in India," from * *Treasury of Christian Literature,* p. 92; Mark 16:17-28.
3. **Choral:** Lord, Who at Cana's Wedding Feast. *LH* 620.

B. ENGLISH

1. **Oral:** Report on silent readings above; how to introduce a friend.
2. **Written:** Report on a church wedding observed; "going steady."
3. **Vocabulary and Spelling:** engagement, wedding, divorce, courtship, nuptial.
4. **Handwriting:** l — love, L — Love.

C. SOCIAL SCIENCES

1. **Home and Family:** Good manners in the home, between boys and girls; What causes delinquency?
2. **Community and Nation:** Junior Walther League; Should young people hang around the corner drugstore? Why?
3. **History:** Family life in the period being studied.

D. PHYSICAL SCIENCES

1. **Nature Study:** Plant and animal reproduction.
2. **Geography:** Family in the area studied.
3. **Health:** Why do many states require a doctor's certificate before issuing a marriage license?
4. **General Science:** Discuss the laws of heredity; relate to Genesis 1.

E. ARITHMETIC

Develop problems in the four fundamentals using statistics on family size, marriage, divorce.

F. ART

Sketch with pencil or charcoal a family scene.

G. MUSIC

Learn to sing the hymn "Oh, Blest the House Whate'er Befall." *LH 625.*

UNIT
7

THE HONEST LIFE

Seventh Commandment

•

I. Scope and Importance

"Next to our own persons and our wedded companions our temporal treasures are dearest to us." (LLC)

The right way of obtaining property and the right way of using property is here under consideration. The distinction between mine and thine, between public and private property. The majority of court cases grow out of violations of this law.

In the midst of an industrial community, where many live by trade and commerce, Luther's words still apply: "Insist in an especial manner on such Commandments or other parts as seem to be most of all misunderstood or neglected by your people. It will, for example, be necessary that you should enforce with the utmost earnestness the Seventh Commandment, which treats of stealing, when you are teaching workmen, dealers, and even farmers and servants, inasmuch as many of these are guilty of various dishonest and thievish practices." (LSC, Preface)

II. Aim

A. KNOWLEDGE

Insight, understanding: Aim to stimulate observation and thinking which will develop clear, vivid, and correct ideas about property rights and property responsibilities; clarify the concept of stealing from man and from God. Teach recognition of sin and of virtue with reference to property, wages, salaries, stewardship of money. Familiarize with related vocabulary. Memorize for use (for quoting) suggested memory materials.

B. ATTITUDE

Sharpen the conscience on the taking or withholding of little things. Foster a willingness to confess sins of dishonesty to God and to God's representatives. Stimulate the feeling of gratitude for having a Savior from sin. Be in dead earnest. Your own attitudes and values will imperceptibly carry over. Appeal to their conscience. Sin is terrible. The faith-born practice of stewardship of money and property is glorious! Foster right group morale. Aim to have these attitudes to carry over to the playground, the home, the church, the community.

C. HABITS, SKILLS

Willful behavior: make an end to any roughing in the school. Train in taking good care of own and school property. Inaugurate a program of property improvement in and around school, on the church premises. Get a school mission offering under way. Put a stop to wasteful habits. Train in habits of thrift, industry, and careful spending; returning promptly and in good condition when they borrow. Train in returning found articles. Train in proportionate giving. Encourage tithing.

D. ANTICIPATED OUTCOME IN TERMS OF SANCTIFIED CHARACTERS

Boys and girls who are honest in all their affairs; who take good care of their own and other people's property; who are not afraid of work. Young people in whom parents rejoice, and adults who make an honest living, support themselves, and share with others; and who do not rob God. Christ-centered personalities. Jesus-like characters with reference to material possessions.

THE HONEST LIFE – Unit 7

III. Curriculum Material

A. BIBLE STUDIES

DATE USED

- *The Robbers Near Jericho. *Luke 10:25-37.*
- *God Hates Thievery! (Achan.) *Joshua 7:16-26.*
- They Brought More Than Enough! *Ex. 36:1-7.*
- *Judas, the Thief. *John 12:1-9.*
- *Gehazi's Fraud. *2 Kings 5:20-24.*
- *Abraham's Generosity in the Interest of Peace. *Gen. 13:1-12.*
- A "Big Brother" Comes to the Rescue (Abraham and Lot). *Gen. 14:12-16.*
- Admonition to the Rich. *James 5:1-4.*
- Good Stewards are Happy and Blessed. *Deut. 26:11-19.*
- Shrewd Stewardship. *Luke 16:1-9.*
- On Contentment and on Duty of the Rich. *1 Tim. 6:6-10, 17-19.*
- Will a Man Rob God? *Mal. 3:8-12.*
- Talents and Faithful Stewardship of Money. *Matt. 25:14-30.*
- A Glorious Promise to the Liberal. *Is. 58:8-12.*
- Practical Christianity. *James 2:14-17.*
- Helping Strangers in a Strange Land. *Gen. 46:31-47—47:6.*
- Upon the First Day of the Week. *1 Cor. 16:1, 2.*
- God Frowns on Laziness. *Prov. 13:1-11.*
- What is Meant by Restitution? *Luke 19:1-10.*

B. LUTHER'S SMALL CATECHISM

Questions 66, 67.

C. MEMORY MATERIAL

1. Bible Texts

GRADE

1   If any would not work, neither should he eat. *2 Thess. 3:10.* (2)

2   The wicked borroweth and payeth not again. *Ps. 37:21.* (2)

3   Whoso is partner with a thief hateth his own soul. *Prov. 29:24.* (3)

4   Whatsoever ye would that men should do to you, do ye even so to them. *Matt. 7:12.*

GRADE

   Give to him that asketh thee, and from him that would borrow of thee turn not thou away. *Matt. 5:42.* (3)

5 He that hath pity upon the poor lendeth unto the Lord; and that which he hath given will He pay him again. *Prov. 19:17.* (5)

   Out of the heart proceed evil thoughts, murders, adulteries, fornications, thefts, false witness, blasphemies. *Matt. 15:19.*

6 To do good and to communicate forget not; for with such sacrifices God is well pleased. *Heb. 13:16.* (5)

   Ye shall do no unrighteousness in judgment, in meteyard, in weight, or in measure. *Lev. 19:35.*

7 Let him that stole, steal no more; but rather let him labor, working with his hands the thing which is good, that he may have to give to him that needeth. *Eph. 4:28.*

   If thou meet thine enemy's ox or his ass going astray, thou shalt surely bring it back to him again. *Ex. 23:4.*

8 Woe unto him that buildeth his house by unrighteousness and his chambers by wrong; that useth his neighbor's service without wages and giveth him not for his work! *Jer. 22:13.* (8)

   Charity envieth not . . . seeketh not her own. *1 Cor. 13:4, 5.*

2. *Luther's Small Catechism*

1–2 The Seventh Commandment. Expl. 3–8.
6–8 The Fourth Petition.

3. *Hymns*

1–2 Take my silver and my gold,
   Not a mite would I withhold;
   Take my intellect and use
   Every power as Thou shalt choose.   *LH 400:4*

3–4 Jesus, Jesus, only Jesus,
    Can my heartfelt longing still.
   Lo, I pledge myself to Jesus
    What He wills alone to will.
   For my heart, which He hath filled,
   Ever cries, Lord, as Thou wilt.   *LH 348:1*

5–6 Steal not; all usury abhor
   Nor wring their life-blood from the poor,
   But open wide thy loving hand
   To all the poor in the land.
    Have mercy, Lord!   *LH 287:8*

THE HONEST LIFE — Unit 7

GRADE
7–8

> And let me with all men,
>   As far as in me lieth,
> In peace and friendship live.
> And if Thy gift supplieth
>   Great wealth and honor fair,
> Then this refuse me not,
> That naught be mingled there
>   Of goods unjustly got.
>
> LH 395:5

4. Prayers

Forgive, O holy God, where we have ever taken our neighbor's money or goods, or obtained them by false ware or dealing. With Thy gracious assistance, may we henceforth help him to improve his property and business. Amen.

Lord God, Thou Giver of all good gifts, we are unworthy of any good things; yet, for Jesus' sake, we pray: Give us this day our daily bread. Grant us everything that we need for the support and wants of the body. Lead us to know and remember that these blessings come from Thee. Help us to receive them with thanksgiving. We ask it for Jesus' sake. Amen.

LH 438:1-5; 439:1-6; p. 107, No. 48, For Grace to Use Our Gifts; p. 106, No. 42–45, Thanksgiving.

Collects for the 9th Sunday after Trinity.

D. SUMMARY OUTLINE FOR THE CHALKBOARD

Ownership: Private and Public Property; Stewardship.

It is a *sin*

  to take other people's property

  a) by force: robbery, kidnaping, extortion, blackmailing, racketeering

  b) secretly: theft, forgery, embezzlement, shoplifting

  c) fraudulently: false pretenses, under-paying, under-working, gypping, hooking

  d) by chance: gambling, betting, raffle, slot machine

  e) by borrowing and not returning; installment buying and not paying

  to destroy or neglect property; waste; squander

  to idolize property; regard it as an end instead of a means to an end

  to fail to regard or use property as God requires.

   Have mercy, Lord!

  Let us as God's children and faithful stewards
    acquire property by industry and thrift (ant, bee, beaver)

regard our incomes and possessions as a trust
use them as good and faithful stewards
- a) to provide ourselves and others with necessities
- b) to help build God's Kingdom (church, missions, schools, colleges)
- c) to alleviate human suffering (charity).

All for Jesus sake!

IV. Instructional Methods and Materials

A. PROBLEM AND APPROACH

What do you really own? How did you get it? Is it right to own something? Dishonesty is a growing problem in our country. What can we do about it?

B. SUGGESTED TEACHING UNIT

1. Devotion

Hymn: That Man a Godly Life Might Live. *LH* 287:1-8.
Scripture Reading: Matt. 25:14-30
Prayer: * *Teen-Agers Pray*, p. 42.

2. Bible Story

Joshua 7:16-26.

3. Memory Passages

Eph. 4:28: Let him that stole.
Jer. 22:13: Woe to him that buildeth his house.
2 Thess. 3:10: If any would not work.
Steal not; all ursury abhor. *LH* 287:8.
The 7th Commandment.
The 4th Petition.
Table of Duties: To Servants.

4. Luther's Small Catechism

Questions 66—67.

5. Liturgy

The Litany. *LH* p. 110.

C. AIDS TO LEARNING

1. **Visual:** *The Seventh Commandment* from *The Ten Commandments* visualized — 79-101 — 10 filmstrips.
   Spending Money — film.

THE HONEST LIFE – Unit 7

    Ahab, The Pouting King — film.
    Learning About Money — 79-5739 — sound filmstrip.
2. **Audio:** "From God Shall Naught Divide Me" — *LH* 393 — (A Mighty Fortress) Word, W-4017 (Stereo WST-9003).
3. **Objects:** Coins and bills in various denominations; repaired toys.
4. **Workbook:** * *The New Life,* Unit VII.
    * * *Learning About God,* Unit VII.
    * * *Growing in Faith,* Unit VII.
    * * *Growing in Grace,* Unit VII.
    * * *Growing in Christ,* Unit 7.
5. **Bulletin Board:** Pictures and clippings about robbery, vandalism.
6. **Chalkboard:** Summary outline.
7. **Group Activity:** Collect and repair broken toys and other objects.
8. **Music:** Prepare to sing hymn *LH* 287 at a parents' meeting.
9. **Art:** "Man with a Hoe" — Millet.
10. **Library:** S. Roth and W. Kramer, * *The Church Through the Ages.* Luther's Large Catechism.

D. EVALUATION

Have we developed the concept of money as one of God's gifts? To be earned and used in His service?

V. Suggestions for Correlations with Other Subjects

A. READING
1. **Silent:** Prov. 13:1-11; Luke 19:1-10.
2. **Oral:** "So You're Going to High School," from * *Treasury of Christian Literature,* page 19.
3. **Choral:** Take My Life and Let It Be. *LH* 400.

B. ENGLISH
1. **Oral:** Report on silent readings above; How I earn and use money.
2. **Written:** Misleading advertising is stealing.
3. **Vocabulary and Spelling:** robbery, bribery, embezzle, lottery, stewardship.
4. **Handwriting:** m — money, M — Mammon.

C. SOCIAL SCIENCES
1. **Home and Family Life:** The family budget; allowances.
2. **Community and Nation:** The unemployment problem; equal work opportunities for all.
3. **History:** The story of banks and banking; savings and loan associations.

D. PHYSICAL SCIENCES
1. **Nature Study:** Thrift in the animal kingdom.
2. **Geography:** Living standards around the world.
3. **Health:** Work and your health; physical fitness.
4. **General Science:** Automation — good or bad?

E. ARITHMETIC
Charts and graphs on unemployment; keeping a bank account; writing checks and balancing accounts.

F. ART
"The Gleaners" — Millet.

G. MUSIC
The Litany. *LH*, p. 110.

UNIT
8

THE CHARITABLE LIFE

Eighth Commandment

•

I. Scope and Importance

If you lose your money, you lose much. If you lose your reputation, you lose more. If you lose God, you lose all. Sins of the tongue are vicious. A good reputation is a priceless possession.

Keep watch on your words, my darlings; For words are
 wonderful things.
They are sweet like the bees' fresh honey, Like the bees they
 have terrible stings.
They can bless like the warm, glad sunshine And brighten
 a lonely life;
They can cut in the strife of anger Like a cruel two-edged knife.
Keep them back if they are cold and cruel, Under bar and lock
 and seal,
For the wounds they make, my darlings, Are always slow to heal.
May peace guard your lips forever; From the time of your
 early youth
May the words that you daily utter Be the beautiful words
 of truth.

Institutions and individuals spend thousands to be favorably and well known.

This commandment is of special importance to persons who appear in court: judges, lawyers, witnesses, accusers and accused.

"Knowledge of sin does not entitle the right to judge it. Though I see and know my neighbor's sin, I am not commanded to report it. If I recklessly pass sentence upon him, I commit a greater sin than he. Concerning that sin which you recognize, you must maintain silence and secrecy until rightful authority to judge and punish has been conferred upon you." (LLC)

Matthew Eighteen! How much better social relations in the home, among relatives, in the neighborhood, in school, in the congregation, among nations, if this procedure were always followed.

II. Aim

A. KNOWLEDGE

Insight, understanding: Develop clear, vivid, correct thinking in matters of "witnessing." Recognize value of a good reputation. Increase familiarity with related vocabulary. Thoroughly memorize for use choice selections from the memory materials.

B. ATTITUDE

Develop feeling of shame and guilt for sins against this commandment. Cause to blush with shame for sins of omission: Failing to say the right thing at the right time in the right way. Awaken felt need for cleansing grace of God in Christ. Develop appreciation of the Cross and what it stands for. Awake desire, will, and determination to refrain from unethical thinking and uncharitable practices. Create desirable group sentiment, public opinion.

C. HABITS, SKILLS

Develop the habit of speaking favorably of individuals, of nations, races, institutions. Form the habit of refraining from speaking about the shortcomings of others. Practice saying what

THE CHARITABLE LIFE — Unit 8

you mean and meaning what you say. Stamp out tattling in school.

D. ANTICIPATED OUTCOME IN TERMS OF JESUS-LIKE CHARACTERS

Boys and girls who are kind, charitable, disposed to say good things, reluctant to reveal bad things about others. Young men and women who readily recognize rumors, propaganda, gossip and habitually shrug their shoulders at them. Adults who are very fair though frank, who avoid and discourage where they can the custom of gossiping and spreading false and harmful rumors.

III. Curriculum Material

A. BIBLE STUDIES

DATE USED

- *False Witnesses Against Jesus. *Matt. 26:59-61.*
- *Jezebel and Naboth. *1 Kings 21:5-14.*
- *Whence Camest Thou, Gehazi? *2 Kings 5:20-27.*
- *A Malicious Betrayal of a Secret (Doeg). *1 Sam. 22:9-19.*
- *What Money Will Do (Judas). *Matt. 26:14-16.*
- *A Conspiracy of Silence. *1 Sam. 22:6-9.*
- *Shielding Someone Against False Accusations (Jonathan). *1 Sam. 19:1-7.*
- *A Case of "Speaking Well of Him." *Luke 7:1-5.*
- The Tongue Can No Man Tame. But God Can. *James 3.*
- A Soft Answer Turneth Away Wrath. *Proverbs 15:1-18.*
- Deceitful Deception Desperately Despicable. *Jer. 9:1-11.*
- He That Speaketh Lies Shall Not Escape. *Proverbs 19:1-13.*
- The Father of Lies and of Liars. *Gen. 3:1-5.*
- A Son Who Belied His Father (Absalom). *2 Sam. 15:1-6.*
- Whisperers and Backbiters Have Wicked Minds. *Rom. 1:28-32.*
- A Case of Hatred, Slander, and Murder (Haman). *Esther 3:5-15.*

DATE USED

.... Pray for Them Which Despitefully Use You.
Luke 23:32-34.

.... Be Slow to Sit in Judgment on Others. *Rom. 14:1-5.*

.... The Famous Charity Chapter. *1 Cor. 13.*

.... They Flatter with Their Tongues. *Psalm 5:8-10.*

.... How a Queen Opened Her Mouth for the Dumb.
Esther 7:1-10.

.... Brother Must Not Bring Lawsuit Against Brother.
1 Cor. 6:1-8.

.... A Righteous Man Hateth Lying. *Proverbs 13:1-12.* (5)

B. LUTHER'S SMALL CATECHISM

Questions 68, 69.

C. MEMORY MATERIAL

1. Bible Texts

GRADE

1   A false witness shall not be unpunished. *Prov. 19:5.* (4)

2   He that speaketh lies shall not escape. *Prov. 19:5.* (1)

3   Speak not evil one of another, brethren. *James 4:11.* (2)

4   Let none of you imagine evil in your hearts against his neighbor. *Zech. 8:17.* (3)

5   A talebearer revealeth secrets; but he that is of a faithful spirit concealeth the matter. *Prov. 11:13.* (5)
Judge not, and ye shall not be judged; condemn not, and ye shall not be condemned. *Luke 6:37.* (4)

6   Charity shall cover the multitude of sins. *1 Peter 4:8.*
If thy brother shall trespass against thee, go and tell him his fault between thee and him alone. *Matt. 18:15.*

7   Putting away lying, speak every man truth with his neighbor; for we are members one of another. *Eph. 4:25.* (3)
Charity believeth all things, hopeth all things, endureth all things. *1 Cor. 13:7.* (5)

8   Thou givest thy mouth to evil, and thy tongue frameth deceit. Thou sittest and speakest against thy brother; thou slanderest thine own mother's son. These things hast thou done, and I kept silence; thou thoughtest that I was altogether such an one as thyself. But I will reprove thee and set them in order before thine eyes. Now consider this, ye that forget God, lest I tear you in pieces and there be none to deliver. *Ps. 50:19-22.*
Open thy mouth for the dumb in the cause of all such as are appointed to destruction. Open thy mouth, judge righteously, and plead the cause of the poor and needy. *Prov. 31:8, 9.* (6)

THE CHARITABLE LIFE — Unit 8

GRADE

2. Luther's Small Catechism

1–2 The Seventh Commandment. Expl. 3–8.

5–8 The Fifth Petition.

3. Hymns

1–2 Jesus, Savior, wash away
All that has been wrong today;
Help me every day to be
Good and gentle, more like Thee.   *LH 653:2*

3–4 Take my voice and let me sing
Always, only, for my King;
Take my lips and let them be
Filled with messages from Thee.   *LH 400:3*

5–6 Bear not false witness nor belie
Thy neighbor by foul calumny.
Defend his innocence from blame;
With charity hide his shame.
    Have mercy, Lord!   *LH 287:9*

7–8 Oh, let me never speak
    What bounds of truth exceedeth;
Grant that no idle word
    From out my mouth proceedeth;
And then, when in my place
    I must and ought to speak,
My words grant power and grace
    Lest I offend the weak.   *LH 395:3*

4. Prayers

Forgive, O gracious God, where I may have deceitfully belied, betrayed, slandered, or defamed my neighbor. Grant me Thy Holy Spirit, that I may henceforth defend him (her), and always charitably put the best construction on everything. I ask it for Jesus' sake. Amen.

LH pp. 108, 109, Nos. 69, 62, 74, 71. Use appropriate prayers created by teacher and by pupils.

Collect for Gospel of 4th Sunday after Trinity.

D. SUMMARY OUTLINE FOR THE CHALKBOARD

A GOOD REPUTATION — A PRICELESS POSSESSION

    It is a *sin*
        to bear false witness in court (perjury)
        to withhold the truth maliciously
        to slander, insinuate, cast reflections
        to gossip about a person, a family, a race, an institution
        to imagine evil; be unduly suspicious

to betray, reveal secrets, be a tattletale
to be two-faced, hypocritical; to mislead; put on a false front
to make propaganda against anyone; to fail to carry out the positive command.
Have mercy, Lord!

Let us as Christians
defend those who are falsely accused
not judge prematurely; not jump at conclusions
give the accused the benefit of the doubt
speak well or not at all about persons, races, institutions
charitably put the best construction on everything
speak to the offender; say what we mean and mean what we say; be charitable.
For Jesus' sake and in imitation of Jesus.

IV. Instructional Methods and Materials

A. PROBLEM AND APPROACH

Stores, factories, and businesses spend large sums of money for advertising in newspapers and magazines, on radio and television. Why? Is it really worth all the thousands of dollars to be well known?

B. SUGGESTED TEACHING UNIT

1. *Devotion*

Hymn: That Man a Godly Life Might Live. *LH* 287:1-9.
Scripture Reading: 1 Kings 2:5-14.
Prayer: The Morning Prayer. Luther's Small Catechism, p. 22.

2. *Bible Story*

1 Sam. 19:1-7

3. *Memory Passages*

Prov. 19:5: A false witness.
Prov. 11:13: A talebearer revealeth secrets.
Matt. 18:15: If thy brother shall trespass.
Bear not false witness nor belie. *LH* 287:9.
The 8th Commandment.
The 5th Petition.

4. *Luther's Small Catechism*

Questions 68—69.

5. *Liturgy*

Introit for Jubilate Sunday. *LH*, p. 70.

THE CHARITABLE LIFE — Unit 8

C. AIDS TO LEARNING
1. **Visual:** *The Eighth Commandment* from *The Ten Commandments visualized* — 79-101 — 10 filmstrips.
   Turn the Other Cheek — film.
2. **Object:** Diorama of a courtroom; poster.
3. **Workbook:** * *The New Life,* Unit VIII.
   * *Learning About God,* Unit VII.
   * *Growing in Faith,* Unit VII.
   * *Growing in Grace,* Unit VII.
   * *Growing in Christ,* Unit 8.
4. **Bulletin Board:** Pictures and clippings from court scenes; ads from magazines or newspapers.
5. **Chalkboard:** Summary outline.
6. **Group Activity:** Visit a court in session; dramatize a situation that calls for sensitivity to other people's feelings.
7. **Music:** LH 395:3
8. **Art:** Poster — Guard your tongue.
9. **Library:** Maud Petersham, *David* (Macmillan). (Gr. 3—5)
   Joseph and His Brothers (Macmillan). (Gr. 3—5)

D. EVALUATION
Have you changed your attitude toward anyone?

V. Suggestions for Correlations with Other Subjects

A. READING
1. **Silent:** Matt. 26:59-61; 1 Sam. 22:9-19; 1 Sam. 22:6-9.
2. **Oral:** Rom. 1:28-32; Prov. 15:1-18.
3. **Choral:** James 3.

B. ENGLISH
1. **Oral:** Report on silent readings above; report on visit to a courtroom.
2. **Written:** Report on Esther 3:5-15; 3-paragraph composition on the topic "How a Rumor Grows."
3. **Vocabulary and Spelling:** perjury, slander, libel, propaganda, oath.
4. **Handwriting:** s — slander, S — Silence.

C. SOCIAL SCIENCES
1. **Nature Study:** Protective coloring in birds and animals.
2. **Geography:** Is there a "master race"?
3. **Health:** Can slander cause illness? see Prov. 16:24.
4. **General Science:** Can the "scientific method" support truth? see 1 Tim. 6:20.

D. ARITHMETIC

Can figures (numbers) lie?

E. ART

Make a poster about gossiping; make a diorama of a courtroom.

F. MUSIC

Beati Pauperes *LH* 668.

UNIT
9

THE CONTENTED LIFE

Ninth and Tenth Commandments

•

I. Scope and Importance

There is a jewel which no Indian mines
Can buy, no chymic art can counterfeit.
It makes men rich in greatest poverty,
Makes water wine, turns wooden cups to gold,
The homely whistle to sweet music's strain.
Seldom it comes, to few, from Heaven sent,
That much in little, all in naught — *Content.*

"Aequam animam in arduis rebus servare." ("To preserve a steady, unruffled mind in the midst of difficult situations.") That is a Stoic idea. Stoic thinking and secular literature are much concerned about contentment. Avarice, greed, selfishness, covetousness, envy, jealousy — these are the inborn human traits that stand in the way of ideal new social and new economic orders. They cause strife, lawsuits, wars.

"There was need of these commandments because of the fact that under Jewish rule men-servants and maid-servants were not free, as now, to serve for wages at their own pleasure; in body and in all they had they were their master's property, the same as his cattle and other possessions." (LLC)

"Such is human nature that no one of us desires the other to possess as much as himself, and each secures as much as he can, without regard to his neighbor's interests. Yet we want to be thought upright; we dress ourselves up to conceal our roguery. We seek and invent ingenious devices and clever frauds, such as are now daily contrived with cunning skill, under the guise of justice." (LLC)

"Let us understand these commandments to be directed particularly against envy and wretched avarice, God's purpose being to remove the cause and source of our injuries to our neighbor." (LLC)

II. Aim

A. KNOWLEDGE

Follow, identify, and ferret out sin to its innermost source and fountain, the hidden spring of human motivation: Selfishness. Covetousness is sin; Paul: "I had not known sin but by the Law: for I had not known lust except the Law had said: Thou shalt not covet." Help the learners to know themselves. A bit of psychology is required. Distinguish between proper and improper ambition. Familiarize with related vocabulary. Memorize quotable items in the memory materials.

B. ATTITUDE

Create feeling of horror, disgust, and shame against every form of covetousness, greed, avarice, discontent; particularly as the learner discovers these in himself. Create a felt need for God's mercy and for a new spirit. Develop a yearning desire for the spirit of contentment; kindle the wish that they might be as contented as Jesus, and as carefree as the birds and lilies of the field. Make strong, fervent, captivating appeals on the basis of Bible story and Bible verse facts.

C. HABITS, SKILLS

Practice speaking hopefully. Frequently and joyfully sing songs of rejoicing and of praise to God for blessings received.

THE CONTENTED LIFE – Unit 9

Practice daily to cross the bridge when you get there. End the practice of carrying three bags at one time: The one containing the burdens and cares of yesterday, those of tomorrow, and those of today. Sufficient unto the day is the evil thereof.

D. ANTICIPATED OUTCOME IN TERMS OF SANCTIFIED PERSONALITIES

Boys and girls who have learned to curb their wishing and who have adjusted it to what is possible. Happy, contented, singing boys and girls. Young people who will not allow futile ambitions to gnaw away at their inner life. Adult Christians who have found in Jesus the One Thing Needful and who value Jesus as their greatest Treasure.

III. Curriculum Material

A. BIBLE STUDIES

DATE USED

- A Dinner of Herbs with Love. *Prov. 15:13-20.*
- Be Content with Such Things as Ye Have. *Heb. 13:1-6.*
- The Mind of a Mature Man. *Psalm 131.*
- Onesimus, Go Back to Your Job! *Philemon 12*
- °A Pouting King: Heavy and Displeased. *1 Kings 21:1-16.*
- °Shame on David. *2 Sam. 11:2-4.*
- °Absalom Steals Hearts. *2 Sam. 15:1-6.*
- A Good Investment. *Matt. 6:19-24.*
- Sufficient Unto the Day Is the Evil Thereof! *Matt. 6:24-34.* (34)
- Behold the Fowls of the Air. *Matt. 6:25-34.* (26)
- Covetousness Is Foolish. *Luke 12:15-21.*
- Your Gold and Silver Is Cankered. *James 5:1-6.*
- The Covetous Called to Repentance. *Jer. 6:1-17.* (13)
- Against Farm Foreclosures. *Mic. 2:1-3.*
- Zion Shall Be Plowed! Why? *Mic. 3:8-12.* (11)
- What Will Ye Give Me? *Matt. 26:14-16.*
- Holy Anger Against Those Who Underpay. *Mal. 3:1-6.* (5)

B. LUTHER'S SMALL CATECHISM
Questions 70—78.

C. MEMORY MATERIAL
1. Bible Texts

GRADE
1. By love serve one another. *Gal. 5:13.* (1)
2. Be ye therefore perfect, even as your Father which is in heaven is perfect. *Matt. 5:48.* (2)
3. Ye shall be holy; for I, the Lord, your God, am holy. *Lev. 19:2.*
4. Delight thyself also in the Lord; and He shall give thee the desires of thine heart. *Ps. 37:4.* (6)
5. I had not known lust except the Law had said, Thou shalt not covet. *Rom. 7:7.*
6. Woe unto them that join house to house, that lay field to field, till there be no place, that they may be placed alone in the midst of the earth. *Is. 5:8.* (8)
7. Woe unto you, scribes and Pharisees, hypocrites! For ye devour widows' houses and for a pretense make long prayer; therefore ye shall receive the greater damnation. *Matt. 23:14.* (8)
8. Having food and raiment, let us be therewith content. But they that will be rich fall into temptation and a snare and into many foolish and hurtful lusts, which drown men in destruction and perdition. For the love of money is the root of all evil, which while some coveted after, they have erred from the faith and pierced themselves through with many sorrows. *1 Tim. 6:8-10.* (8)

2. *Luther's Small Catechism*

1–2 The Ninth and Tenth Commandments. Expl. 3—8.
6–8 Table of Duties: To Servants; To Employers.
5–8 The Seventh Petition.

3. *Hymns*

1-2 The Lord my Shepherd is,
     I shall be well supplied.
  Since He is mine and I am His,
     What can I want beside?   LH 426:1

3–4 Jesus, Jesus, only Jesus,
     Can my heartfelt longing still.
  Lo, I pledge myself to Jesus
     What He wills alone to will.
  For my heart, which He hath filled,
  Ever cries, Lord, as Thou wilt.   LH 348:1

THE CONTENTED LIFE — Unit 9

GRADE

5–6   Thy neighbor's house desire thou not,
     His wife, nor aught that he hath got,
     But wish that his such good may be
       As thy heart doth wish for thee.
        Have mercy, Lord!   *LH* 287:10

7–8   What is the world to me
       With all its vaunted pleasure
     When Thou, and Thou alone,
       Lord Jesus, art my Treasure!
     Thou only, dearest Lord,
       My soul's Delight shalt be;
     Thou art my Peace, my Rest, —
       What is the world to me!   *LH* 430:1

4. Prayers

Forgive, O merciful Lord, where I may have craftily tried to get something that belonged to my neighbor, or where I may have tried to get something by a show of right. Grant me Thy Holy Spirit that I, as Thy child, may henceforth help and be of service to my neighbor in keeping his property. I ask it for Jesus' sake. Amen.

Collects for 1st and 15th Sunday after Trinity; *LH* 516:1-2, "In the Hour of Trial"; 524:1-3, "In Thee, Lord"; p. 109, No. 74, For Peace; p. 107, No. 56, For Grace.

D. SUMMARY OUTLINE FOR THE CHALKBOARD

Contentment:

It is *sinful:*

    to covet what is beyond our reach

    to be miserly, like Scrooge

    to be greedy — "The Goose That Laid the Golden Egg"

    to be discontented — King Midas

    to worry, fret, pout

    to fail in meeting the positive command.

       Have mercy, Lord!

Let us as redeemed, sanctified and therefore immensely rich people

    be grateful, cheerful, contented with such things as we have (Jesus, lilies, birds)

    be liberal and generous, faithful and good stewards.

       All for Jesus' sake and in imitation of Jesus.

IV. Instructional Methods and Materials

A. PROBLEM AND APPROACH

The number of persons in mental hospitals grows daily. Why? Some reasons are worry and envy. Is mental illness avoidable? How?

B. SUGGESTED TEACHING UNIT

1. Devotion
Hymn: That Man a Godly Life Might Live. *LH* 287:1-10.
Scripture Reading: Matt. 6:24-34.
Prayer: * *Teen-Agers Pray*, p. 44.

2. Bible Story
1 Kings 21:1-16.

3. Memory Passages
1 Tim. 6:8-10: Having food and raiment.
Psalm 37:4: Delight thyself also in the Lord.
Lev. 19:2: Ye shall be holy.
Thy neighbor's house desire thou not. *LH* 287:10
The 9th and 10th Commandments.
The 7th Petition.

4. Luther's Small Catechism
Questions 70—78.

5. Liturgy
The Nunc Dimittis. *LH* p. 29.

C. AIDS TO LEARNING

1. **Visual:** *The Ninth and Tenth Commandments* from *The Ten Commandments* visualized — 79-101 — 10 filmstrips.
   Ahab, The Pouting King — film.
   A Bigger Reward — film.
2. **Audio:** "Jesu, Joy of Man's Desiring" — (The Beloved Choruses) Columbia, ML-5364 (Stereo MS-6058).
   "Jesus, Priceless Treasure" — *LH* 347 — (Let The Earth Rejoice) KFUO, HA 61.
3. **Objects:** Models of war implements.
4. **Workbook:** * *The New Life*, Unit IX.
   * *Learning About God*, Unit VII.
   * *Growing in Faith*, Unit VII.
   * *Growing in Grace*, Unit VII.
   * *Growing in Christ*, Unit 9
5. **Bulletin Board:** Clippings and pictures of war, contented or dissatisfied persons, lawsuits.
6. **Chalkboard:** Summary outline.
7. **Group Activity:** Dramatize Midas and the Golden Touch.
8. **Music:** Listen to recordings listed above.
9. **Art:** "Song of the Lark" — Breton.
10. **Library:** *Aesop's Fables*.

THE CONTENTED LIFE — Unit 9   81

D. EVALUATION

Do we really trust the Lord completely? Have we made progress toward this goal?

V. Suggestions for Correlations with Other Subjects

A. READING

1. **Silent:** "The Heavens Declare," from ° *Treasury of Christian Literature,* p. 208; Luke 12:15-21; James 5:1-6.
2. **Oral:** Psalm 146.
3. **Choral:** Prov. 31:10-31.

B. ENGLISH

1. **Oral:** Report on silent readings above.
2. **Written:** The time I was really worried.
3. **Vocabulary and Spelling:** covetous, envious, contented, avarice, ambitious.
4. **Handwriting:** j — jealous, J — Jesus.

C. SOCIAL SCIENCES

1. **Home and Family Life:** Avoiding quarrels with brothers and sisters.
2. **Community and Nation:** Discuss "keeping up with the Joneses."
3. **History:** What causes war?

D. PHYSICAL SCIENCES

1. **Nature Study:** Plant and animal partnership.
2. **Geography:** Natural resources as a potential cause for war.
3. **Health:** Can a person be "worried to death"?
4. **General Science:** How does automation contribute to the world's problems?

E. ARITHMETIC

Make charts and graphs to compare the costs of war with costs of education in the U. S.

F. ART

"The Gleaners" — Millet; make posters urging contentment.

G. MUSIC

Jubilate Deo. *LH* 666.

UNIT
10

THE PENITENT LIFE

Close of Commandments, Purpose of Law, Sin, Repentance

•

I. Scope and Importance

"It will be long before a doctrine or rule of life equal to the Ten Commandments is constructed, because they are beyond human power to fulfill unaided. Whoever does fulfill them is a holy, angelic being, superior to all holiness on earth. Occupy yourself with them, trying with all your ability and power to obey them; you will find therein so much to do that you will not seek or need any other work or another kind of holiness." (LLC)

"My opinion is that we shall have our hands full in keeping these commandments — in practicing gentleness, patience, love towards our enemies, chastity, kindness, and whatever other virtues they may include. Such works, however, are not important in the eyes of the world; for they are not restricted to particular times and places, customs and ceremonies, but are common, everyday duties toward our neighbor, with no show about them." (LLC)

"These words contain a threat of wrath and a promise of grace, to terrify and warn us and allure and persuade us to accept and prize God's Word as an expression of divine earnestness. For He declares how intensely He has these commandments and our obedience of them at heart, and how severely he will punish those who scorn and violate them; while, on the other hand, he will richly reward, bless, and grant all good things to those who prize them and cheerfully act and live in accordance with them." (LLC)

Sin brings the soul into hell and hell into the soul. — Sin still lives in the Christian but the Christian no longer lives in sin. — If Christ is sweet to thee, sin will be bitter to thee. Sin is a burden, a canker, a debt, a disease, a poison, slavery. Little sins are seeds of great sins.

II. Aim

A. KNOWLEDGE

Foster thinking that leads to clear, vivid, and correct knowledge of the Law, its threefold purpose; God's anger and punishment because of sin; the origin, nature, kinds, curse, and cure of sin; God's rewards of grace to those who strive to obey the Law for Jesus' sake. Develop familiarity with related vocabulary.

B. ATTITUDE

Foster deep conviction that God is really in earnest about sin; that punishment is certain and terrible even though delayed; that God earnestly desires the salvation of every sinner, through acceptance of Christ's merit.

C. HABITS, SKILLS

Train in the habit of frequent and frank self-examination; of humble confession of sins of commission and sins of omission; of pleading for mercy and of pleading to live a more holy life.

D. ANTICIPATED OUTCOMES IN TERMS OF TRULY SANCTIFIED CHARACTERS

Boys and girls who are fully conscious of sin and punishment and are in dead earnest about becoming more and more like

Jesus; young people who strive prayerfully to continue in the Christian way of life; men and women who continue to live a life of daily repentance and daily renewal, who hate sin in all its forms and who strive for growth in holiness. Mature men and women who are "living epistles."

III. Curriculum Material

A. BIBLE STUDIES

DATE USED

------------------- When Impenitent Sinners Were Destroyed in a Flood. *Gen. 7.*

------------------- Bomb Shelters Do Not Protect Against the Wrath of God. *Gen. 19:23-25.*

------------------- Fire From Heaven. Why? *Gen. 19:13, 23-26.*

------------------- God Fulfills His Threats. *2 Kings 24:10-20.*

------------------- Jesus Wept Because of Impenitence. *Luke 19:41-44.*

------------------- Two Worshipers. What a Difference! *Luke 18:9-14.*

------------------- Whence Came Sin and Suffering? *Gen. 3:1-19.*

------------------- Wicked as Soon as They are Born. *Ps. 58:1-5.*

------------------- Alas! "In His Own Likeness." *Gen. 5:1-8.* (3)

------------------- Comfort Ye My People. *Is. 40:1-11.*

------------------- An Intercessory Prayer for War Prisoners. *1 Kings 8:46-50.*

------------------- Redeemed from the Curse of the Law. *Gal. 3:1-13.*

------------------- What Think Ye of Christ? *Matt. 22:34-46.* (42)

------------------- Salvation Is a Gift of God. *Gal. 3:13-19.*

------------------- Your Photograph — Before and After. *Eph. 2:1-22.*

------------------- A Lifelong Conflict. *Rom. 7:14-25.*

------------------- You Are Servants of Righteousness. *Rom. 6:11-23.*

------------------- Psalms of Penitence: *51, 25, 31, 32, etc.*

------------------- Sections of *Psalm 119.*

------------------- Joy in Heaven. *Luke 15:1-10.*

------------------- Pastors and Teachers as Examples. *Phil. 3:12-21.*

B. LUTHER'S SMALL CATECHISM

Questions 79—99.

THE PENITENT LIFE — Unit 10 85

C. MEMORY MATERIAL

1. Bible Texts

GRADE

1 The wages of sin is death. *Rom. 6:23.* (1)

2 By the Law is the knowledge of sin. *Rom. 3:20.* (3)
   By one man sin entered into the world. *Rom. 5:12.*

3 There is not a just man upon earth that doeth good and sinneth not. *Eccl. 7:20.* (3)
   When lust hath conceived, it bringeth forth sin. *James 1:15.*
   He that committeth sin is of the devil. *1 John 3:8.*

4 Ye were dead in trespasses and sins. *Eph. 2:1.* (4)
   I know that in me (that is, in my flesh) dwelleth no good thing. *Rom. 7:18.* (4)
   Christ is the end of the Law. *Rom. 10:4.*

5 To him that knoweth to do good and doeth it not, to him it is sin. *James 4:17.* (3)
   We are all as an unclean thing, and all our righteousnesses are as filthy rags. *Is. 64:6.* (5)
   Not as though I had already attained, either were already perfect; but I follow after, if that I may apprehend that for which also I am apprehended of Christ Jesus. *Phil. 3:12.*
   Wherewithal shall a young man cleanse his way? By taking heed thereto according to Thy Word. *Ps. 119:9.*
   Enter not into judgment with Thy servant, for in Thy sight shall no man living be justified. *Ps. 143:2.*
   Thy Word is a lamp unto my feet, and a light unto my path. *Ps. 119:105.*

6 The imagination of man's heart is evil from his youth. *Gen. 8:21.* (6)
   Godliness is profitable unto all things, having promise of the life that now is and of that which is to come. *1 Tim. 4:8.* (7)
   Out of the heart proceed evil thoughts, murders, adulteries, fornications, theft, false witness, blasphemies. *Matt. 15:19.*

7 Christ hath redeemed us from the curse of the Law, being made a curse for us; for it is written, Cursed is everyone that hangeth on a tree. *Gal. 3:13.* (8)
   The soul that sinneth, it shall die. The son shall not bear the iniquity of the father, neither shall the father bear the iniquity of the son; the righteousness of the righteous shall be upon him, and the wickedness of the wicked shall be upon him. *Ezek. 18:20.* (8)
   I had not known lust, except the Law had said, Thou shalt not covet. *Rom. 7:7.*

GRADE	
	Put off concerning the former conversation the old man, which is corrupt according to the deceitful lusts. *Eph. 4:22.*
8	Whosoever shall keep the whole Law and yet offend in one point, he is guilty of all. *James 2:10.* (8)
	The natural man receiveth not the things of the Spirit of God, for they are foolishness unto him; neither can he know them, because they are spiritually discerned. *1 Cor. 2:14.* (8)
	The carnal mind is enmity against God. *Rom. 8:7.* (8)
	Cursed is every one that continueth not in all things which are written in the book of the law to do them. *Gal. 3:10.*

2. *Luther's Small Catechism*

3–8	The Conclusion.
4–8	What is Confession?
5–8	What Sins Should We Confess? Which Are These?
6–8	The General Confession.
7–8	Christian Questions.

3. *Hymns*

1–2	Oh, that the Lord would guide my ways
	  To keep His statutes still.
	Oh, that my God would grant me grace
	  To know and do His will!
		LH 416:1

3–4	Lord, help us ever to retain The Catechism's doctrine plain As Luther taught the Word of Truth In simple style to tender youth.	LH 288:1

5–6	Jesus sinners doth receive;
	  Oh, may all this saying ponder
	Who in sin's delusions live
	  And from God and heaven wander!
	Here is hope for all who grieve —
	Jesus sinners doth receive.
		LH 324:1

7–8	From depths of woe I cry to Thee, Lord, hear me, I implore Thee. Bend down Thy gracious ear to me, My prayer let come before Thee. If Thou rememb'rest each misdeed, If each should have its rightful meed, Who may abide Thy presence?	LH 329:1

4. *Prayers*

O most merciful God, who hast given Thine only-begotten Son to die for us, have mercy upon us and for His sake grant us remission of all our

THE PENITENT LIFE — Unit 10 87

sins; and by Thy Holy Spirit increase in us true knowledge of Thee and of Thy will and true obedience to Thy Word, to the end that by Thy grace we may come to everlasting life; through Jesus Christ, our Lord. Amen.
(*LH*, p. 6, The Confession)

Collects for 10th, 11th, and 18th Sundays after Trinity.

Also *LH*, p. 16, O Almighty God, etc.; p. 109, No. 70. Use teacher's and pupil's own prayer.

D. SUMMARY OUTLINE FOR THE CHALKBOARD

The Penitent Life.

Sin:

    meaning: "Sin is the transgression of the Law"

    origin: devil, flesh, world

    kinds: original, actual; commission, omission; conscious, unconscious; willful, out of weakness

    consequences: anger of God; temporal punishment; social ostracism; frowns; disasters; eternal damnation

    confession: necessary, before God

    cure: Jesus, cleanse me from its guilt and power!

    avoidance: for Jesus' sake and in imitation of Jesus. Sanctification.

IV. Instructional Methods and Materials

A. PROBLEM AND APPROACH

"Is your throat sore? Do your muscles ache? Do you have a fever? Then take .... for fast relief." So goes a commercial for a particular drug. The commercial lists several symptoms of a beginning illness. What are the tests for the sickness of sin?

B. SUGGESTED TEACHING UNIT

1. Devotion

Hymn: Jesus Sinners Doth Receive. *LH* 324.
Scripture Reading. Is. 40:1-11.
Prayer: Psalm 25.

2. Bible Story

Luke 15:1-10.

3. Memory Passages

Gal. 2:13: Christ hath redeemed us.
Psalm 119:9: Wherewithal shall a young man.
Phil. 3:12: Not as though I had already attained.
Jesus sinners doth receive. *LH* 324:1.
Close of the Commandments.
Confession.

4. *Luther's Small Catechism*
Questions 77—99.

5. *Liturgy*
The Litany. *LH* 661.

C. AIDS TO LEARNING

1. **Visual:** Introductory Filmstrip from *The Ten Commandments* visualized — 79-101 — 10 filmstrips.
The Ten Commandments — film.
2. **Audio:** "Woe Unto Them Who Forsake Him" and "The Thunder of The Law" — Mendelssohn: *Elijah* — Angel, 3558-C.
"All We Like Sheep Have Gone Astray" — Handel: *The Messiah* — RCA, LD-6409.
"Alas, My God, My Sins Are Great" — *LH* 317 — (A Mighty Fortress) Word, W-4017 (Stereo WST-9003).
3. **Objects:** Mirror, ruler, fence.
4. **Workbook:** * *The New Life,* Unit X.
   * *Learning About God,* Unit III.
   * *Growing in Faith,* Unit III.
   * *Growing in Grace,* Unit III.
   * *Growing in Christ,* Unit 10, 11.
5. **Bulletin Board:** Pictures and clippings illustrating penitence and forgiveness.
6. **Chalkboard:** Summary outline.
7. **Group Activity:** Class discussion on the topic "Forgive us our trespasses as we forgive others."
8. **Music:** The De Profundis. *LH* 664.
9. **Art:** "The Lost Sheep" — Soord.
10. **Library:** Walther, * *Law and Gospel* (for teachers).
Lindberg and Beck, * *A Book of Advent.*

D. EVALUATION

Use the Christian Questions (Luther's Small Catechism, page 31) for a self-examination.

V. Suggestions for Correlations with Other Subjects

A. READING

1. **Silent:** Gen. 7.
2. **Oral:** Is. 40:1-11.
3. **Choral:** Psalm 51; The Christian Questions.

THE PENITENT LIFE — Unit 10

B. ENGLISH
1. **Oral:** Panel discussion — Is "everybody does it" a reason to disobey certain laws?
2. **Written:** An original prayer or litany.
3. **Vocabulary and Spelling:** penitent, confess, remorse, holiness.
4. **Handwriting:** p — penitent, P — Paul.

C. SOCIAL SCIENCES:
1. **Home and Family Life:** Confess faults one to another; forgive each other for wrongs.
2. **Community and Nation:** What can we do to curb the rise in crime?
3. **History:** Communism and Christianity.

D. PHYSICAL SCIENCES
1. **Nature Study:** Natural phenomenon as God's judgment for sin. See Gen. 7; Job 1.
2. **Geography:** Man's carelessness — a cause for wasting natural resources.
3. **Health:** Discuss: disobeying God's natural laws causes pain.
4. **General Science:** Using science in fighting crime, disease.

E. ARITHMETIC
Use fractions, decimals, percent, charts, and graphs to compare crime rates in several years; cost of fighting crime with cost of spreading the Gospel.

F. ART
Make a poster illustrating God's mercy and forgiveness; make a chart or poster showing God's hand in nature.

UNIT 11

GOD AND CREATION

•

I. Scope and Importance

Did the world and man evolve? Or were they created? The answer has very far-reaching implications on one's whole philosophy of life.

"The Creed teaches us everything that we must expect and receive from God. This teaching is intended to help us to follow the Ten Commandments. — If we could, of our own strength, rightly keep the Ten Commandments we should not need anything further, neither Creed nor Lord's Prayer." (LLC)

"Whoever looks upon this universe without wonder, without humble admiration and faith is like a pair of spectacles without eyes to see through them." (Carlyle)

"Each new discovery which science makes in the realm of nature, like the steps of one who climbs a mountain, enlarges our views of the goodness, the greatness, the wisdom, and the power of God the Creator." (Guthrie)

"The laws of nature are not iron chains by which God, so to say, is bound hand and foot but rather elastic cords which he can lengthen or shorten at his sovereign will." (P. Schaff)

GOD AND CREATION – Unit 11

II. Aim

A. KNOWLEDGE

Insight, understanding: Stimulate observation and thinking that leads to clear, correct, and vivid ideas about the origin, nature, and eventual destiny of the universe; of mankind; and more especially of each pupil. Distinguish between those who believe in God as the Creator and Preserver and those who believe merely in matter and motion; evolution. Arouse interest in the origin of species. Pupils shall learn to differentiate between man and monkey. Foster familiarity with related vocabulary. Memorize thoroughly usable Scripture passages.

B. ATTITUDE

Atmosphere, philosophy of life: Guide pupils to take sides with those who believe in the Biblical account of creation; who see God the Creator in His creation; strengthen faith in God; foster attitude of awe and admiration before any and all forms of life: plant, animal, man. Foster right, sustained, and serious interest in nature and natural science. Foster awareness that we *do* live in a changing world. In some respects our world *is* improvable.

C. HABITS, SKILLS

Train pupils in close, intelligent observation of their natural environment, with variations in the seasons; instances of adjustment to environment (color, temperature, form); heavenly bodies: moon, stars, sun, comets. Provide opportunity for direct observation of nature; train for use of Bible quotations in speaking to others of God and creation. Lead pupils to regard their own body with all its organs as the gift of God and consequently to take the best of care of them (teeth, lungs, heart, hands, eyes, etc.).

D. ANTICIPATED OUTCOMES IN TERMS OF PERSONS WHO HAVE THE BIBLICAL "WELTANSCHAUUNG"

Bible-believing boys and girls who observe and admire the natural world; young people who can and who will defend their faith in God the Creator; adults who have a Christian philosophy of the origin, nature, and destiny of the universe, who regard God as the determining factor in individual and racial survival.

III. Curriculum Material

A. BIBLE STUDIES

DATE USED

- *How Things Began. *Gen. 1.*
- What the Skies Tell Us. *Psalm 19.*
- What Was First. *John 1:1-6.*
- Our God is in the Heavens. *Psalm 115.* (3)
- I am the Lord — There Is None Else. *Is. 45:5-18.*
- God Revealed Himself in Nature. *Rom. 1:18-25.*
- Zion Heard and was Glad. *Psalm 97.* (8)
- He Left Not Himself Without Witness. *Acts 14:8-18.* (17)
- Through Faith We Understand. *Heb. 11:1-7.*
- *A Soldier with a Strong Faith. *Luke 7:1-10.*
- *A Nobleman Who Believed. *John 4:47-53.*
- *The Story of a Mother with a Great Faith. *Matt. 15:21-28.*
- *Saving Faith is a Personal Matter (Virgins). *Matt. 25:8-12.*

B. LUTHER'S SMALL CATECHISM

Questions 100—107.

C. MEMORY MATERIAL

1. Bible Texts

GRADE

1 In the beginning God created the heaven and the earth. *Gen. 1:1.* (1)

2 Thy faith hath saved thee; go in peace. *Luke 7:50.* (2)

3 Commit thy way unto the Lord; trust also in Him; and He shall bring it to pass. *Ps. 37:5.* (3)

GOD AND CREATION – Unit 11

GRADE

4 By Him were all things created that are in heaven and that are in earth, visible and invisible. *Col. 1:16.* (4)

I trusted in Thee, O Lord; I said, Thou art my God. *Ps. 31:14.*

5 I ascend unto My Father and your Father, and to My God and your God. *John 20:17.*

How shall they believe in Him of whom they have not heard? *Rom. 10:14.* (4)

6 The just shall live by his faith. *Hab. 2:4.* (1)

So, then, faith cometh by hearing, and hearing by the Word of God. *Rom. 10:17.* (4)

7 Have we not all one Father? Hath not one God created us? *Mal. 2:10.* (8)

Faith is the substance of things hoped for, the evidence of things not seen. *Heb. 11:1.* (7)

8 For this cause I bow my knees unto the Father of our Lord Jesus Christ, of whom the whole family in heaven and earth is named. *Eph. 3:14, 15.*

Thou believest that there is one God; thou doest well; the devils also believe and tremble. *James 2:19.* (8)

Through faith we understand that the worlds were framed by the word of God, so that things which are seen were not made of things which do appear. *Heb. 11:3.* (8)

2. *Luther's Small Catechism*

1 The First Article. Expl. 2–8.

1–8 The First Commandment.

5–8 The Introduction to the Lord's Prayer.

3. *Hymns*

1–2 We sing the almighty power of God,
    Who bade the mountains rise,
Who spread the flowing seas abroad
    And built the lofty skies.   *LH 43:1*

3–4 Oh, that I had a thousand voices
    To praise my God with thousand tongues!
My heart, which in the Lord rejoices,
    Would then proclaim in grateful songs
To all, wherever I might be,
What great things God hath done for me.   *LH 30:1*

5–6 Praise to the Lord, the Almighty, the King of creation!
O my soul, praise Him, for He is thy Health and Salvation!
Join the full throng; Wake, harp and psalter and song;
Sound forth in glad adoration!   *LH 39:1*

GRADE
7–8
    All praise to God, who reigns above,
        The God of all creation,
    The God of wonders, power, and love,
        The God of our salvation!
    With healing balm my soul He fills,
    The God who every sorrow stills, —
        To God all praise and glory!   *LH* 19:1

4. Prayers

To Thee, O great Creator, we humbly give thanks for all Thy wonderful works. Lead us into all truth that we may know whence we are, why we are here, and whither we are going. We ask it in Jesus' name. Amen.

The Morning Prayer. The Evening Prayer. *LH*, p. 106, No. 42, Thanksgiving.

Also Nos. 43 to 45.

D. SUMMARY OUTLINE FOR THE CHALKBOARD

God and Creation

The Creator: revealed in nature, in conscience, in the Bible.

Created: made out of nothing by mere word — "very good."

The Creation:
    invisible: heaven, angels
    visible: heavenly bodies, earth
    inorganic: minerals, gases
    organic: plants, animal, man

Let us observe and study nature intelligently and reverently
    in order to have dominion over the forces and resources of nature
        in order thus to glorify God and cause others to know and glorify Him (Missions)
    contribute toward human welfare.

IV. Instructional Methods and Materials

A. PROBLEM AND APPROACH

Where did the universe come from? What is it made of? These are questions scientists have been asking for many years, and they are still seeking the answers. There are many different ideas, but no scientist is really sure of them.

B. SUGGESTED TEACHING UNIT

1. Devotion

Hymn: Praise to the Lord, the Almighty. *LH* 39:1.
Scripture Reading: Gen. 1.
Prayer: Extempore.

GOD AND CREATION – Unit 11

2. **Bible Story**

   Gen. 2.

3. **Memory Passages**

   Heb. 11:3: Through faith we understand.
   Col. 1:16: By Him were all things created.
   Psalm 37:5: Commit thy way unto the Lord.
   We all believe in one true God. *LH* 251:1.
   The First Article.
   The 1st Commandment.
   Introduction to the Lord's Prayer.

4. **Luther's Small Catechism**

   Questions 100—107.

5. **Liturgy**

   Levavi Oculos. *LH* 665.

C. AIDS TO LEARNING

1. **Visual:** *Creation* — Part of *The Apostles' Creed* series — 79-102 — filmstrip.
   God's Wonders in Growing Things — film.
2. **Audio:** "Praise to the Lord, the Almighty" — *LH* 39 — (A Mighty Fortress) RCA, LM 2199.
   "The Heavens Are Telling," from *The Creation* (Haydn) — (Great Sacred Choruses) RCA, LM-1117; also Columbia, ML 5364.
   "We All Believe in One True God" — *LH* 251 — (Sing Unto The Lord) KFUO, HA60.
3. **Object:** Compass; plants.
4. **Workbook:** * *The New Life*, Unit XI
   * *Learning About God*, Unit II.
   * *Growing in Faith*, Unit I, II.
   * *Living for God*, Unit II.
   * *Building for Eternity*, Unit II.
   * *Growing in Grace*, Unit II.
   * *Growing in Christ*, Unit 12.
5. **Bulletin Board:** Pictures and clippings showing nature's wonders.
6. **Chalkboard:** Summary outline.
7. **Group Activity:** Visit a planetarium; observe stars and constellations.
8. **Music:** The Te Deum. *LH*, p. 35.
9. **Art:** "Spring" — Botticelli.
10. **Library:** T. Graebner, * *God and the Cosmos*.
    F. A. Callies, * *God's Stars*.

D. EVALUATION

Do you understand God's role in nature better?

V. Suggestions for Correlations with Other Subjects

A. READING
1. **Silent:** John 1:1-6; Psalm 97.
2. **Oral:** Psalm 115; Rom. 1:18-25.
3. **Choral:** Psalm 19.

B. ENGLISH
1. **Oral:** Report on the topic "How plants grow."
2. **Written:** An original prayer or poem.
3. **Vocabulary and Spelling:** biology, astronomy, Creator, astronaut, cosmonaut.
4. **Handwriting:** c — creatures, C — Creator.

C. SOCIAL SCIENCES
1. **Home and Family Life:** Caring for plants and pets at home.
2. **Community and Nation:** Keeping the countryside beautiful.
3. **History:** Different ideas concerning the start of it all: creation and evolution.

D. PHYSICAL SCIENCES
1. **Nature Study:** God's hand in nature.
2. **Geography:** Conserving natural resources; national parks and monuments.
3. **Health:** Nature's healing powers; physical fitness.
4. **General Science:** Replenish, subdue, have dominion. See Gen. 2:28.

E. ARITHMETIC

Develop problems using space exploration as the topic; prepare charts and graphs comparing the natural resources of the U. S. with other leading countries.

F. ART

"Avenue of Trees" — Hobbema.

G. MUSIC

The Te Deum. *LH*, p. 35.

UNIT
12

ANGELS

•

I. Scope and Importance

Angels play an important role in the Bible. In both the Old and the New Testaments they are prominent.

"One angel is mightier than the whole world." (Luther)

"For every member of my congregation I wish an angel's heart to love their God and Savior, angels' lips to praise their Maker and Redeemer, angels' willingness to serve God and their fellow men, and angels' bliss to dwell forever in the mansions of their Father in Heaven." (Caspari)

The devil is called the father of lies (John 8:44), the god of this world (2 Cor. 4:4), the old serpent (Rev. 12:9); sometimes he transforms himself into an angel of light (2 Cor. 11:14).

II. Aim

A. KNOWLEDGE

Develop thinking which leads to clear, correct, Biblical ideas concerning angels; good, bad; Michael, Gabriel, Satan; their origin, history, nature, work. Familiarize with related vocabulary. Memorize usable texts.

B. ATTITUDE

Foster implicit faith in Jesus, that He will send His angel to protect His child. Place the emphasis on trust in the good angels.

Foster wariness, alertness against the attack of Satan and his angels.

C. HABITS, SKILLS

Train pupils to do bravely, courageously, and fearlessly what duty bids them do, trusting that the guardian angel will give protection as he did in the case of Daniel and others.

D. ANTICIPATED OUTCOME IN TERMS OF SANCTIFIED PERSONALITIES

Boys and girls who derive comfort from truth set forth in the picture in their bedroom: Guardian Angel; who strive in conduct to be angelic. Young people who retain their faith in angel-beings who are on guard for us. Adults who are on the alert against the Wicked One and who derive comfort and strength from their faith in good angels.

III. Curriculum Material

A. BIBLE STUDIES

DATE USED

    *One Against 185,000. *2 Kings 19:20-36.*
    *Angels as Broadcasters of Good News. *Luke 2:8-14.*
    *An Angel Rescues a Prisoner. *Acts 12:1-10.*
    *An Angel Holds a Lion's Mouth Shut. *Dan. 6:18-23.*
    *An Angel Carries a Saved Soul into Heaven. *Luke 16:19-22.*
    *Satan Transformed Into an Angel of Light. *2 Cor. 11:13-15.*
    When Angels Will Appear in the Skies. *Matt. 25:31-46.*
    Fear Not; His Angels Will Protect You. *Ps. 91.* (11)
    *About the Leader of the Bad Angels. *Gen. 3:1-6.*
    *Jesus, Stronger Than Satan. *Matt. 4:1-11.*
    *Satan Tries to Mislead a Strong Man of God. *Job 2.*
    God's Strong Messengers. *Psalm 103.* (20)
    Angels Are Not as Great as Jesus. *Heb. 1.*

B. LUTHER'S SMALL CATECHISM

Questions 108—111.

ANGELS — Unit 12

C. MEMORY MATERIAL
1. Bible Texts
GRADE

1. Bless the Lord, ye His angels, that excel in strength. *Ps. 103:20.*

2. In heaven their angels do always behold the face of My Father which is in heaven. *Matt. 18:10.* (3)

3. Suddenly there was with the angel a multitude of the heavenly host. *Luke 2:13.*

4. When the Son of Man shall come in His glory and all the holy angels with Him, then shall He sit upon the throne of His glory. *Matt. 25:31.*

5. Are they not all ministering spirits, sent forth to minister for them who shall be heirs of salvation? *Heb. 1:14.* (5)

6. Thousand thousands ministered unto Him, and ten thousand times ten thousand stood before Him. *Dan. 7:10.*

   He shall give His angels charge over thee to keep thee in all thy ways. They shall bear thee up in their hands lest thou dash thy foot against a stone. *Ps. 91:11, 12.* (3)

7. Bless the Lord, ye His angels that excel in strength, that do His commandments, hearkening unto the voice of His word. Bless ye the Lord, all ye His hosts; ye ministers of His, that do His pleasure. *Ps. 103:20, 21.*

   Be sober, be vigilant; because your adversary, the devil, as a roaring lion walketh about, seeking whom he may devour; whom resist steadfast in the faith. *1 Peter 5:8, 9.* (5)

8. (The devil) was a murderer from the beginning and abode not in the truth, because there is no truth in him. When he speaketh a lie, he speaketh of his own; for he is a liar, and the father of it. *John 8:44.*

   We wrestle not against flesh and blood, but against principalities, against powers, against the rulers of the darkness of this world, against spiritual wickedness in high places. *Eph. 6:12.* (8)

   God spared not the angels that sinned, but cast them down to hell and delivered them into chains of darkness, to be reserved unto Judgment. *2 Peter 2:4.*

2. Luther's Small Catechism
1   The First Article. Expl. 3—8.
6–8 The Sixth Petition.
7–8 The Third Petition.

3. Hymns
1–2 Through the long night-watches
     May Thine angels spread
   Their white wings above me,
     Watching round my bed.   *LH 654:6*

GRADE

3–4   Lord Jesus, who dost love me,
      Oh, spread Thy wings above me
         And shield me from alarm!
      Though evil would assail me,
      Thy mercy will not fail me:
         I rest in Thy protecting arm.   *LH 554:5*

5–6   Songs of praise the angels sang,
      Heaven with alleluias rang,
      When creation was begun,
      When God spake and it was done.   *LH 35:1*

7–8   Jesus, Brightness of the Father,
      Life and Strength of all who live,
      For creating guardian angels
         Glory to Thy name we give
      And Thy wondrous praise rehearse,
      Singing in harmonious verse.   *LH 257:1*

4. *Prayers*

O everlasting God, who hast ordained and constituted the services of angels and men in a wonderful order, mercifully grant that, as Thy holy angels always do Thee service in heaven, so by Thy appointment may they succor and defend us on earth through Jesus Christ, Thy Son, our Lord, who liveth and reigneth forever one God, world without end. Amen.

The Morning Prayer. The Evening Prayer. *LH*, p. 118. For Aid Against Temptation. *LH*, p. 107, No. 57.

D. SUMMARY OUTLINE FOR THE CHALKBOARD

Angels: Messengers — Spirits.

      Good: a) forever happy
               b) praise God
               c) minister: serve God and His people.

Therefore: Be unafraid when on the path of duty.

      Bad: a) forever rejected
              b) enemies of God and man
              c) with Satan as leader, they seek to destroy and hinder God's word and work.

Therefore: Watch, and pray.

IV. Instructional Methods and Materials

A. PROBLEM AND APPROACH

Are angels real? If so, where are they? What do they do? Do they help or harm you?

B. SUGGESTED TEACHING UNIT

1. Devotion

ANGELS — Unit 12

Hymn: Songs of Praise the Angels Sang. *LH* 35:1.
Scripture Reading: 2 Kings 19:20-36.
Prayer: Luther's Morning Prayer.

2. *Bible Story*

Daniel 6:18-23.

3. *Memory Passages*

Psalm 103:20: Bless the Lord, ye His angels.
Matt. 18:10: In heaven their angels.
1 Peter 5:8-9: Be sober, be vigilant.
Songs of praise the angels sang. *LH* 35:1.
The First Article.
The 6th Petition.

4. *Luther's Small Catechism*

Questions 108—111.

5. *Liturgy*

The Proper Preface for the season and The Sanctus. *LH*, p. 25—26.

C. AIDS TO LEARNING

1. **Visual:**
2. **Audio:** "For He Shall Give His Angels Charge Over Thee" — Mendelssohn: *Elijah* — Angel, 3558-C.
   "The Lord of Hosts" and "Let All the Angels of God Worship Him" — Handel: *The Messiah* — RCA, LD-6409.
3. **Objects:** Sound waves, light waves, can you see them? Are they real? Sound and images on TV.
4. **Workbook:** * *The New Life,* Unit XII.
   * *Learning About God,* Unit II.
   * *Growing in Faith,* Unit II.
   * *Living for God,* Unit II.
   * *Growing in Grace,* Unit II.
   * *Growing in Christ,* Unit 13.
5. **Bulletin Board:** Pictures of angels.
6. **Chalkboard:** Summary outline.
7. **Group Activity:** Study the use of angels in church art and architecture.
8. **Music:** See Audio Aids above.
9. **Art:** "Angels and Shepherds" — Plockhorst.
10. **Library:** W. A. Kramer, * *Living for Christ.*
    H. W. Gockel, * *What Jesus Means to Me.*

D. EVALUATION

Do you have a clearer concept of angels?

V. Suggestions for Correlations with Other Subjects

A. READING
1. **Silent:** John 1:1-6; * *The Church Through the Ages*, chapter 1.
2. **Oral:** Matt. 4:1-11.
3. **Choral:** Psalm 91; Matt. 4:1-11; Rev. 12:7-12.

B. ENGLISH
1. **Oral:** Report on silent readings.
2. **Written:** Report on the various appearances of angels recorded in the O. T., the N. T.
3. **Vocabulary and Spelling:** Gabriel, angelic, spirit, messenger.
4. **Handwriting:** a — angel, A — Angelus.

C. SOCIAL SCIENCES
1. **Family and Home Life:** Read Matt. 18:10, Ps. 91:11-12. What difference can this make in family life?
2. **Community and Nation:** Find examples of an angel's action on behalf of a nation. Use your concordance. Can the term "angel of mercy" be applied to a Christian? How?
3. **History:** Civil law sometimes refers to "an act of God." What does this term mean?

D. PHYSICAL SCIENCES
1. **Nature Study:** Report on movement of electric current, light and sound waves; transmitting radio and TV signals.
2. **Geography:** Prepare a map of the Holy land and locate places where angels appeared.
3. **Health:** Find examples of angels saving human life. Use your concordance.
4. **General Science:** Debate: Can a Christian be a scientist?

E. ARITHMETIC
How many angels make "12 legions of angels"? What is a "legion"? Compare Biblical measures with those used in our country.

F. ART
"Angels' Heads" — Reynolds.

G. MUSIC
Learn the Introit for St. Michael's and All Angels' Day. *LH*, p. 92.

UNIT
13

MAN

•

I. Scope and Importance

Man is the most important of all organic beings. Other living creatures are but a means to an end. Man is an end. The worth of the individual is paramount. Adam was created in the image of God. Man is endowed with reason, intelligence, emotion, will, speech, erect walk, and with an immortal soul. People Come First. State motto of Missouri.

The origin, nature, purpose, and destiny of mankind and of each individual person is a matter of tremendous consequence. Man or monkey? God or gorilla? In the image of God or a mere ambitious animal? A fallen saint or a cultured brute? This is a very important unit.

In this unit the learners should receive an overview of man: creation, fall, redemption, sanctification, final salvation in heaven.

II. Aim

A. KNOWLEDGE

Insight, understanding: Stimulate thinking which leads to a clear, correct, Biblical concept concerning the human race and each person: origin, nature, purpose, destiny. Develop Biblical world view. Find right answers to: Whence am I? Why am I? Whither am I going? Familiarity with related vocabulary. Memorize thoroughly a limited number of usable Bible quotations.

B. ATTITUDE

Foster a serious and sustained interest in and concern for man's temporal and eternal welfare; create a desire to do and serve; create humility because of the fall of man and of his sinful heart and actions. Eliminate prejudice and pride over against humans who are of a different color or language. Regard as very important each individual human being. Foster tolerance. Encourage interest in social service.

C. HABITS, SKILLS

Train pupils in thinking of their bodies as creations of God and as temples of the Spirit of God; take good care of their body and its organs; wholesome, balanced diet; clean and sound teeth; health habits that include eating, drinking, elimination, care of teeth, skin, hands and fingernails, eyes, ears, heart, lungs; posture in sitting and walking; train also in habits that express belief in the soul and its daily needs. Train in habits of providing and taking good care of food, clothing, shelter, etc. Train in habit of thanking God and His representatives for providing us with food, shelter, clothing, and protection.

D. ANTICIPATED OUTCOME IN TERMS OF SANCTIFIED PERSONALITIES

Individuals who are humbly and gratefully aware of their dignity, origin, purpose and destiny; who are actively concerned about the welfare and happiness of every other human being, in time and hereafter. Adults who are somewhat conversant with physiology, hygiene, sociology, anthropology, and psychology.

III. Curriculum Material

A. BIBLE STUDIES

DATE USED

```
_____  Man, Evolved or Created? Gen. 1:26-31.
_____  When Man Lived in Paradise. Gen. 2:8-17.
_____  Adam Receives a Helpmate. Gen. 2:18-25.
_____  Why Man Was Driven from Paradise. Gen. 3.
_____  Dare Anyone Say: He Made Me Not?
                  Is. 29:13-17. (16)
_____  Threescore Years and Ten. Ps. 90:1-12. (10)
```

MAN — Unit 13

DATE USED

No Self-made Men! *Dan. 4:29-33.*
Man is Weak — But God Is Strong to Save. *Is. 40:1-11.*
Some Persons Will Never Die. *John 8:48-59.* (51)
Why Christians Are Not Afraid of Death.
1 Cor. 15:35-58.
Redeemed and Born Again (Twice-born Man).
1 Peter 1:18-25.
Believers May Look Forward to a Tearless Eternity.
Rev. 7:9-17.

B. LUTHER'S SMALL CATECHISM

Questions 112—115.

C. MEMORY MATERIAL

1. Bible Texts

GRADE

1 I will praise Thee; for I am fearfully and wonderfully made; marvelous are Thy works; and that my soul knoweth right well. *Ps. 139:14.* (4)

2 I will praise Thee; for I am fearfully and wonderfully made; marvelous are Thy works; and that my soul knoweth right well. *Ps. 139:14.* (4)

3 The Lord God formed man of the dust of the ground and breathed into his nostrils the breath of life; and man became a living soul. *Gen. 2:7.* (4)

4 Put on the new man, which after God is created in righteousness and true holiness. *Eph. 4:24.* (4)

5 (Adam) begat a son in his own likeness, after his image. *Gen. 5:3.*

6 I will behold Thy face in righteousness; I shall be satisfied, when I awake, with Thy likeness. *Ps. 17:15.* (5)

7 (Ye) have put on the new man, which is renewed in knowledge after the image of Him that created him. *Col. 3:10.*

8 God said, Let Us make man in Our image, after Our likeness; and let them have dominion over the fish of the sea and over the fowl of the air and over the cattle and over all the earth and over every creeping thing that creepeth upon the earth. So God created man in His own image, in the image of God created He him; male and female created He them. *Gen. 1:26, 27.*

2. Luther's Small Catechism

1   The First Article. Expl. 3—8.
6—8 The Second Article
7—8 The Third Article.
6—8 The Seventh Petition.

3. Hymns

GRADE

1–2   Oh, bless the Lord, my soul!
       Let all within me join
     And aid my tongue to bless His name
       Whose favors are divine.   LH 27:1

3–4   Take my life and let it be
     Consecrated, Lord, to Thee;
     Take my moments and my days,
       Let them flow in ceaseless praise.   LH 400:1

5–6   A pilgrim and a stranger,
       I journey here below;
     Far distant is my country,
       The home to which I go.
     Here I must toil and travail,
       Oft weary and opprest;
     But there my God shall lead me
       To everlasting rest.   LH 586:1

7–8   O Love, who madest me to wear
       The image of Thy Godhead here;
     Who soughtest me with tender care
       Through all my wanderings wild and drear, —
     O Love, I give myself to Thee,
       Thine ever, only Thine, to be.   LH 397:1

4. Prayers

Almighty God, who hast given Thine only Son to be unto us both a Sacrifice for sin and also an Ensample of godly life, give us grace that we may always most thankfully receive this His inestimable benefit and also daily endeavor ourselves to follow the blessed steps of His most holy life; through the same Jesus Christ, Thy Son, our Lord. Amen.
LH, p. 108, No. 62

(*LH*, p. 110, The Litany; p. 115, The Morning Suffrages; p. 105, Nos. 36, 37, For the Sick; No. 38, For Mothers; p. 107, Nos. 55, 56, For Grace to Love and Serve God; No. 661, The Litany.)

D. SUMMARY OUTLINE FOR THE CHALKBOARD

Man
     created — not evolved
     in God's image — in holiness, with reason, immortal soul, speech
     fallen — not good by nature
     redeemed — not saved by self
     sanctified and serving — the image partly restored
     in heaven — singing praises unto the Lamb; God's image fully restored.

MAN — Unit 13

IV. Instructional Methods and Materials

A. PROBLEM AND APPROACH
Cemeteries are filled with gravestones. Each stone marks the resting place of some person. Is this the end for each person, or is there something else to come?

B. SUGGESTED TEACHING UNIT

1. **Devotion**

   Hymn: Now Thank We All Our God. *LH* 36.
   Scripture Reading: Gen. 1:26-31.
   Prayer: The Morning Suffrages. *LH*, p. 115.

2. **Bible Story**

   Rev. 7:9-17.

3. **Memory Passages**

   Psalm 139:14: I will praise Thee.
   Psalm 17:15: I will behold Thy face.
   Eph. 4:24: Put on the new man.
   O Love, who madest me to wear. *LH* 397:1.
   The 1st Article.

4. **Luther's Small Catechism**

   Questions 112—115.

5. **Liturgy**

   The Venite. *LH*, p. 33.

C. AIDS TO LEARNING

1. **Visual:** *Creation* — 79-102 — filmstrip.
   The Fall of Man — 79-232 — filmstrip.
2. **Audio:** "The Creation" — (Speak Four Trio), Word, W-4013.
   (This is a speech choir rendering of Genesis 1; 2:1-3)
3. **Object:** Skeleton of a man or animal (a plastic model may be used).
4. **Workbook:** ° *The New Life,* Unit XIII.
   ° *Learning About God,* Unit II.
   ° *Growing in Grace,* Unit II.
   ° *Growing in Christ,* Unit 14.
5. **Bulletin Board:** Pictures and clippings of individuals and family groups, babies; various races; men and women at various occupations.
6. **Chalkboard:** Summary outline.
7. **Group Activity:** Visit a welfare institution.
8. **Music:** The Magnificat. *LH*, p. 43.

9. **Art:** "Man With a Hoe."
10. **Library:** J. W. Klotz, * *Modern Science in the Christian Life.*
    * *Challenge of the Space Age.*

D. EVALUATION

Have I found a Scriptural and satisfying answer to the questions "Who am I, where did I come from, and where am I going?"

V. Suggestions for Correlations with Other Subjects

A. READING

1. **Silent:** Gen. 2:18-25; Is. 40:10, 11.
2. **Oral:** Psalm 90; selections from * *The Lutheran Annual.*
3. **Choral:** Canticle — Benedicite Omnia Opera. *LH* p. 120.

B. ENGLISH

1. **Oral:** Report on silent readings above.
2. **Written:** The most interesting person I know.
3. **Vocabulary and Spelling:** humane, evolution, image, sociology.
4. **Handwriting:** h — human, H — Humanism.

C. SOCIAL SCIENCES

1. **Home and Family Life:** Solving family problems together.
2. **Community and Nation:** Christian race relationships.
3. **History:** The United Nations: an organization for world understanding.

D. PHYSICAL SCIENCES

1. **Nature Study:** Prepare an illustrated chart showing the various classifications for living things.
2. **Geography:** Natural resources and our standard of living: how they are related.
3. **Health:** Our bodies — God's temples.
4. **General Science:** How changes take place in living things.

E. ARITHMETIC

Make charts and graphs showing the growth of the world's population and that of the U. S.

F. ART

Make symbols for the Creator, such as the Creator's Hand.

G. MUSIC

The Litany. *LH* 661.

UNIT
14

GOD'S GOVERNMENT AND PRESERVATION

A Thanksgiving or New Year Unit

•

I. Scope and Importance

God preserves His creation, usually by natural means and methods, if necessary by supernatural means and methods. Where God guides, He also provides. While on the path of duty we may rest assured that God goes with us. A thorough appreciation of this unit should contribute toward a happy life.

Items mentioned in the Fourth Petition may well be integrated with this unit.

II. Aim

A. KNOWLEDGE

Insight, Understanding: Stimulate thinking that leads to clear, vivid, and correct ideas about God's government of the world and the preservation of all creatures; understanding that human effort and human ingenuity, intelligence and skill, have a place, but a subordinate place, in the preservation of creation. Even a sparrow does not die without the permission of God the Preserver. Such knowledge makes for courage and good cheer. Familiarity with laws of nature. Discover design and purpose in nature and history. Familiarize with related vocabulary. Commit to memory well selected and appreciated memory gems.

B. ATTITUDE

Seek to engender faith and implicit trust in the God who has revealed Himself in nature, conscience, and the Bible. Encourage learners to cast all their cares upon Him, seeing that He careth for them. Foster the spirit of joyful gratitude to God for His preservation and care. Cultivate appreciation of the part which human work, ingenuity, skill, and love (all gifts of God) play in this matter. Induce sincere consecration to the Living God. The hymns will help you to create atmosphere, sentiment, group morale.

C. HABITS, SKILLS

Train pupils to sing joyous songs of gratitude, confidence, and trust, "Now Thank We All Our God." Train the children in habits of industry, honest work, thrift, saving. Train pupils to view history and science in the light of the important truth of God's government and preservation.

D. ANTICIPATED OUTCOME IN TERMS OF SANCTIFIED PERSONALITIES

Persons who understand, believe, and rejoice in the truth that God lives, and that God's people need not fret or fear unduly. Happy, industrious, carefree, God-fearing and God-trusting boys and girls, men and women, who praise God by their songs, attitudes, and conduct. Well-poised, well-adjusted, happy, positive, buoyant personalities.

III. Curriculum Material

A. BIBLE STUDIES

DATE USED

- _____ Jesus Will Not Let His People Starve. *Matt. 14:15-21.*
- _____ God Preserves His Creation. *Gen. 8:15; 9:1-7.*
- _____ *God Provides for the Survival of His Creation. *Gen. 9:1-3.*
- _____ *In Days of Depression We May Look to the Lord (Israel). *Deut. 8.*
- _____ *Even in Hard Times We May Share and yet Not Want (Elijah). *1 Kings 17:1-16.*

GOD'S GOVERNMENT AND PRESERVATION — Unit 14

DATE USED

- *Believe It: No Evil Shall Befall Thee (Lot). Gen. 19:12-26.
- *God Helps His People Free from Every Need. Exodus 13:11-22.
- *Great Help Comes to a Great Believer (Centurion). Luke 7:1-10.
- The Lord Guides and He Provides. Psalm 23.
- Do Not Worry! Psalm 37:23-26.
- God Does Shelter His Own. Matt. 2:11-15.
- Consider the Lilies, Ye of Little Faith! Matt. 6:24-34. (28).
- God's Greatest Proof of His Great Love for You. Rom. 8:28-39.
- Make a Joyful Noise unto the Lord. Psalm 100.
- *Our Great God Guides and Provides. Psalm 104.
- Great Is Our God. Psalm 147.

B. LUTHER'S SMALL CATECHISM
Questions 116—120.

C. MEMORY MATERIAL
1. Bible Texts

GRADE

1. Cast all your care upon Him; for He careth for you. 1 Peter 5:7. (2)

2. Oh, give thanks unto the Lord, for He is good; because His mercy endureth forever. Ps. 118:1.

3. Commit thy way unto the Lord; trust also in Him; and He shall bring it to pass. Ps. 37:5.

4. Like as a father pitieth his children, so the Lord pitieth them that fear Him. Ps. 103:13. (3)

5. The eyes of all wait upon Thee; and Thou givest them their meat in due season. Thou openest Thine hand and satisfiest the desire of every living thing. Ps. 145:15, 16.

6. There shall no evil befall thee, neither shall any plague come nigh thy dwelling. Ps. 91:10. (6)

7. Are not two sparrows sold for a farthing? And one of them shall not fall on the ground without your Father. But the very hairs of your head are all numbered. Matt. 10:29, 30. (6)

   Ye thought evil against me; but God meant it unto good, to bring to pass, as it is this day, to save much people alive. Gen. 50:20. (7)

GRADE

8   I am not worthy of the least of all thy mercies and of all the truth which Thou hast showed unto Thy servant. *Gen. 32:10.* (7)

What shall I render unto the Lord for all His benefits toward me? *Ps. 116:12.*

2. *Luther's Small Catechism*

1   The First Article. Expl. 4—8.
5–8   Introduction to the Lord's Prayer.
7–8   The Seventh Petition and the Fourth Petition.

3. *Hymns*

1–2   The Lord my pasture shall prepare
And feed me with a shepherd's care;
His presence shall my wants supply
And guard me with a watchful eye;
My noonday walks He shall attend
And all my midnight hours defend.   *LH* 368:1

3–4   Now thank we all our God
   With heart and hands and voices,
Who wondrous things hath done,
   In whom His world rejoices;
Who from our mother's arms
   Hath blessed us on our way
With countless gifts of love,
   And still is ours today.   *LH* 36:1

5-6   O God, forsake me not!
   Thy gracious presence lend me;
Lead Thou Thy helpless child;
   Thy Holy Spirit send me
That I my course may run.
   Be Thou my Light, my Lot,
My Staff, my Rock, my Shield, —
   O God, forsake me not!   *LH* 402:1

7–8   Thee will I love, my Strength, my Tower;
   Thee will I love, my Hope, my Joy;
Thee will I love with all my power,
   With ardor time shall ne'er destroy.
Thee will I love, O Light Divine,
So long as life is mine.   *LH* 399:1

4. *Prayers*

O Lord, I sing with lips and heart (*LH* 569:1-7). The Morning Prayer. The Evening Prayer (*LH*, p. 118). For the Civil Authorities (*LH*, p. 104). Thanksgiving (*LH*, p. 106, Nos. 42—45). The Litany (*LH*, pp. 110, 111).

GOD'S GOVERNMENT AND PRESERVATION – Unit 14

The Bidding Prayer (*LH*, p. 116). Collects for the 7th Sunday after Trinity. Collects for the New Year.

Use throughout day appropriate short prayers at the beginning or at the end of a lesson. Use extempore as well as teacher's and pupils' written prayers.

D. SUMMARY OUTLINE FOR THE CHALKBOARD

Where God guides, He provides.
>God *created* all
>God *preserves* all, by *natural means;* if necessary, by *supernatural means*
>God's *goodness prompts Him*
>Everyone should *praise* God
>God's people may *trust* God

IV. Instructional Methods and Materials

A. PROBLEM AND APPROACH

Does man's survival depend on man alone? Does it depend on his intelligence, physical fitness, or a combination of several characteristics?

B. SUGGESTED TEACHING UNIT

1. Devotion

Hymn: The Lord My Pasture Shall Prepare. *LH* 368:1.
Scripture Reading: Matt. 6:24-34.
Prayer: ° *Teen-Agers Pray,* p. 19.

2. Bible Story

1 Kings 17:1-16.

3. Memory Passages

1 Peter 5:7: Cast all your care.
Gen. 50:20: Ye thought evil against me.
Psalm 37:5: Commit thy way unto the Lord.
The Lord my pasture shall prepare. *LH* 368:1.
The 1st Article.
The 4th Petition.

4. Luther's Small Catechism

Questions 116—120.

5. Liturgy

Levavi Oculos. *LH* 665.

C. AIDS TO LEARNING

1. **Visual:** *Creation* — 79-102 — filmstrip.
2. **Audio:** "If Thou But Suffer God to Guide Thee" — *LH* 518 — (Let the Earth Rejoice) KFUO, HA 61.
   "Oh, Rest in the Lord," "He Watches Over Israel," "Be Not Afraid," and "Lift Thine Eyes" — Mendelssohn: *Elijah*. Angel, 3558-C.
3. **Object:** human hairs, bird(s).
4. **Workbook:** * *The New Life*, Unit XIV.
   * *Learning About God*, Unit II.
   * *Growing in Faith*, Unit II.
   * *Living for God*, Unit II.
   * *Building for Eternity*, Unit II.
   * *Growing in Grace*, Unit II.
   * *Growing in Christ*, Unit 15.
5. **Bulletin Board:** Pictures and clippings of people at work, government agencies; religious pictures illustrating God's protection.
6. **Chalkboard:** Summary outline.
7. **Group Activity:** Visit a government agency; visit a natural forest.
8. **Music:** See Audio Aids above.
9. **Art:** "Harvest" — Parrish.
10. **Library:** H. W. Gockel, * *My Hand in His*.
    Meindert De Jong, *The Mighty Ones, Great Men and Women of Early Bible Days* (Harper & Row). (Gr. 6—9)

D. EVALUATION

Do we have a clearer understanding of God's creation and preservation? Do we have a new appreciation for honest work?

V. Suggestions for Correlations with Other Subjects

A. READING

1. **Silent:** Matt. 6:24-34.
2. **Oral:** Psalm 23; "Dawn," from * *Treasury of Christian Literature*, p. 169
3. **Choral:** Psalm 100.

B. ENGLISH

1. **Oral:** Panel discussion — The Christian and his government.
2. **Written:** Write an original story, poem, or prayer about God's care and protection.
3. **Vocabulary and Spelling:** preservation, Noah, government, anxiety, careless, fearless.
4. **Handwriting:** s — security, S — Savior.

GOD'S GOVERNMENT AND PRESERVATION – Unit 14

C. SOCIAL SCIENCES

1. **Home and Family Life:** Prepare a family devotion on the topic "God Cares for Our Family."
2. **Community and Nation:** Discuss what makes a good government; prepare a report on causes of unemployment.
3. **History:** Report on the basic differences between democracy and Communism; the origin of Thanksgiving Day.

D. PHYSICAL SCIENCES

1. **Nature Study:** Prepare a map showing the length of the growing season in various parts of the U. S.
2. **Geography:** Need anyone go hungry? How can we help other less fortunate countries?
3. **Health:** Is overeating harmful? What are the basic 7 foods?
4. **General Science:** How has science increased life expectancy in the U. S.? What inventions have contributed to more efficient food storage?

E. ARTHMETIC

Examine various tax forms. Make charts and graphs to show how local, state, and federal tax monies are spent.

F. ART

"Feeding Her Birds" — Millet.

G. MUSIC

Sing the Cantate Domino, *LH* 667, at a children's worship service.

UNIT
15

JESUS CHRIST
Son of God and Son of Man

(1)

A Christmas or Advent Unit

•

I. Scope and Importance

O blest the land, the city blest,
Where Christ the Ruler is confessed!
O happy hearts and happy homes
To whom this King in triumph comes!
The cloudless Sun of Joy He is,
Who bringeth pure delight and bliss.
We praise Thee, Spirit, now,
Our Comforter art Thou!

Jesus Christ is the world's most important person. No soul can afford to live or die without knowledge of Him and faith in Him.

"Take Christ out of the Scriptures, and what will you find remaining in them?" (Luther)

"All other things are but chaff when compared with Christ, the Son of God." (Luther)

Jesus is the Way, the Truth, and the Life. He that has

seen Him has seen the Father. Jesus is the Savior of sinners and the Example for saints.

All eternity will hear the hymns of praise addressed to Jesus.

II. Aim

A. KNOWLEDGE

Stimulate thinking which leads to clear, vivid, and Biblical ideas about Jesus. God manifest in the flesh. The story of the incarnation is the historical event which is second to none in importance for the human race. Familiarity with related vocabulary.

B. ATTITUDE

Group sentiment: Throughout this and the following five units the instructor should keep in mind that the personal appeal to acknowledge, receive, accept, and believe in Jesus is the focal point in each lesson. The Holy Spirit will kindle a fervent, personal faith in the hearts of the learners, but He has chosen to do that through the Word. Avoid mere intellectualism. Knowledge, information, familiarity with facts are important and indispensable. But these are only a means to an end. Faith, hope, and charity, these are the end objectives at which the teacher with insight will aim. Aim at developing willingness to participate in choir work, soul-winning and soul-keeping endeavors.

"Let every heart prepare a throne and every voice a song."
"Jesus, Savior, come to me; Let me ever be with Thee."

C. HABITS, SKILLS

Since the Bible was written that men might believe in Jesus, the Son of God, and, believing, have life eternal, the pupils should be trained in the habit of always finding Jesus as the core and center of the Bible; of asking: How is that story or verse connected with Jesus? Ability to quote pertinent Bible text. Skill in winning others for Christ, inviting them to church, school, Sunday school, confirmation instruction. Develop skill in speaking or writing an original prayer. Foster the habit of assembling for worship, to give on the first day of the week as the Lord has prospered. 1 Cor. 16:1, 2.

D. ANTICIPATED OUTCOME IN TERMS OF
CHRIST-CENTERED PERSONALITIES

Boys and girls, men and women, who are sincerely and affectionately in faith attached to Jesus; who rejoice in His love, are grateful to Him, strive to follow in His footsteps, and tell others convincingly of Him.

III. Curriculum Material

A. BIBLE STUDIES

DATE USED

_____	*Immanuel — God with Us. *Matt. 1:18-25.*
_____	The Annunciation. *Luke 1:26-38.*
_____	*The Savior of the World is Born. *Luke 2:1-11.*
_____	*In the Beginning Was the Word. *John 1:1-18.*
_____	He that Hath Seen Me Hath Seen the Father. *John 14:8-11.*
_____	*The Man with the Power of God over Death (Lazarus). *John 11:32-46.*
_____	Jesus and His Father Are One. *John 10:27-39.*
_____	*He is Risen. *Matt. 28:1-8.*
_____	*The One to Whom All Power is Given. *Matt. 28:18-20.*
_____	Worshiping the King of the Jews. *Matt. 2:1-10.*
_____	Gentiles Shall Also Worship Jesus. *Is. 60:1-6.*
_____	"I Am from Above." *John 8:21-25.*

B. LUTHER'S SMALL CATECHISM

Questions 121—124; 128; 135—137.

C. MEMORY MATERIAL

1. Bible Texts

GRADE

1 Let all the angels of God worship Him. *Heb. 1:6.*
   This is the true God and eternal Life. *1 John 5:20.* (3)
   All men should honor the Son even as they honor the Father. He that honoreth not the Son honoreth not the Father, which hath sent Him. *John 5:23.*

2 The Son of Man hath power on earth to forgive sins. *Matt. 9:6.* (2)
   Lo, I am with you alway, even unto the end of the world. *Matt. 28:20.* (2)

JESUS CHRIST, Son of God and Son of Man — Unit 15

GRADE

All power is given unto Me in heaven and in earth. *Matt. 28:18.* (2)

3   She shall bring forth a Son, and thou shalt call His name Jesus; for He shall save His people from their sins. *Matt. 1:21.*
This is the true God and eternal Life. *1 John 5:20.* (3)
God so loved the world, that He gave His only-begotten Son, that whosoever believeth in Him should not perish, but have everlasting life. *John 3:16.*

4   Unto us a Child is born, unto us a Son is given; and the government shall be upon His shoulder; and His name shall be called Wonderful, Counselor, The Mighty God, The Everlasting Father, The Prince of Peace. *Is. 9:6.* (4)
Jesus Christ the same yesterday and today and forever. *Heb. 13:8.* (3)
Lord, Thou knowest all things. *John 21:17.* (1)

5   Neither is there salvation in any other; for there is none other name under heaven given among men whereby we must be saved. *Acts 4:12.* (5)
God, Thy God, hath anointed Thee with the oil of gladness above Thy fellows. *Ps. 45:7.*
This is life eternal that they might know Thee the only true God, and Jesus Christ, whom Thou hast sent. *John 17:3.*

6   God anointed Jesus of Nazareth with the Holy Ghost and with power. *Acts 10:38.*
There is one God, and one Mediator between God and men, the man Christ Jesus. *1 Tim. 2:5.* (7)
(He upholds) all things by the word of His power. *Heb. 1:3.*

7   In the beginning was the Word, and the Word was with God, and the Word was God. The same was in the beginning with God. *John 1:1, 2.*
(The Father) hath given Him authority to execute judgment. *John 5:27.*
All things were made by Him; and without Him was not anything made that was made. *John 1:3.*
Let this mind be in you which was also in Christ Jesus, who, being in the form of God, thought it not robbery to be equal with God; but made Himself of no reputation and took upon Him the form of a servant and was made in the likeness of men; and being found in fashion as a man, He humbled Himself and became obedient unto death, even the death of the cross. *Phil. 2:5-8.* (8)

8   He that believeth not the Son shall not see life, but the wrath of God abideth in him. *John 3:36.*
I know whom I have believed and am persuaded that He is able

GRADE

to keep that which I have committed unto Him against that day. *2 Tim. 1:12.*

Behold, a voice out of the cloud, which said, This is My beloved Son, in whom I am well pleased; hear ye Him. *Matt. 17:5.*

Behold My hands and My feet, that it is I Myself; handle Me and see; for a spirit hath not flesh and bones, as ye see Me have. *Luke 24:39.*

My soul is exceeding sorrowful, even unto death. *Matt. 26:38.*

2. *Luther's Small Catechism*

1–8   The Second Article. Expl. 3–8.

5–8   The Second Petition.

3. *Hymns*

1–2
To you this night is born a child
Of Mary, chosen virgin mild;
This little child, of lowly birth,
Shall be the joy of all the earth.   LH 85:2

3–4
All my heart this night rejoices
   As I hear Far and near
Sweetest angel voices.
"Christ is born," their choirs are singing
   Till the air Ev'rywhere
Now with joy is ringing.   LH 77:1

5–6
Come, Thou precious Ransom, come,
   Only Hope for sinful mortals!
Come, O Savior of the world!
   Open are to Thee all portals.
Come, Thy beauty let us see;
Anxiously we wait for Thee.   LH 55:1

7–8
O Lord, how shall I meet Thee,
   How welcome Thee aright?
Thy people long to greet Thee,
   My Hope, my heart's Delight!
Oh, kindle, Lord, most holy,
   Thy lamp within my breast
To do in spirit lowly
   All that may please Thee best.   LH 58:1

4. *Prayers*

Stir up our hearts, O Lord, to make ready the way of Thine only-begotten Son, so that by His coming we may be enabled to serve Thee with pure minds; through the same Jesus Christ, Thy Son, our Lord, who liveth and reigneth with Thee and the Holy Ghost, ever one God, world without end. Amen.   (*LH*, p. 54)

JESUS CHRIST, Son of God and Son of Man — Unit 15

Most Merciful God (*LH*, p. 55 — Other Collects for Advent). Almighty and Everlasting God (*LH*, p. 57). Collects for the Annunciation, Collects for Advent Sundays, Collects for Christmas.

D. SUMMARY OUTLINE FOR THE CHALKBOARD

Christmas

1) O. T. Promises: Messiah, Anointed, Christ
2) N. T. Fulfillment: Jesus, Helper
   Conceived
   Born: Christmas, Bethlehem
      Personal Union
      Incarnation
   O Come, Let Us Adore Him!

IV. Instructional Methods and Materials

A. PROBLEM AND APPROACH

Jesus once asked His hearers this question: "What do you think of the Christ? Whose son is He?" Each of them had differing ideas and opinions. Have you ever tried to answer that question? What do YOU think about it?

B. SUGGESTED TEACHING UNIT

1. *Devotion*

Hymn: Come, Thou Precious Ransom, Come. *LH* 55:1.
Scripture Reading: Matt. 1:18-25.
Prayer: ° *Teen-Agers Pray*, p. 27.

2. *Bible Story*

Luke 2:1-11.

3. *Memory Passages*

John 3:16: God so loved the world.
Is. 9:6: Unto us a Child is born.
John 1:1: In the beginning was the Word.
O blest the land, the city blest. *LH* 73:3.
The Second Article.
The Second Petition.
The Nicene Creed.

4. *Luther's Small Catechism*

Questions 121—124; 135—137.

5. *Liturgy*

The Gloria in Excelsis. *LH*, p. 7.

C. AIDS TO LEARNING

1. **Visual:** *Redemption* — 79-103 — 2 filmstrips.
   The Glory of The Lord — 79-5243 — sound filmstrip.
2. **Audio:** "From Heaven Above to Earth I Come" — *LH* 85 — (The Lutheran Hour) RCA, LPM-1863 (Stereo LSP-1863).
   "Praise God the Lord, Ye Sons of Men" — *LH* 105 — (Christmas Carols) Word, W-4020.
   "Once He Came in Blessing" — *LH* 74 — (Sing Unto the Lord) KFUO, HA 60; also Word, W-4017.
   Christmas portions of *The Messiah* — RCA, LD-6409.
3. **Objects:** Creche (or diorama).
4. **Workbook:** * *The New Life*, Unit XV.
   * *Learning About God*, Unit I.
   * *Growing in Christ*, Unit 16.
5. **Bulletin Board:** Christmas pictures.
6. **Chalkboard:** Summary outline.
7. **Group Activity:** Sing carols at home for aged, homes of "shut-ins."
8. **Music:** The Hallelujah Chorus from Handel's *Messiah*.
9. **Art:** "Star in the East" — Dore.
10. **Library:** Various Christmas stories; R. E. Haugen, *Christmas* (Augsburg).

D. EVALUATION

Have you come to know Christ as your Savior? Is it Christmas everyday in your life?

V. Suggestions for Correlations with Other Subjects

A. READING

1. **Silent:** John 8:12-25: "The Story of the Messiah," from * *Treasury of Christian Literature*, p. 147.
2. **Oral:** Is. 60:1-6.
3. **Choral:** Psalm 2.

B. ENGLISH

1. **Oral:** Report on Christmas customs of other lands.
2. **Written:** An original Christmas story or poem.
3. **Vocabulary and Spelling:** Christmas, Immanuel, Noel, incarnation.
4. **Handwriting:** c — cheer; C — Christmas.

C. SOCIAL SCIENCES

1. **Home and Family Life:** Help plan for your family's Christmas celebration.
2. **Community and Nation:** Prepare a Christmas display for your school or church lawn.

JESUS CHRIST, Son of God and Son of Man — Unit 15

3. History: The first Christmas tree in America; different Christmas customs.

D. PHYSICAL SCIENCES
1. **Nature Study:** Nature at Christmas.
2. **Geography:** How Christmas is celebrated in other lands.
3. **Health:** Discuss Mal. 4:2. How does this relate to celebrating Christmas?
4. **General Science:** Astronomy: from the wise men to the present.

E. ARITHMETIC
Christmas savings clubs; find articles and clippings that tell about the amount of money spent for Christmas gifts.

F. ART
Prepare a display for the school or church lawn. Study the "Sistine Madonna" by Raphael.

G. MUSIC
Sing Christmas carols from various lands; listen to the Christmas portions of *The Messiah*.

UNIT 16

JESUS CHRIST
Son of God and Son of Man

(2)
A Christmas or Epiphany Unit

•

I. Scope and Importance

This is a continuation and further elaboration of the preceding unit. Every lesson throughout the school year should be Christo-centric. However, it is very important, too, that we have a series of units in which Christ Jesus is definitely and solely made the subject of teaching and learning.

"Like a precious perfume the name of Jesus is diffused throughout the whole Scripture. All the leaves of Holy Writ smell of it, not only those that were written after His coming, but also those that were written before." (Leighton)

Jesus is light to the eye, honey to the taste, music to the ear, and joy to the heart.

II. Aim

A. KNOWLEDGE

Stimulate thinking which will lead to clear, well-defined, Biblical ideas concerning Jesus Christ as the God-Man Savior of sinners. The personal union of the two natures in one

JESUS CHRIST, Son of God and Son of Man — Unit 16

person is a great mystery indeed and can never be fathomed, and yet even a child can rejoice in "the mystery of godliness," God manifest in the flesh. The reason why the Savior should be both true God and true man is stressed in this unit. Why did God become man?

B. ATTITUDE

Aim to foster sincere faith in and affectionate attachment to Jesus. The pupils who have learned to appreciate, value, love, and admire Jesus will show also desirable social attitudes over against others: schoolmates, superiors, rivals. Foster a group sentiment which is permeated with Jesus.

C. HABITS, SKILLS

Train pupils in the art of quoting Scriptures to defend their faith. To defend their own faith, to convince and win others is an art which requires thorough familiarity with pertinent Scripture passages. Train pupils in making their own oral and written prayers centered about Jesus. Develop skill in locating pertinent Scripture chapters and verses.

D. ANTICIPATED OUTCOME IN TERMS OF CHRIST-CENTERED PERSONALITIES

Persons who have one unifying purpose and joy in life: to serve Jesus; to follow in His footsteps; to be Christ-minded.

III. Curriculum Material

A. BIBLE STUDIES

DATE USED

- Kiss the Son. *Psalm 2.*
- Behold Your God! *Is. 40:9-11.*
- On Seeing the Father in the Son. *John 14:1-14.*
- *Every Tongue Shall Confess It. *Phil. 2:5-11.*
- How the Invisible Became Visible. *John 1:1-18.*
- *About Some Men Who Forsook All and Followed Jesus. *Luke 5:1-11.*
- When the Disciples Saw Jesus Only. *Mark 9:1-10.*
- Before Abraham Was, I Am. *John 8:46-59.*
- One God and Lord Jesus Christ. *1 Cor. 8:4-6.*

DATE USED

                 A Great Light for Those Sitting in Darkness. *Is. 9:2-6.*
                 Whom Say Ye That I Am? *Matt. 16:13-20.*
                 °A Very Great Discovery. *John 1:43-51.*
                 Do We Look for Another? *Matt. 11:1-6.*
                 Jesus' Second Miracle. *John 4:46-54.*
                 °Jesus Meets a Woman at the Well. *John 4:1-6.*
                 °How Someone Brought His Brother to Jesus. *John 1:35-42.*
                 The Boy Who was Obedient to Both His Father in Heaven and His Parents. *Luke 2:41-52.*
                 The Chief Cornerstone in Zion. *1 Peter 2:4-8.*
                 The Power that Changed Water into Wine at a Wedding. *John 2:1-11.*
                 The Vine and the Branches. *John 15:1-10.*
                 One with Authority to Forgive and Power to Heal. *Matt. 9:1-8.*
                 The Great Physician. *Mark 7:31-37.*
                 What Manner of Man Is This? *Luke 8:22-25.*
                 °A Mighty Choral Union. *Rev. 5:11-14.*

B. LUTHER'S SMALL CATECHISM

    Questions 125—127; 129—131.

C. MEMORY MATERIAL

    1. Bible Texts

GRADE

1   Lord, Thou knowest all things. *John 21:17.* (1)

     The blood of Jesus Christ, His Son, cleanseth us from all sin. *1 John 1:7.* (1)

2   The Son of Man hath power on earth to forgive sins. *Matt. 9:6.* (2)

     All power is given unto Me in heaven and in earth. *Matt. 28:18.* (2)

3   Lo, I am with you alway, even unto the end of the world. *Matt. 28:20.* (2)

     This is the true God and eternal Life. *1 John 5:20.* (3)

4   Jesus Christ the same yesterday and today and forever. *Heb. 13:8.* (3)

     Unto us a Child is born, unto us a Son is given; and the government shall upon His shoulder; and His name shall be called Wonderful, Counselor, The Mighty God, The Everlasting Father, The Prince of Peace. *Is. 9:6.*

JESUS CHRIST, Son of God and Son of Man — Unit 16

GRADE

5 In Him dwelleth all the fullness of the Godhead bodily. *Col. 2:9.* (5)

Christ hath abolished death. *2 Tim. 1:10.* (5)

6 (Ye) killed the Prince of Life. *Acts 3:15.*

Without controversy great is the mystery of godliness: God was manifest in the flesh. *1 Tim. 3:16.*

7 When the fullness of the time was come, God sent forth His Son, made of a woman, made under the Law, to redeem them that were under the Law, that we might receive the adoption of sons. *Gal. 4:4, 5.* (8)

There is one God, and one Mediator between God and men, the man Christ Jesus. *1 Tim. 2:5.* (7)

Thanks be to God, which giveth us the victory through our Lord Jesus Christ. *1 Cor. 15:57.*

8 The Word was made flesh and dwelt among us (and we beheld His glory, the glory as of the Only-begotten of the Father), full of grace and truth. *John 1:14.* (7)

The Son of Man came, not to be ministered unto, but to minister and to give His life a ransom for many. *Mark 10:45.*

Forasmuch, then, as the children are partakers of flesh and blood, He also Himself likewise took part of the same, that through death He might destroy him that had the power of death, that is, the devil. *Heb. 2:14.*

2. Luther's Small Catechism

1 The Second Article. Expl. 2—8.

3. Hymns

1-2 All hail the power of Jesus' name!
    Let angels prostrate fall;
    Bring forth the royal diadem
    And crown Him Lord of all.   *LH 339:1*

3-4 As with gladness men of old
    Did the guiding star behold;
    As with joy they hailed its light,
    Leading onward, beaming bright,
    So, most gracious Lord, may we
    Evermore be led by Thee!   *LH 127:1*

5-6 Hark, the herald angels sing,
    "Glory to the newborn King;
    Peace on earth and mercy mild,
    God and sinners reconciled!"
    Joyful, all ye nations rise,

GRADE

> Join the triumph of the skies;
> With th' angelic host proclaim,
> "Christ is born in Bethlehem!"
> Hark! the herald angels sing,
> "Glory to the newborn King!" *LH 94:1*

7–8
> O Jesus, King of Glory,
> Both David's Lord and Son!
> Thy realm endures forever,
> In heaven is fixed Thy throne.
> Help that in earth's dominions,
> Throughout from pole to pole,
> Thy reign may spread salvation
> To each benighted soul. *LH 130:1*

4. Prayers

Merciful God and Father, we thank Thee that Thou hast caused the Sun of Righteousness to rise upon those that dwelt in darkness; and we beseech Thee, graciously break the power of darkness in our hearts, that we may continually increase in the knowledge of Thy truth, and serve Thee in righteousness and true holiness, through Jesus Christ, Thy Son, our Lord, who liveth and reigneth with Thee and the Holy Ghost, ever one God, world without end. Amen. Collects for First Sunday in Advent.

Collects for Third Sunday in Advent. Collects for Fourth Sunday in Advent. Collects for Epiphany. Collects for Twelfth Sunday after Trinity. Collect for Gospel on Judica Sunday.

D. SUMMARY OUTLINE FOR THE CHALKBOARD

Jesus Christ

I. True God:

> names: God, Lord
> attributes: eternal, unchanging, omniscient, etc.
> honor: worship Him

Why: To be an effective Redeemer

> from sin
> from death
> from the devil

II. True Man:

> human names: man, child
> human form and attributes: hands, hungry, born, died

Why: To suffer and die as man's substitute
Appeal: All hail the power of Jesus' name

JESUS CHRIST, Son of God and Son of Man — Unit 16

IV. Instructional Methods and Materials

A. PROBLEM AND APPROACH
Show a picture of Jesus stilling the storm. Discuss the implications the idea illustrated have for us today.

B. SUGGESTED TEACHING UNIT

1. Devotion
Hymn: All Hail the Power of Jesus' Name. *LH* 339.
Scripture Reading: Psalm 2.
Prayer: * *Teen-Agers Pray*, p. 70.

2. Bible Story
Matt. 2:1-12.

3. Memory Passages
Heb. 13:8: Jesus Christ the same yesterday.
John 1:14: The Word was made flesh.
Gal. 4:4-5: When the fullness of time was come.
As with gladness men of old. *LH* 127:1.
The Second Article.
The Second Petition.

4. Luther's Small Catechism
Questions 125—127; 129—131.

5. Liturgy
The Magnificat. *LH*, p. 43.

C. AIDS TO LEARNING
1. **Visual:** *Redemption* — 79-103 — two filmstrips.
2. **Audio:** "How Brightly Beams the Morning Star" — *LH* 343 — (Great Lutheran Hymns) Lutheran Records, RF-6903.
3. **Objects:** Electric switch, lamp.
4. **Workbook:** * *The New Life*, Unit XVI.
   * *Learning About God*, Unit I.
5. **Bulletin Board:** Pictures and clippings of mission activity.
6. **Chalkboard:** Summary outline.
7. **Group Activity:** Dramatize "What a Friend We Have in Jesus" (Walther League).
8. **Music:** Cantate Domino. *LH* 667.
9. **Art:** "Flight into Egypt" — Rubens.
10. **Library:** J. E. Hermann, *Stewardship Topics*. (Stewardship Dept.)

D. EVALUATION
Have we gained a clearer understanding of Jesus' divine and human natures? What topic needs further clarification?

V. Suggestions for Correlations with Other Subjects

A. READING

1. **Silent:** Mission articles and reports in * *The Lutheran Witness;* "Founders of Lutheranism," "James Hudson Taylor, Missionary" from * *Treasury of Christian Literature,* pp. 385, 423.
2. **Oral:** Is. 40:1-11.
3. **Choral:** Psalm 2.

B. ENGLISH

1. **Oral:** Role playing — inviting neighborhood friends to attend church with you.
2. **Written:** Write letters to Concordia Tract Mission for tracts to give to unchurched neighbors.
3. **Vocabulary and Spelling:** Epiphany, missionary, pagan.
4. **Handwriting:** d — divine, D — Deity.

C. SOCIAL SCIENCES

1. **Home and Family Life:** Discuss — Jesus, the Head of our family, the unseen Guest at every meal.
2. **Community and Nation:** "The Saxons Come to America," from * *The Church Through the Ages.*
3. **History:** "Builders of the Kingdom," from * *The Church Through the Ages.*

D. PHYSICAL SCIENCES

1. **Nature Study:** Nature points to God, the Scriptures to Christ. Discuss and give examples.
2. **Geography:** From Jerusalem to the world, the spread of Christianity.
3. **Health:** Discuss your family doctor's role and that of the Great Physician.
4. **General Science:** Science and Jesus' miracles.

E. ARTHMETIC

Make a table showing the growth of the Missouri Synod in the last 10 years. See the *Statistical Yearbook.*

F. ART

Prepare a poster on the theme "What Will You Do with Jesus?"

G. MUSIC

Choose an Epiphany hymn from your hymnal; learn to sing it in two parts for a worship service or parents' meeting.

UNIT
17

THE OFFICE AND WORK OF CHRIST AS PROPHET, PRIEST, AND KING

A Pre-Palm Sunday or an Epiphany Season Unit

•

I. Scope and Importance

The status and office of Jesus as a prophet, a priest, and a king; the threefold kingdom in which Jesus rules; the manner in which He did and in which He does now perform His role as prophet, priest, and king.

Here is a great source of faith-strengthening comfort and consolation.

"In His life Christ is an example, showing us how to live; in His death He is a sacrifice, atoning for our sins; in His resurrection a conqueror; in His ascension a King; in His intercession a High Priest." (Luther)

"As in some of the sunny islands of the Southern Pacific one tree supplies the people with all that they need for their simple wants, fruits for their food, leaves for their houses, stoves, thread, needles, clothing, drink, everything, so Jesus Christ the Tree of Life is Himself the Sum of all the Promises, and having Him, we have everything that we need." (Maclaren)

"He that preaches a God to me that died not for me

the death on the cross, such a God I will not receive." (Luther)

"The moment I make of myself and Christ two, I am all wrong; but when I see that we are one, all is rest and peace." (Luther)

A personal faith in Jesus makes us members of His mystical body, the church.

II. Aim

A. KNOWLEDGE

Stimulate thinking which leads to clear, vivid, and correct ideas about the status and role of a prophet, a priest, and a king; and which leads to mental pictures of Jesus as our Prophet, Priest, and King. Familiarize with related vocabulary.

B. ATTITUDE

Presentation of these truths should lead to great reverence for Jesus as a teacher, great comfort derived from Jesus as our Substitute and Intercessor; and to joyful adoration of Jesus as the heavenly King. Such hymns as "O Jesus, King Most Wonderful," "Jesus, Priceless Treasure!" "O Savior, Precious Savior," "Crown Him with Many Crowns," "Beautiful Savior" should now be sung with fervor and enthusiasm. Singing of such songs helps to create atmosphere. And school atmosphere has great educational value.

C. HABITS, SKILLS

Train children in speaking with reverence of Jesus, of His sacrifice for humanity, His great power, and His great blessing. The ability to quote pertinent Scripture passages concerning the work and service of Jesus at the right time, in the right words, and in the right spirit is an art which ordinarily requires much practice. The skill to find appropriate references through the help of a concordance and parallel references likewise needs motivation and frequent practice. To sing praises of the Savior in the choir requires skill, training, and whole-souled participation on the part of choir members.

THE OFFICE AND WORK OF CHRIST – Unit 17

D. ANTICIPATED OUTCOME IN TERMS OF CHRIST-CENTERED PERSONALITIES

Graduates who will speak highly of their school because there they learned thoroughly to know and love and admire the Redeemer, the beautiful Savior; who will gratefully remember their pastors and teachers because these taught them through the Word to know, love, and rejoice in the Savior; young and old believers whose lives are buoyed up, ennobled, enriched by Christian faith, Christian hope, Christian patience, Christian love and life.

III. Curriculum Material

A. BIBLE STUDIES

DATE USED

- .... A Teacher with Unusual Authority. *Matt. 7:24-29.*
- .... Why Many Believed in Jesus. *John 7:14-31.*
- .... God Spoke to Us by His Son. *Heb. 1:1-6.*
- .... Lift Up Your Heads. *Psalm 24.*
- .... Strange but Good News: With His Stripes We are Healed. *Is. 53:4-9.*
- .... A Royal Reception. *Matt. 21:1-16.*
- .... Redeemed with the Precious Blood of Christ. *1 Peter 1:18-23.*
- .... Thou Hast Made Me to Serve with Thy Sins. *Is. 43:22-25.*
- .... Jesus Our Mediator. *Heb. 9:11-15.*
- .... Christ the Model Teacher. *Matt. 13:33-35.*
- .... The Nazarene Thrust Out of Nazareth. *Luke 4:16-32.*
- .... The Good Friday Psalm. *Psalm 22:1-19.*
- .... Jesus, King of Kings and Lord of Lords. *1 Tim. 6:11-16.*
- .... °He Showed Forth His Glory. *John 2:1-11.*
- .... °Superhuman Power. *John 11:32-46.*
- .... °Strange Powers. *John 18:1-6.*

B. LUTHER'S SMALL CATECHISM

Questions 132—134.

C. MEMORY MATERIAL

1. Bible Texts

GRADE

1   Christ died for our sins according to the Scriptures. *1 Cor. 15:3.* (3)

GRADE

2   This is My beloved Son, in whom I am well pleased; hear ye Him. *Matt. 17:5.* (3)

3   All power is given unto Me in heaven and in earth. *Matt. 28:18.*

4   He that heareth you heareth Me; and he that despiseth you despiseth Me; and he that despiseth Me despiseth Him that sent Me. *Luke 10:16.*

5   The Lord, thy God, will raise up unto thee a Prophet from the midst of thee, of thy brethren, like unto me; unto Him ye shall hearken. *Deut. 18:15.* (6)

6   When the fullness of the time was come, God sent forth His Son, made of a woman, made under the Law, to redeem them that were under the Law, that we might receive the adoption of sons. *Gal. 4:4, 5.* (8)

    The Lord shall deliver me from every evil work and will preserve me unto His heavenly kingdom; to whom be glory forever and ever. Amen. *2 Tim. 4:18.* (6)

7   If any man sin, we have an Advocate with the Father, Jesus Christ, the Righteous; and He is the Propitiation for our sins; and not for ours only, but also for the sins of the whole world. *1 John 2:1, 2.* (7)

    The Law was given by Moses, but grace and truth came by Jesus Christ. No man hath seen God at any time; the only-begotten Son, which is in the bosom of the Father, He hath declared Him. *John 1:17, 18.*

8   Such an High Priest became us who is holy, harmless, undefiled, separate from sinners, and made higher than the heavens; who needed not daily, as those high priests, to offer up sacrifice, first for His own sins and then for the people's; for this He did once when He offered up Himself. *Heb. 7:26, 27.*

    Jesus answered, My kingdom is not of this world. If My kingdom were of this world, then would My servants fight that I should not be delivered to the Jews. But now is My kingdom not from hence. Pilate therefore said unto Him, Art Thou a king, then? Jesus answered, Thou sayest that I am a king. To this end was I born, and for this cause came I into the world, that I should bear witness unto the truth. Everyone that is of the truth heareth My voice. *John 18:36, 37.*

    Let this mind be in you which was also in Christ Jesus, who, being in the form of God, thought it not robbery to be equal with God; but made Himself of no reputation and took upon Him the form of a servant and was made in the likeness of men; and being found in fashion as a man, He humbled Himself and became obedient unto death, even the death of the cross. *Phil. 2:5-8.* (8)

THE OFFICE AND WORK OF CHRIST — Unit 17

GRADE

2. Luther's Small Catechism

1   The Second Article. Expl. 2—8.

3. Hymns

1–2
> Oh, for a thousand tongues to sing
>   My great Redeemer's praise,
> The glories of my God and King,
>   The triumphs of His grace!

                                                           LH 360:1

3–4
> O Jesus, King most Wonderful,
>   Thou Conqueror renowned,
> Thou Sweetness most ineffable,
>   In whom all joys are found!

                                                           LH 361:1

5–6
> Jesus I will never leave,
>   Who for me Himself hath given;
> Firmly unto Him I'll cleave
>   Nor from Him be ever driven.
> Life from Him doth light receive, —
> Jesus I will never leave.

                                                           LH 365:1

7–8
> Jesus, priceless Treasure,
> Fount of purest pleasure,
>   Truest Friend to me.
> Ah, how long in anguish
> Shall my spirit languish,
>   Yearning, Lord, for Thee?
> Thou art mine, O Lamb divine!
> I will suffer naught to hide Thee,
> Naught I ask beside Thee.

                                                           LH 347:1

4. Prayers

    Almighty and everlasting God, who hast sent Thy Son, our Savior Jesus Christ, to take upon Him our flesh, and to suffer death upon the cross, that all mankind should follow the example of His great humility: mercifully grant that we may both follow the example of His patience and also be made partakers of His resurrection; through the same Jesus Christ, our Lord, who liveth and reigneth with Thee and the Holy Ghost, ever one God, world without end. Amen.

    Collects for Palm Sunday; Collects for Holy Week; Collects for Misericordias Sunday.

D. SUMMARY OUTLINE FOR THE CHALKBOARD

(May be placed and left on chalkboard for this week.)

Our Most Wonderful Servant: JESUS

1. As *Prophet:*
    He revealed Himself as God's Son and Savior — how?
    He still reveals Himself — how?

2. As *Priest:*

> He fulfilled the Law perfectly as our substitute
> He sacrificed Himself
> He still intercedes for the believers

3. As *King:*

> He rules over all creation — in the kingdom of power
> He rules in His Church — in the kingdom of grace
> He rules in heaven — in the kingdom of glory

Appeal: Is He enthroned in your heart? Does He have His way in your daily life?

Today He calls for "unconditional surrender."

Surrender NOW: Say: "Take my life and let it be Consecrated, Lord, to Thee."

IV. Instructional Methods and Materials

A. PROBLEM AND APPROACH

In the south Pacific islands, there is a tree that supplies native peoples with all they need. Luther says Christ is like that tree. Do you agree with him? Why?

B. SUGGESTED TEACHING UNIT

1. *Devotion*

   Hymn: Oh, Jesus King Most Wonderful. *LH* 361.
   Scripture Reading: Heb. 1:1-6.
   Prayer: ° *Teen-Agers Pray,* p. 72.

2. *Bible Story*

   John 18:1-6.

3. *Memory Passages*

   Luke 10:16: He that heareth you.
   1 John 2:1-2: If any man sin.
   Phil. 2:5-8: Let this mind be in you.
   Oh, Jesus, King most wonderful. *LH* 361:1.
   The Second Article.

4. *Luther's Small Catechism*

   Questions 132—134.

5. *Liturgy*

   The Te Deum. *LH,* p. 35.

C. AIDS TO LEARNING

1. **Visual:** *Redemption* — 79-103 — two filmstrips.
   Why Do We Live — 79-644 — filmstrip.

THE OFFICE AND WORK OF CHRIST – Unit 17   137

2. **Audio:**
   Prophetic Office
   "He Shall Feed His Flock" and "His Yoke Is Easy" — Handel: *The Messiah* — RCA, LD-6409.
   "Jesus, Priceless Treasure" — *LH* 347 — (Let the Earth Rejoice) KFUO, HA61.
   Priestly Office
   "Behold the Lamb of God" — Handel: *The Messiah* — RCA, LD-6409.
   "O Sacred Head, Now Wounded" — *LH* 172 — (Great Lutheran Hymns) — Lutheran Records, RF-6903; also KFUO, HA60; and RCA, LPM-1863.
   Kingly Office
   "Rejoice Greatly, Thy King Cometh," "Lift Up Your Heads, O Ye Gates," and "Hallelujah Chorus" — Handel: *The Messiah* — RCA, LD-6409.
   "Wake, Awake, For Night Is Flying" — *LH* 609 — (The Lutheran Hour) RCA, LPM-1863, also Lutheran Records, RF-6903.
3. **Objects:** Cross, crucifix.
4. **Workbook:** * *The New Life*, Unit XVII.
   * *Learning About God*, Unit IV.
   * *Living for God*, Unit IV.
   * *Building for Eternity*, Unit IV.
   * *Growing in Grace*, Unit IV.
   * *Growing in Christ*, Unit 16.
5. **Bulletin Board:** Pictures of Christ's ministry to people; pictures of pastor, teacher, lawyer, head of a government.
6. **Chalkboard:** Summary outline.
7. **Group Activity:** Select a mission project the class can carry out, such as "Stamps for Missions."
8. **Music:** "Behold the Lamb of God," from *The Messiah*.
9. **Art:** "Christ Entering Jerusalem" — Plockhorst.
10. **Library:** * *The Lutheran Witness*.
    G. W. Hoyer, *I Think I'll Be* . . . (LLL).
    C. W. Hall, *Adventurers for God* (Harper & Row). (Gr. 8)

D. EVALUATION
Have we reached our objectives? What needs further study?

V. Suggestions for Correlations with Other Subjects

A. READING
1. **Silent:** John 7:14-31; one or more hymns of your own selection.
2. **Oral:** Psalm 24; Ps. 22:1-19.
3. **Choral:** Send Thou, O Lord, to Every Place. *LH* 506.

B. ENGLISH

1. **Oral:** Recite all or part of your favorite hymn; tell why you have chosen it.
2. **Written:** Write a letter to Synod's Mission Department asking for the mission projects catalog.
3. **Vocabulary and Spelling:** prophet, priest, substitute.
4. **Handwriting:** k — kings, K — King.

C. SOCIAL SCIENCES

1. **Home and Family Life:** Plan a family singing time; select several suitable hymns.
2. **Community and Nation:** Make an outline map of your town; locate the various churches on the map.
3. **History:** Study the Declaration of Independence; what influence of Christianity do you find in it?

D. PHYSICAL SCIENCES

1. **Nature Study:** How animals care for their young.
2. **Geography:** Has the Gospel reached into every country? Where does our church have mission stations?
3. **Health:** How do medical missions help spread the Gospel?
4. **General Science:** Report on the training and work of a psychiatrist. Discuss — Can a Christian Be a Psychiatrist?

E. ARITHMETIC

Prepare charts showing the growth of our foreign missions; compare the foreign mission budget of Synod with its total budget.

F. ART

Study the painting "Christ and Peter," by Hofmann. Make a mural illustrating Christ's threefold office.

G. MUSIC

The Kyrie, *LH*, p. 17; The Nunc Dimittis, *LH*, p. 29.

UNIT
18

THE STORY OF REDEMPTION

A Lenten Unit

•

I. Scope and Importance

"He suffered under Pontius Pilate, was crucified, dead, and buried."

"The cross of Christ is our *spes unica,* our only hope." (Spurgeon)

This story of Jesus' suffering, trial, condemnation, and death is so important for us that a special church season each year (Lent) is set aside when Christians assemble in their house of worship to meditate upon Christ's Passion, to learn to appreciate anew the Cross with all its blessings and to bring others nearer to the Cross.

Let us not be ashamed to have a cross on our church, to sign ourselves with the cross in our service and devotional life, to wear a cross. It stands for Christ crucified and risen again. It is a reminder of God's redeeming love.

II. Aim

A. KNOWLEDGE

Stimulate thinking and meditating which leads to clear, vivid, and Biblical concepts concerning Jesus our Redeemer. Main events in the story of Lent and sufficient detail to make the story realistic and meaningful. Place and time settings of the story should receive attention. The meaning and significance of Christ's innocent suffering and death for each individual pupil needs to be brought into clear light. Show that "redeem" means "buy back." Emphasize that Jesus actually paid a "price" to save us. Familiarity with related vocabulary and with relevant elements in the liturgy.

B. ATTITUDE

Certainly, sympathy with Jesus, righteous indignation against the enemies, scorn for His weak friends and disciples have a place in the application of these Lententide truths. However, a feeling of shame, humility, repentance because of one's own sin needs to be stressed. Strong appeals on the basis of Jesus' great self-denying love for each pupil may be made. Foster a feeling of gratitude and of affectionate attachment to Jesus. Kindle a keen desire to show appreciation to Jesus in tangible ways. Awaken the desire to follow Jesus in His self-denial, His self-sacrifice for others, even though others do not deserve it.

C. HABITS, SKILLS

Pupils should receive some specific training in sacrificial living and sacrificial giving. The habits of special self-denials, particularly faithful and frequent attendance at public worship, of private devotional readings, and of prayers may be fostered in this season especially.

D. ANTICIPATED OUTCOME IN TERMS OF CHRIST-CENTERED PERSONALITIES

Pupils, graduates to whom the Cross is really meaningful, significant as a source of comfort, strength, and guidance.

III. Curriculum Material

A. BIBLE STUDIES

DATE USED

- _____ Jesus Suffers Great Agony in Gethsemane. *Matt. 26:36-46.*
- _____ Judas Betrays Jesus with a Kiss. *Matt. 26:47-56.*
- _____ Slapped in the Face. *Matt. 26:57-68.*
- _____ A Case of Cowardice and of Timely Repentance. *Matt. 26:69-75.*

THE STORY OF REDEMPTION – Unit 18   141

DATE USED
---------------- A Case of Evading Responsibility. *Matt. 27:11-26.*
---------------- Innocent and Yet Condemned to Die. *Matt. 27:27-31.*
---------------- Crucified and Dead. *Matt. 27:32-50.*
---------------- He Bore My Griefs. *Is. 53:4-9.*
---------------- °A Worm and No Man. *Psalm 22:6-8.*
---------------- °In Great Distress. *Psalm 22:11-16.*
---------------- A Man of Sorrows. *Is. 53:1-5.*
---------------- °Vinegar to Drink. *Psalm 69:17-21.*
---------------- °Praise Him! He Redeemed Us with His Blood! *Rev. 5:9-13.*
---------------- Appraisal and Application. *1 Cor. 6:18-20.*
---------------- °No Room in the Inn. *Luke 2:7.*
---------------- °Worshiped by Some; Persecuted by Others, even in Infancy. *Matt. 2:11-18.*
---------------- °Push Him Off the Precipice! *Luke 4:16-32.*
---------------- °Almost Pelted with Stones. *John 8:48-59.*
---------------- °Such Love Holds Us Forever to God. *Rom. 8:31-39.*
---------------- °Now Salvation Is Come. *Rev. 12:10-12.*
---------------- °Even Satan Is Conquered. *1 Peter 5:8-11.*

B. LUTHER'S SMALL CATECHISM
Questions 138–147.

C. MEMORY MATERIAL
1. *Bible Texts*
GRADE
1   The Son of Man is come to save that which was lost. *Matt. 18:11.* (1)

2   The foxes have holes, and the birds of the air have nests; but the Son of Man hath not where to lay His head. *Matt. 8:20.*
    Behold the Lamb of God, which taketh away the sin of the world. *John 1:29.* (2)

3   He whom God raised again saw no corruption. *Acts 13:37.*
    He died for all. *2 Cor. 5:15.* (3)

4   With His stripes we are healed. *Is. 53:5.*
    He is despised and rejected of men; a man of sorrows and acquainted with grief; and we hid, as it were, our faces from Him; He was despised, and we esteemed Him not. *Is. 53:3.*
    Ye seek to kill Me, a man that hath told you the truth, which I have heard of God. *John 8:40.*

5   Our Savior, Jesus Christ . . . hath abolished death and hath brought life and immortality to light. *2 Tim. 1:10.* (5)

GRADE

He hath made Him to be sin for us who knew no sin, that we might be made the righteousness of God in Him. *2 Cor. 5:21.* (5)

I will put enmity between thee and the woman, and between thy seed and her seed. It shall bruise thy head, and thou shalt bruise his heel. *Gen. 3:15.* (5)

(They deny) the Lord that bought them and bring upon themselves swift destruction. *2 Peter 2:1.*

6 Though He was rich, yet for your sakes He became poor, that ye through His poverty might be rich. *2 Cor. 8:9.* (6)

This is a faithful saying and worthy of all acceptation, that Christ Jesus came into the world to save sinners; of whom I am chief. *1 Tim. 1:15.*

Pilate therefore took Jesus and scourged Him. And the soldiers platted a crown of thorns and put it on His head; and they put on Him a purple robe and said, Hail, King of the Jews! And they smote Him with their hands. *John 19:1-3.*

About the ninth hour Jesus cried with a loud voice, saying, . . . My God, My God, why hast Thou forsaken Me? *Matt. 27:46.*

7 For this purpose the Son of God was manifested, that He might destroy the works of the devil. *1 John 3:8.* (7)

Surely He hath borne our griefs and carried our sorrows; yet we did esteem Him stricken, smitten of God, and afflicted. But He was wounded for our transgressions, He was bruised for our iniquities; the chastisement of our peace was upon Him; and with His stripes we are healed. *Is. 53:4, 5.* (7)

O death, where is thy sting? O grave, where is thy victory? The sting of death is sin, and the strength of sin is the Law. But thanks be to God, which giveth us the victory through our Lord Jesus Christ. *1 Cor. 15:55-57.* (7)

He is the Propitiation for our sins; and not for ours only, but also for the sins of the whole world. *1 John 2:2.*

Then delivered he Him therefore unto them to be crucified. And they took Jesus and led Him away. And He, bearing His cross, went forth into a place called the place of a skull, which is called in the Hebrew Golgotha, where they crucified Him. *John 19:16-18.*

8 Christ hath redeemed us from the curse of the Law, being made a curse for us; for it is written, Cursed is everyone that hangeth on a tree. *Gal. 3:13.*

(Christ) His own self bare our sins in His own body on the tree, that we, being dead to sins, should live unto righteousness; by whose stripes ye were healed. *1 Peter 2:24.*

Forasmuch, then, as the children are partakers of flesh and blood, He also Himself likewise took part of the same that through

THE STORY OF REDEMPTION — Unit 18

GRADE

death He might destroy him that had the power of death, that is, the devil, and deliver them who through fear of death were all their lifetime subject to bondage. *Heb. 2:14, 15.*

Ye know that ye were not redeemed with corruptible things, as silver and gold, from your vain conversation received by tradition from your fathers, but with the precious blood of Christ, as of a lamb without blemish and without spot. *1 Peter 1:18, 19.*

2. Luther's Small Catechism

1   The Second Article. Expl. 2—8.

4—8   The Sacrament of the Altar: What It Is; Benefits; Power.

3. Hymns

1—2   Glory be to Jesus,
        Who in bitter pains
  Poured for me the life-blood
        From His sacred veins!   *LH 158:1*

3—4   In the Cross of Christ I glory,
        Tow'ring o'er the wrecks of time.
  All the light of sacred story
        Gathers round its head sublime.   *LH 354:1*

5—6   Christ, the Life of all the living,
        Christ, the Death of death, our foe,
  Who, Thyself for me once giving
        To the darkest depths of woe,—
  Through Thy sufferings, death, and merit
  I eternal life inherit:
        Thousand, thousand thanks shall be,
        Dearest Jesus, unto Thee.   *LH 151:1*

7—8   O sacred Head, now wounded,
        With grief and shame weighed down,
  Now scornfully surrounded
        With thorns, Thine only crown.
  O sacred Head, what glory,
        What bliss, till now was Thine!
  Yet, though despised and gory,
        I joy to call Thee mine.   *LH 172:1*

4. Prayers

Almighty and everlasting God, who hast sent Thy Son, our Savior Jesus Christ, to take upon Him our flesh, and to suffer death upon the cross, that all mankind should follow the example of His great humility: mercifully grant that we may both follow the example of His patience, and also be made partakers of His resurrection; through the same Jesus Christ, our Lord, who liveth and reigneth with Thee and the Holy Ghost, ever one God, world without end. Amen.

Collects for Lent.

D. SUMMARY OUTLINE FOR THE CHALKBOARD

The Story of Redeeming Love
    All were *lost* in sin
    None could *save* himself
    God *loved all*
    He sent *Jesus* to be a Savior for all

Jesus Fully REDEEMED All Sinners
    NOT by ordinary material values but by His *innocent life, suffering, blood,* and *death*

FROM:
    sin: guilt, punishment, dominion
    death: eternal death and fear of temporal death
    devil: his power

THEREFORE:
    ALL, everyone, everywhere, should NOW, NOW!
    repent — feel deep sorrow over sin
    accept Jesus — believe
    resolve to sin no more — won't *you* renounce sin, devil, and world?
    For Jesus' sake?!

IV. Instructional Methods and Materials

A. PROBLEM AND APPROACH

Many Christians wear a cross on their coat, ring, or chain around their necks. Why? What does wearing a cross mean?

B. SUGGESTED TEACHING UNIT

1. *Devotion*

Hymn: In the Cross of Christ I Glory. *LH* 354.
Scripture Reading: Is. 53:4-9.
Prayer: * *Teen-Agers Pray,* p. 3.

2. *Bible Story*

Matt. 27:27-31.

3. *Memory Passages*

John 1:29: Behold the Lamb of God.
1 Tim. 1:15: This is a faithful saying.
Is. 53:4-5: Surely He hath borne our griefs.
We all believe in Jesus Christ. *LH* 252:2.
The Second Article.

4. *Luther's Small Catechism*

Questions 138—147.

THE STORY OF REDEMPTION — Unit 18

5. **Liturgy**
   The Agnus Dei. *LH*, p. 28.

C. AIDS TO LEARNING

1. **Visual:** *Redemption* — 79-103 — two filmstrips.
   Jesus Before the High Priest — 79-5306 — sound filmstrip.
   Trial Before Pilate — 79-5307 — sound filmstrip.
2. **Audio:** "O Sacred Head, Now Wounded" — *LH* 172 — (Great Lutheran Hymns) Lutheran Records, RF-6903; also KFUO, HA60; and RCA, LPM-1863.
   Passion portions of Handel: *The Messiah* — RCA, LD-6409.
3. **Objects:** Crosses, crucifixes.
4. **Workbook:** * *The New Life*, Unit XVIII.
   * *Learning About God*, Unit IV.
   * *Building for Eternity*, Unit IV.
   * *Growing in Grace*, Unit IV.
   * *Growing in Christ*, Unit 17, 18.
5. **Bulletin Board:** Pictures of Christ's passion.
6. **Chalkboard:** Summary outline.
7. **Group Activity:** Prepare a hymn or anthem to be sung at a Lenten service.
8. **Music:** The Litany. *LH* 661.
9. **Art:** "The Last Supper" — Da Vinci.
10. **Library:** A. R. Kretzmann. * *Symbols*.
    F. R. Webber. * *Church Symbolism*.

D. EVALUATION

Have we gained a clearer understanding of Christ's atonement for our sins? Of God's grace and mercy?

V. Suggestions for Correlations with Other Subjects

A. READING

1. **Silent:** Matt. 27:27-31; "Easter Meanings and Customs," from * *Treasury of Christian Literature*, p. 66.
2. **Oral:** Rev. 5:9-13.
3. **Choral:** Mark 15:1-20.

B. ENGLISH

1. **Oral:** Report on silent readings above.
2. **Written:** Write an original prayer or poem of thanks for God's mercy in Jesus.

3. **Vocabulary and Spelling:** ransom, Redeemer, atonement, Calvary, Pilate, Golgotha.
4. **Handwriting:** r — redeem, R — Redeemer.

C. SOCIAL SCIENCES
1. **Home and Family Life:** Panel discussion on the topic — "Living as Redeemed Children of God in the Home."
2. **Community and Nation:** How did your congregation get its start?
3. **History:** What effect does the Cross have in the world today? Find examples in the newspaper.

D. PHYSICAL SCIENCES
1. **Nature Study:** How God used earthquakes and eclipses.
2. **Geography:** Make a large map of Jerusalem; trace Jesus' movements during Holy Week.
3. **Health:** Children's responsibility for supporting aging parents.
4. **General Science:** Prepare a pictorial chart illustrating constructive use of atomic power.

E. ARITHMETIC
Make charts comparing Biblical weights, measures, money, and divisions of time with ours.

F. ART
Illustrate the main events of Holy Week in picture or symbols. Study "What Happened to Your Hands" by Anderson, or "The Last Supper" by Da Vinci.

G. MUSIC
The Litany, *LH* 661; The Agnus Dei, *LH*, p. 28.

UNIT
19

THE EXALTED JESUS
Descent, Resurrection, Ascension

An Easter Unit

•

I. Scope and Importance

"Christ's resurrection gives us a certified Christianity, an accredited salvation." (Hallock)

"With Christ's resurrection Christianity stands or falls. If you pull out that keystone, down comes the arch." (Maclaren)

"The best proof of Christ's resurrection is a living Church, which itself is walking in a new life and drawing life and new strength and hope from Him who hath overcome.

"Christ has conquered sin, death, and the devil and delivered all men from their spiritual foes. His victory on that first memorable Easter morn marked the beginning of a world conquest. Before Him kings and emperors, races and nations, have bent the knee in the course of the past twenty centuries. And even today He is leading His forces on to victory and peaceful conquest, manifesting His omnipotence, love and grace, drawing to Himself from all quarters on earth thousands upon thousands who yield Him homage." (Bretscher)

II. Aim

A. KNOWLEDGE

Familiarize children with the facts and significance of His descent, His resurrection, and of His ascent into Heaven. Familiarity with a related vocabulary will prove helpful in developing vivid, clear, and Biblical ideas of these three important events and their significance for us today.

B. ATTITUDE

Atmosphere, group sentiment: A joyous, buoyant, victorious atmosphere should be allowed to prevail in the classroom during the teaching and learning of this important unit. When Luther once was in a sad and depressed mood, he gained new courage by writing on the table and the walls of his room the words: Vivit! Vivit! (He lives). Appropriate art work and poster display in the room will help to create this atmosphere.

C. HABITS, SKILLS

Cultivate behavior patterns that reflect the presence of Jesus, the Living Savior, in the classroom and on the playgrounds. The art of "going and telling" should be practiced. Bring that unchurched friend to church next Sunday. The school chorus offers a unique opportunity to participate in joyously telling others about the Living Savior.

D. ANTICIPATED OUTCOME IN TERMS OF CHRIST-CENTERED CHARACTERS

Boys and girls, men and women who live the buoyant, victorious life to which believers are inspired by the Easter and Ascension truths. Living testimonies to the Living God. Zealous personal missionaries who will speak in a self-evident and conversational tone to others of the Living Lord whom they worship and adore. Christians of whom the Lord will eventually say: "Well done, thou good and faithful Steward!"

III. Curriculum Material

A. BIBLE STUDIES

DATE USED

_____ Buried in a Tomb Hewn Out of Rock. *Matt. 27:57-61.*

_____ *A Futile Attempt to Fight Against God. *Matt. 27:62-66.*

THE EXALTED JESUS — Unit 19

DATE USED

*He Lives, He Lives Who Once Was Dead. *Matt. 28:1-5.*
*Sorrow Changed Into Rejoicing. *Mark 16:1-15.*
*Why Seek Ye the Living Among the Dead? *Luke 24:1-12.*
Did Not Our Heart Burn Within Us? *Luke 24:13-32.*
*And Ye Are Witnesses of These Things. *Luke 24:33-51.*
*Why Weepest Thou? *John 20:11-18.*
*That Ye Might Believe. *John 20:19-31.*
In Christ Shall All Be Made Alive. *1 Cor. 15:12-22.*
*A Measure of Your Love to Jesus. *John 21:15-19.*
*Ascended into Heaven. *Luke 24:50-53.*
*Why Stand Ye Gazing into Heaven? *Acts 1:1-11.*
Ascended, But Near Us with His Gifts. *Eph. 4:7-15.*
The Name Above Every Name. *Phil. 2:9-11.*
A Victory Parade. *Col. 2:9-15.*
Our Ascended Lord Is King Over All. *Ps. 47:1-9.*

B. LUTHER'S SMALL CATECHISM
Questions 148—153.

C. MEMORY MATERIAL
1. Bible Texts
GRADE

1 Destroy this temple, and in three days I will raise it up. *John 2:19.*

2 Because I live, ye shall live also. *John 14:19.*

3 I will come again and receive you unto Myself, that where I am, there ye may be also. *John 14:3.*

4 I am the Resurrection and the Life. He that believeth in Me, though he were dead, yet shall he live; and whosoever liveth and believeth in Me shall never die. *John 11:25, 26.* (4)

   If Christ be not raised, your faith is vain; ye are yet in your sins. *1 Cor. 15:17.* (4)

5 (He was) declared to be the Son of God with power, according to the spirit of holiness, by the resurrection from the dead. *Rom. 1:4.*

   (Christ) was delivered for our offenses and was raised again for our justification. *Rom. 4:25.*

6 He that descended is the same also that ascended up far above all heavens. *Eph. 4:10.*

GRADE

7   (Christ was) put to death in the flesh, but quickened by the spirit; by which also He went and preached unto the spirits in prison. *1 Peter 3:18, 19.*

   Father, I will that they also whom Thou hast given Me be with Me where I am, that they may behold My glory. *John 17:24.*

8   He rose again the third day according to the Scriptures; and ... was seen of Cephas, then of the Twelve; after that He was seen of above five hundred brethren at once, of whom the greater part remain unto this present, but some are fallen asleep. After that He was seen of James, then of all the Apostles. And last of all He was seen of me also, as of one born out of due time. *1 Cor. 15:4-8.*

   God also hath highly exalted Him and given Him a name which is above every name, that at the name of Jesus every knee should bow, of things in heaven and things in earth and things under the earth, and that every tongue should confess that Jesus Christ is Lord, to the glory of God the Father. *Phil. 2:9-11.* (8)

2. *Luther's Small Catechism*

1   The Second Article. Expl. 2—8.

3. *Hymns*

1–2   I know that my Redeemer lives;
      What comfort this sweet sentence gives!
      He lives, He lives, who once was dead;
      He lives, my everliving Head.   LH 200:1

3–4   "Christ the Lord is risen today,"
      Sons of men and angels say.
      Raise your joys and triumphs high;
      Sing, ye heavens, and, earth, reply.   LH 193:1

5–6   Draw us to Thee,
      For then shall we
        Walk in Thy steps forever
      And hasten on
      Where Thou art gone
        To be with Thee, dear Savior.   LH 215:1

7–8   Awake, my heart, with gladness,
        See what today is done;
      Now, after gloom and sadness,
        Comes forth the glorious Sun.
      My Savior there was laid
      Where our bed must be made
      When to the realms of light
      Our spirit wings its flight.   LH 192:1

THE EXALTED JESUS — Unit 19

4. Prayers

Grant, we beseech Thee, Almighty God, that we, who celebrate the solemnities of the Lord's resurrection, may by the renewal of Thy Holy Spirit rise again from the death of the soul; through the same Jesus Christ, our Lord. Amen. (Collect for Easter)

Almighty God, who hast raised Thy dear Son to Thy right hand in the heavens, grant that, as we do joyfully believe and this day celebrate His ascension, so we may even in this present world live in heavenly things, seeking only the things which are eternal, that we may in the end be made partakers of the glory of Thy Son, Jesus Christ, our Lord, who liveth and reigneth with Thee and the Holy Ghost, ever one God, world without end. Amen. (Collect for Ascension)

D. SUMMARY OUTLINE FOR THE CHALKBOARD

The Exalted Jesus
    descended into hell — to triumph over His enemies
    rose from the dead and thus
    convincingly proved that
        He is the Son of God
        His doctrines are true
        His Father is satisfied
        His disciples (believers) will also arise to everlasting life and joy
Believe this
Live this
    Arise, now, unto a new and better life!

IV. Instructional Methods and Materials

A. PROBLEM AND APPROACH

Can anyone be sure of forgiveness? Of "inseparable union with God"?

B. SUGGESTED TEACHING UNIT

1. Devotion

Hymn: I Know That My Redeemer Lives. *LH* 200.
Scripture Reading: Mark 16:1-15.
Prayer: ° *Teen-Agers Pray*, p. 30.

2. Bible Story

Luke 24:33-51.

3. Memory Passages

John 11:25: I am the Resurrection and the Life.
Rom. 1:4: He was declared to be the Son of God.
Phil. 2:9-11: God also hath highly exalted Him.
Awake My Heart with Gladness. *LH* 192:1.
The Second Article.

4. ***Luther's Small Catechism***
   Questions 148—155.

5. ***Liturgy***
   The Benedictus. *LH,* p. 38.

C. AIDS TO LEARNING

1. **Visual:** *Redemption* — 79-103 — two filmstrips.
   In Joseph's Garden — 79-5239 — sound filmstrip.
   He Is Risen — 79-5301 — sound filmstrip.
   The Living Christ — 79-5328 — sound filmstrip.

2. **Audio:** "Sounds, From the Mission Fields — Africa and New Guinea," 79-9364 (CPH).
   "Christ Is Arisen" — *LH* 187 — (A Mighty Fortress) Word, W-4017.
   "Christ Jesus Lay in Death's Strong Bands" — *LH* 195, and "Jesus Christ Is Risen Today, Alleluia" — *LH* 199 — (Great Lutheran Hymns) Lutheran Records, RF-6903.

3. **Objects:** Idols.

4. **Workbook:** ° *The New Life,* Unit XIX.
   ° *Learning About God,* Unit IV.
   ° *Living for God,* Unit IV.
   ° *Building for Eternity,* Unit IV.
   ° *Growing in Grace,* Unit IV.
   ° *Growing in Christ,* Unit 19.

5. **Bulletin Board:** Pictures of the first Easter; pictures and clippings about Easter today; pictures and clippings about idols and idol worship.

6. **Chalkboard:** Summary outline.

7. **Group Activity:** Take part in a mission fair.

8. **Music:** *The Messiah.*

9. **Art:** "Women at the Tomb" — Plockhorst.

10. **Library:** ° *Basic Mission Studies.*

D. EVALUATION

What other questions do you have about our Lord's resurrection? about the church's real mission?

V. Suggestions for Correlations with Other Subjects

A. READING

1. **Silent:** Matt. 28:1-5; select 2 hymns from the Easter and Ascension section (187—223) in ° *The Lutheran Hymnal.*

2. **Oral:** Read one of the hymns you selected to your class.

3. **Choral:** Hymn 200.

THE EXALTED JESUS — Unit 19

B. ENGLISH
1. **Oral:** Report on mission work in one of our church's mission fields.
2. **Written:** Write a short essay on the topic "How I Can Witness to My Faith."
3. **Vocabulary and Spelling:** Easter, Ascension, regeneration.
4. **Handwriting:** e — eternal, E — Easter.

C. SOCIAL SCIENCES
1. **Home and Family Life:** Plan an Easter devotion that can be used at your family's devotion.
2. **Community and Nation:** Write a short report on how your community observes Easter; evaluate the observance in your report.
3. **History:** Easter customs around the world.

D. PHYSICAL SCIENCES
1. **Nature Study:** The arrival of spring; early arrivals of plants and birds.
2. **Geography:** How do people observe Easter in the area you are now studying?
3. **Health:** Is there such a thing as "spring fever"? Plan your physical fitness program for spring.
4. **General Science:** How things live and grow.

E. ARITHMETIC
Plan an Easter budget: clothing, flowers, church offerings, etc.

F. ART
Study the picture "Disciples Running to the Tomb" by Burnand. Make an Easter to Ascension mural.

G. MUSIC
Listen to the "Hallelujah Chorus," from *The Messiah*.

UNIT
20

THE EXALTED JESUS
Sitting at Right Hand, Return to Judgment

Last Week in Church Year or Second Week in Advent

•

I. Scope and Importance

Christ *is set* at the Father's right hand in heavenly places. What does that mean for you and me here and now?

Christ will return for Judgment. What implications has that for you and me here in our school today?

"Judgment Day is God's day of settlement with a world that has had a long credit. It is the winding up of earth's bankrupt estate and each man's individual interests. It is the closing of an open account that has been running on ever since the Fall." (Moody)

"We are like operators in a telegraph office touching keys here which make impressions in a land beyond the sea. And when we get there, we shall have to read what we have written here." (Maclaren)

II. Aim

A. KNOWLEDGE

Stimulate thinking and meditation which results in clear, vivid, and Biblical knowledge of facts concerning Christ sitting at the right hand of God, controlling all things, and of His return to Judgment. Make this Catechism section meaningful. Foster familiarity with related vocabulary. Place the Bible texts into meaningful situations. Memorize pertinent texts thoroughly for use.

B. ATTITUDE

Do not foster a slavish fear of the Day of Judgment; rather create alertness and a joyous anticipation of complete redemption (Luke 21:28). Sensitize the conscience. Let the facts reach into the area of fears and hopes, ambitions, plans, values. School atmosphere impregnated with these facts will be different. It should make for kindliness, fervency of spirit, industry, anxiety to work while it is day. It should tremendously accelerate soul-winning efforts.

C. HABITS, SKILLS

Train children to think, wish, speak, act as if Christ would return tomorrow. The unit should provide an incentive for "doing with might" whatever their hands find to do. This culminating unit which brings the Second Article to a close here should provide strong motivation to induce sanctified living; living not unto themselves but unto Him who died, rose, and will return again.

D. ANTICIPATED OUTCOME IN TERMS OF CHRIST-CENTERED PERSONALITIES

Boys and girls, men and women, who live out, in school, on the playground, at home, the implications of this verse: Christ is the Head of this house, the Unseen Guest at every meal, the Silent Listener to every conversation.

III. Curriculum Material

A. BIBLE STUDIES

DATE USED

_____ A Scene in the Open Heaven. *John 1:43-51.*

_____ A Glimpse into Heaven. *Rev. 7:9-17.*

_____ "It Is Good for Us to Be Here." (A Foretaste of Heaven.) *Matt. 17:1-9.*

_____ Jesus at the Right Hand of God. *1 Peter 3:18-22.*

156 Luther's Small Catechism — INSTRUCTOR'S MANUAL

DATE USED

_____ Into Heaven Itself. *Heb. 9:24-28.*
_____ The Lamb Worthy of Great Honor. *Rev. 5:1-10.*
_____ Ten Virgins: Five Wise, Five Foolish! *Matt. 25:1-13.*
_____ *When the Son of Man Shall Come in His Glory. *Matt. 25:31-46.*
_____ *"As Lightning Cometh Out of the East." *Matt. 24:3-28.*
_____ *"With a Great Sound of a Trumpet." *Matt. 24:29-35.*
_____ Greet Judgment Day with Joy! *Luke 21:25-33.*
_____ *Watch and Pray. *Matt. 24:42-51.*
_____ Although Unbelievers Scoff, Judgment Day *Will* Come. *2 Peter 3:3-14.*
_____ *The Mystery of Iniquity. *2 Thess. 2.*
_____ *Light for Those Who Sit in Darkness. *Luke 1:67-80.*
_____ The Love of Christ Constraineth Us to Serve. *2 Cor. 5:9-17.*
_____ *The Truly Good Life. *Rom. 12:4-16.*
_____ *The Exalted Jesus. *Eph. 1:19-23.*
_____ *A Strange Footstool. *Psalm 110.*

B. LUTHER'S SMALL CATECHISM

Questions 154—159.

C. MEMORY MATERIAL

1. Bible Texts

GRADE

1 (God) hath appointed a day in the which He will judge the world. *Acts 17:31.*

2 The end of all things is at hand. *1 Peter 4:7.* (2)

3 (He is) ordained of God to be the Judge of quick and dead. *Acts 10:42.* (3)

Behold, He cometh with clouds; and every eye shall see Him, and they also which pierced Him. *Rev. 1:7.*

4 He will judge the world in righteousness by that Man whom He hath ordained. *Acts 17:31.* (4)

This same Jesus which is taken up from you into heaven shall so come in like manner as ye have seen Him go into heaven. *Acts 1:11.* (4)

5 If any man sin, we have an Advocate with the Father, Jesus Christ the Righteous. *1 John 2:1.*

Of that day and that hour knoweth no man, no, not the angels which are in heaven, neither the Son, but the Father. *Mark 13:32.* (5)

THE EXALTED JESUS — Unit 20

GRADE

(Christ) is even at the right hand of God, who also maketh intercession for us. *Rom. 8:34.*

6 He died for all that they which live should not henceforth live unto themselves, but unto Him which died for them and rose again. *2 Cor. 5:15.* (6)

The Lord said unto my Lord, Sit Thou on My right hand till I make Thine enemies Thy footstool. *Matt. 22:44.*

When the Son of Man shall come in His glory, and all the holy angels with Him, then shall He sit upon the throne of His glory. *Matt. 25:31.*

7 The day of the Lord will come as a thief in the night, in the which the heavens shall pass away with a great noise, and the elements shall melt with fervent heat; the earth also and the works that are therein shall be burned up. *2 Peter 3:10.* (7)

We must all appear before the judgment seat of Christ that everyone may receive the things done in his body, according to that he hath done, whether it be good or bad. *2 Cor. 5:10.* (7)

I am crucified with Christ; nevertheless I live; yet not I, but Christ liveth in me; and the life which I now live in the flesh I live by the faith of the Son of God, who loved me and gave Himself for me. *Gal. 2:20.*

8 (God) set Him (Christ) at His own right hand in the heavenly places, far above all principality and power and might and dominion and every name that is named, not only in this world, but also in that which is to come; and hath put all things under His feet and gave Him to be the Head over all things to the Church, which is His body, the fullness of Him that filleth all in all. *Eph. 1:20-23.*

(He) ascended up far above all heavens that He might fill all things. And He gave some, apostles; and some, prophets; and some, evangelists; and some, pastors and teachers; for the perfecting of the saints, for the work of the ministry, for the edifying of the body of Christ. *Eph. 4:10-12.*

That we, being delivered out of the hand of our enemies, might serve Him without fear, in holiness and righteousness before Him, all the days of our life. *Luke 1:74, 75.*

2. *Luther's Small Catechism*

1 The Second Article. Expl. 2—8.

3. *Hymns*

1-2 Let thoughtless thousands choose the road
That leads the soul away from God;
This happiness, dear Lord, be mine,
To live and die entirely Thine.   LH 608:1

GRADE

3–4   While I draw this fleeting breath,
      When mine eyelids close in death,
      When I soar to worlds unknown,
      See Thee on Thy judgment-throne,
      Rock of Ages, cleft for me,
      Let me hide myself in Thee!   LH 376:4

5–6   O Jesus Christ, do not delay,
          But hasten our salvation;
      We often tremble on our way
          In fear and tribulation.
      Then hear us when we cry to Thee;
      Come, mighty Judge, and make us free
          From every evil! Amen.   LH 611:7

7–8   "Wake, awake, for night is flying,"
      The watchmen on the heights are crying;
          "Awake, Jerusalem, arise!"
      Midnight hears the welcome voices
      And at the thrilling cry rejoices:
          "Oh, where are ye, ye virgins wise?
      The Bridegroom comes, awake!
      Your lamps with gladness take!
          Hallelujah!
      With bridal care
      Yourselves prepare
      To meet the Bridegroom, who is near."   LH 609:1

4. Prayers

Stir up our hearts, O Lord, to make ready the way of Thine only-begotten Son, so that by His coming we may be enabled to serve Thee with pure minds; who liveth and reigneth with Thee and the Holy Ghost, ever one God, world without end. Amen.

Collects for Second Sunday in Advent. Collects for 25th, 26th, and 27th Sundays after Trinity.

D. SUMMARY OUTLINE FOR THE CHALKBOARD

The exalted Jesus

1. ascended into heaven
     to fill and rule all things
     to prepare a place for believers
2. sitteth at the right hand of the Father
3. will come again
     a) visibly
     b) soon
     c) suddenly
     d) on God's appointed Day
     e) in great glory

THE EXALTED JESUS — Unit 20

f) not to set up a millennium, but to judge the quick and the dead

4. Therefore: we should
   a) keep our lamps trimmed
   b) watch and pray
   c) strive to be good and faithful servants

IV. Instructional Methods and Materials

A. PROBLEM AND APPROACH

Where is Jesus now? What will things be like when he returns in judgment?

B. SUGGESTED TEACHING UNIT

1. *Devotion*

Hymn: Let Thoughtless Thousands Choose the Road. *LH* 608:1.
Scripture Reading: Matthew 7:1-9.
Prayer: Extempore.

2. *Bible Story*

Matthew 25:1-13.

3. *Memory Passages*

Acts 17:31: He hath appointed a day.
Acts 1:11: This same Jesus.
Eph. 4:10-12: He ascended far up above all heavens.
Wake, awake, for night is flying. *LH* 609:1.
The Second Article

4. *Luther's Small Catechism*

Questions 154—159.

5. *Liturgy*

The Sanctus. *LH*, p. 26.
The Lord's Prayer. *LH*, p. 27.

C. AIDS TO LEARNING

1. **Visual:** *Redemption* — 79-103 — two filmstrips.
2. **Audio:** "Wake, Awake, for Night Is Flying" — *LH* 609 — (The Lutheran Hour) RCA, LPM-1863; also Lutheran Records, RF-6903. Easter portions of Handel: *The Messiah* — RCA, LD-6409.
3. **Objects:** Pictures of sun or moon eclipse.
4. **Workbook:** * *The New Life*, Unit XX.
   * *Learning About God*, Unit IV.

* *Growing in Grace,* Unit IV.
* *Growing in Christ,* Unit 20.
5. **Bulletin Board:** Pictures of Christ's ascension, return.
6. **Chalkboard:** Summary outline.
7. **Group Activity:** Make a mural illustrating Christ's ascension and return in Judgment.
8. **Music:** See Audio Aids above.
9. **Art:** "The Transfiguration" — Raphael.
10. **Library:** Ethel L. Smither, *First to Be Called Christians* (Abingdon). (Gr. 3—5)

D. EVALUATION

Do you have a clearer understanding of your relationship to the glorified Christ? of the judgment?

V. Suggestions for Correlations with Other Subjects

A. READING
1. **Silent:** Joel 2:28-32; Acts 2:1-13.
2. **Oral:** Is. 55:1-7; Matt. 22:1-10.
3. **Choral:** Gal. 5:16-24; John 15:1-10.

B. ENGLISH
1. **Oral:** Report on one of the readings above.
2. **Written:** Write a letter to a friend telling why you believe that Jesus will return as judge of all men.
3. **Vocabulary and Spelling:** Advent, Judgment, eschatology, millennium.
4. **Handwriting:** j — judge; J — Judge.

C. SOCIAL SCIENCES
1. **Home and Family Life:** Make or obtain wall mottoes related to the unit emphasis.
2. **Community and Nation:** Jesus said, "Behold I come quickly!" Discuss what bearing this has on your life as a citizen.
3. **History:** Discuss: To what extent may we say that the rise and fall of nations is controlled by God?

D. PHYSICAL SCIENCES
1. **Nature Study:** What causes an earthquake? an eclipse? Give examples of God's use of these phenomena for His own purposes.
2. **Geography:** Discuss: The Christian and prejudice.

THE EXALTED JESUS — Unit 20

3. **Health:** Read Matt. 25:31-46. Discuss its implications for your school's health program, the city health program.
4. **General Science:** Report on a natural phenomenon that caused great destruction, e. g., the San Francisco earthquake.

E. ARITHMETIC

Make a graph showing the amounts of money spent in your community for various social welfare purposes.

F. ART

Study "The Transfiguration" by Raphael; make a poster showing the Christian motivation for social welfare work.

G. MUSIC

Listen to "The Trumpet Shall Sound" from Handel's *Messiah;* or the Bach cantata "Wake, Awake!"

UNIT
21

THE HOLY GHOST AND HIS WORK

A Pentecost Unit

•

I. Scope and Importance

"So that this treasure (redemption) might not remain buried, but be put to use and enjoyed, God caused His Word to be revealed and proclaimed, in which the Holy Spirit is given to offer and apply to us the treasures of this redemption. Therefore, sanctifying us is simply bringing us to Christ, the Lord, to receive this blessing, which we could not have obtained ourselves (nor anyone else)." (LLC)

"Look at the electric wires; unconnected, they are dead, useless pieces of cord; but connect them with the motive power, whether near at hand or far away, and presently from these dead cords there comes a blaze of glory. What we need is connection with the heavens, direct communication with the Source of light and fire." (Parker)

"Except a man be born again by water and the Spirit he cannot enter into the Kingdom of God."

This unit deals with the changing of sinners into saints: regeneration, conversion, reconstruction, renovation.

THE HOLY GHOST AND HIS WORK — Unit 21

II. Aim

A. KNOWLEDGE

Develop understanding of the person and work of the Holy Ghost. Stimulate thinking, listening, and reading which leads to clear, vivid, and Biblical ideas concerning conversion, regeneration, sanctification, and the part which the means of grace and those who administer the means of grace play in this process. Stress total inability of man and necessity of Holy Spirit's work. Foster familiarity with related vocabulary.

B. ATTITUDE

Apply the truths in such a way that they will foster: Humility: The kind of humbleness of heart which declares: My present state as a child of God is 100 percent the work of the Holy Spirit. I dare not boast of anything. Gratitude: For God's unmerited grace and power. For Christian education. A high regard for the God-appointed means of grace, for every opportunity to use the means of grace. Kindle the desire and zeal gladly to hear and learn the Word of God. Foster zealous interest in missions. Zorn: "We are constantly in danger of having our religion become externalized." The Gospel is the *power* of God. We must vitalize, personalize religious learning lest our students have the form of godliness but lack the power thereof.

C. HABITS, SKILLS

Train in regular habits of using the Word of God. Attending a Christian school, reading and memorizing Scripture passages, singing Christ-centered hymns, attending church regularly; mission-mindedness; bringing others within the walls of the church.

D. ANTICIPATED OUTCOME IN TERMS OF SANCTIFIED PERSONALITIES

Boys and girls who gladly hear and learn the Word; young people who like to attend services, Bible classes, and who appreciate opportunities for participation in Christian service projects; adults who use the means of grace frequently and fervently; spirit-filled Christians, as described in Acts 2:1-47.

III. Curriculum Material

A. BIBLE STUDIES

DATE USED

_____ The Outpouring of the Spirit is Promised. *Joel 2:28-32.*
_____ The Power of the Spirit is Promised. *Acts 1:4-8.*
_____ Good Citizenship of Unbelievers Cannot Fully Please God. *Rom. 8:5-9.*
_____ The Outpouring of Power on Pentecost. *Acts 2:1-13.*
_____ °The Holy Spirit Extends a Wedding Invitation. *Luke 14:15-24.*
_____ Always Everywhere — Faith Only Through the Word. *Rom. 10:14-19.*
_____ °An Invitation Which Must Not Be Turned Down. *Matt. 22:1-10.*
_____ The Most Eloquent Invitation in the World. *Is. 55:1-7.*
_____ °Joy Awaits Those Who Accept the Invitation. *Acts 8:1-8.*
_____ What a Contrast Between Flesh and Spirit! *Gal. 5:16-24.*
_____ °To Happiness Through Faith — Accept the Invitation and Rejoice. *Acts 16:25-34.*
_____ Converted by the Power of God. *Acts 9:1-12.*
_____ To Keep Faith, "Continue in My Word!" *John 8:30-32.*
_____ °A Great Gift from a Poor Widow. *Mark 12:41-44.*
_____ °Saved to Serve. *Mark 14:3-9.*
_____ "Abide in Me and I in You." *John 15:1-10.*
_____ °Different Ways of Serving Jesus. *Luke 10:38-42.*
_____ A Great Sinner Changed into a Great Saint. *Acts 9:1-9.*

B. LUTHER'S SMALL CATECHISM

Questions 160—174.

C. MEMORY MATERIAL

1. *Bible Texts*

GRADE

1 Create in me a clean heart, O God, and renew a right spirit within me. *Ps. 51:10.*

   Know ye not that ye are the temple of God and that the Spirit of God dwelleth in you? *1 Cor. 3:16.*

2 (You) were dead in trespasses and sins. *Eph. 2:1.*

   In Christ Jesus I have begotten you through the Gospel. *1 Cor. 4:15.*

3 The Spirit searcheth all things, yea, the deep things of God. *1 Cor. 2:10.* (3)

GRADE

Turn Thou me, and I shall be turned; for Thou art the Lord, my God. *Jer. 31:18.* (3)

(God) will have all men to be saved and to come unto the knowledge of the truth. *1 Tim. 2:4.* (3)

Without faith it is impossible to please Him (God). *Heb. 11:6.* (3)

Go ye, therefore, and teach all nations, baptizing them in the name of the Father and of the Son and of the Holy Ghost. *Matt. 28:19.*

The Spirit of glory and of God resteth upon you. *1 Peter 4:14.*

4   He which hath begun a good work in you will perform it until the Day of Jesus Christ. *Phil. 1:6.* (4)

No man can say that Jesus is the Lord but by the Holy Ghost. *1 Cor. 12:3.* (4)

In vain they do worship Me, teaching for doctrines the commandments of men. *Matt. 15:9.* (4)

(Ye) are kept by the power of God through faith unto salvation. *1 Peter 1:5.* (4)

If any man be in Christ, he is a new creature. *2 Cor. 5:17.* (4)

The carnal mind is enmity against God. *Rom. 8:7.*

5   We are His workmanship, created in Christ Jesus unto good works, which God hath before ordained that we should walk in them. *Eph. 2:10.* (5)

Whether therefore ye eat or drink, or whatsoever ye do, do all to the glory of God. *1 Cor. 10:31.* (5)

By grace are ye saved, through faith, and that not of yourselves; it is the gift of God; not of works, lest any man should boast. *Eph. 2:8, 9.* (5)

He called you by our Gospel. *2 Thess. 2:14.*

This is the will of God, even your sanctification. *1 Thess. 4:3.*

The Word of God . . . effectually worketh also in you that believe. *1 Thess. 2:13.*

God, who commanded the light to shine out of darkness, hath shined in our hearts to give the light of the knowledge of the glory of God in the face of Jesus Christ. *2 Cor. 4:6.*

6   But ye are washed, but ye are sanctified, but ye are justified in the name of the Lord Jesus and by the Spirit of our God. *1 Cor. 6:11.* (6)

He that abideth in Me and I in him, the same bringeth forth much fruit; for without Me ye can do nothing. *John 15:5.* (6)

As I live, saith the Lord God, I have no pleasure in the death of the wicked; but that the wicked turn from his way and live. *Ezek. 33:11.* (6)

GRADE

In whom (Christ), though now ye see Him not, yet believing, ye rejoice with joy unspeakable. *1 Peter 1:8.*

Faith cometh by hearing. *Rom. 10:17.*

Neither pray I for these alone, but for them also which shall believe on Me through their word. *John 17:20.*

The God of hope fill you with all joy and peace in believing, that ye may abound in hope through the power of the Holy Ghost. *Rom. 15:13.*

7 Ye are a chosen generation, a royal priesthood, an holy nation, a peculiar people, that ye should show forth the praises of Him who hath called you out of darkness into His marvelous light. *1 Peter 2:9.* (7)

By the word of the Lord were the heavens made and all the host of them by the Breath (Spirit) of His mouth. *Ps. 33:6.* (7)

According to His mercy He saved us by the washing of regeneration and renewing of the Holy Ghost. *Titus 3:5.*

If ye love Me, keep My commandments. *John 14:15.*

The Spirit and the bride say, Come. And let him that heareth say, Come. And let him that is athirst come. And whosoever will, let him take the water of life freely. *Rev. 22:17.*

Jesus answered, Verily, verily, I say unto thee, Except a man be born of water and of the Spirit, he cannot enter into the kingdom of God. That which is born of the flesh is flesh; and that which is born of the Spirit is spirit. *John 3:5, 6.*

Being born again, not of corruptible seed, but of incorruptible, by the Word of God, which liveth and abideth forever. *1 Peter 1:23.*

8 (God) hath saved us and called us with an holy calling, not according to our works, but according to His own purpose and grace, which was given us in Christ Jesus before the world began. *2 Tim. 1:9.* (8)

Peter said, Ananias, why hath Satan filled thine heart to lie to the Holy Ghost? Thou hast not lied unto men, but unto God. *Acts 5:3, 4.*

O Jerusalem, Jerusalem, thou that killest the prophets and stonest them which are sent unto thee, how often would I have gathereth thy children together, even as a hen gathereth her chickens under her wings, and ye would not! *Matt. 23:37.*

Wither shall I go from Thy Spirit, or whither shall I flee from Thy presence? If I ascend up into heaven, Thou art there; if I make my bed in hell, behold, Thou art there. If I take the wings of the morning and dwell in the uttermost parts of the sea, even there shall Thy hand lead me, and Thy right hand shall hold me. *Ps. 139:7-10.*

THE HOLY GHOST AND HIS WORK – Unit 21

GRADE

The Lord . . . is not willing that any should perish, but that all should come to repentance. *2 Peter 3:9.*

O Israel, thou hast destroyed thyself; but in Me is thine help. *Hos. 13:9.*

The natural man receiveth not the things of the Spirit of God; for they are foolishness unto him; neither can he know them, because they are spiritually discerned. *1 Cor. 2:14.*

Ye stiff-necked and uncircumcised in heart and ears, ye do always resist the Holy Ghost; as your fathers did, so do ye. *Acts 7:51.*

2. Luther's Small Catechism

1–2   The Third Article. Expl. 3–8.

1–8   The First Commandment

4–8   The First Petition.

3. Hymns

1–2   Holy Ghost, with light divine
Shine upon this heart of mine;
Chase the shades of night away,
Turn the darkness into day.   *LH 234:1*

3–4   Behold a Stranger at the door!
He gently knocks, has knocked before,
Has waited long, is waiting still;
You treat no other friend so ill.

But will He prove a friend indeed?
He will; the very Friend you need;
The Friend of sinners – yes, 'tis He,
With garments dyed on Calvary.   *LH 650:1, 2*

5–6   Come, Holy Ghost; Creator blest,
Vouchsafe within our souls to rest;
Come with Thy grace and heavenly aid
And fill the hearts which Thou hast made.   *LH 233:1*

7–8   O Holy Spirit, enter in
And in our hearts Thy work begin,
    Thy temple deign to make us;
Sun of the soul, Thou Light Divine,
Around and in us brightly shine,
    To joy and gladness wake us
That we, In Thee Truly living,
To Thee giving Prayer unceasing,
May in love be still increasing.   *LH 235:1*

4. Prayers

Almighty God, our heavenly Father, who of Thy tender love towards us sinners hast given us Thy Son that, believing on Him, we might have everlasting life, grant us, we beseech Thee, Thy Holy Spirit that we may continue steadfast in this faith to the end and may come to everlasting life; through Jesus Christ, Thy Son, our Lord. Amen.

General Collects, *LH*, Nos. 1—9; Collects for Whitsunday.

D. SUMMARY OUTLINE FOR THE CHALKBOARD

The Holy Ghost
1) is the Third Person in the Trinity
2) is holy
3) makes sinners holy: brings them to faith in Jesus
    strengthens and keeps their faith in Jesus
4) through the means of grace or the Word:
    In the Bible, the sermon, instruction
    In the sacraments, water and word
        Bread, wine, and word
5) which are administered through the church

Let us now begin to *use* the means of grace and to have *others* also *use* the means of grace.

IV. Instructional Methods and Materials

A. PROBLEM AND APPROACH

There is an old saying that asks "Can a leopard change his spots?" What do you think that means? Can a sinner cleanse himself from sin? Can a new economic order, Communism for example, change the nature of man?

B. SUGGESTED TEACHING UNIT

1. *Devotion*

Hymn: Holy Ghost, with Light Divine. *LH* 234.
Scripture Reading: Acts 2:1-13.
Prayer: Extempore.

2. *Bible Story*

Acts 2:1-47.

3. *Memory Passages*

1 Cor. 3:16: Know ye not.
1 Cor. 12:3: No man can say.
John 3:5-6: Verily, verily, I say unto thee, except a man.
We all confess the Holy Ghost. *LH* 252:3.
The Third Article.

4. *Luther's Small Catechism*

Questions 160—174.

THE HOLY GHOST AND HIS WORK — Unit 21

5. **Liturgy**
   The Offertory. *LH*, p. 22.

C. AIDS TO LEARNING

1. **Visual:** *Sanctification* — 79-104 — 3 filmstrips
2. **Audio:** "Come, Holy Spirit, God and Lord" — *LH* 224; also "Built on a Rock, the Church Doth Stand" — *LH* 467 — (Great Lutheran Hymns) Lutheran Records, RF-6903.
3. **Objects:** Baptismal font, shell; chalice and paten; two lamps, one connected to electric power, the other not connected.
4. **Workbook:** * *The New Life,* Unit XXI.
   * *Learning About God,* Unit V.
   * *Growing in Faith,* Unit V.
   * *Living for God,* Unit V.
   * *Building for Eternity,* Unit V.
   * *Growing in Grace,* Unit V.
   * *Growing in Christ,* Unit 21.
5. **Bulletin Board:** Pictures of the first Pentecost; pictures and clippings about mission activities at home and abroad.
6. **Chalkboard:** Summary outline.
7. **Group Activity:** Attend a Communion service. Discuss the Holy Spirit's activity in the service.
8. **Music:** Select several hymns from the Pentecost section, *LH* 224—236.
9. **Art:** Symbols for the Holy Spirit; for the Trinity.
10. **Library:** Elsa J. Werner, *The Golden Bible, The New Testament* (Golden Press). (Gr. 4—7)

D. EVALUATION

Does the Holy Spirit live in you? How do you know? How does this show itself in your daily life?

V. Suggestions for Correlations with Other Subjects

A. READING

1. **Silent:** Luke 14:15-24.
2. **Oral:** "God Give Us Men" from * *Treasury of Christian Literature,* p. 5.
3. **Choral:** Read hymn 224 or 231 antiphonally.

B. ENGLISH

1. **Oral:** Report on the silent reading above.
2. **Written:** Imagine that you were one of the strangers in Jerusalem that

heard the disciples speak on that first Pentecost Day. Write a letter to a friend telling him about your experience.
3. **Vocabulary and Spelling:** secular, spiritual, regeneration, convert.
4. **Handwriting:** s — sanctify, S — Spirit.

C. SOCIAL SCIENCES

1. **Home and Family Life:** Prepare a devotion centering around the Holy Spirit; use it for home devotions.
2. **Community and Nation:** When was the last time your congregation conducted a community canvass? What did the canvass show? Should another one be conducted? Why or why not?
3. **History:** What role did the Christian church play in the historical period now being studied?

D. PHYSICAL SCIENCES

1. **Geography:** Does the Lutheran church support a mission program in the area being studied? If so, how extensive a program is it?
2. **Health:** Spirit-filled Christians participate in welfare work. Organize a class welfare project such as CARE or UNESCO.
3. **General Science:** Discuss the various evolution theories; compare them with the Biblical account of creation. What is the role of the Holy Spirit in creation?

E. ARITHMETIC

How many new members did your congregation receive last year? What is the ratio between old members and new members?

F. ART

Study "Christ at the Door" by Sallman; make symbols for the Holy Spirit, the Trinity.

G. MUSIC

Listen to recording listed under Audio Aids above.

UNIT
22

THE CHURCH

A Church Anniversary Unit

•

I. Scope and Importance

The church: visible and invisible; militant and triumphant; true and false. Paramount importance of being a real member in the invisible church.

"A person may be a member of *a* church but at the same time not a member of The Church." (Walther)

If the church joins the world, there is no need for the world to join the church. Church members may be divided into three classes: shirkers, jerkers, workers.

"What kind of church would my church be if everyone did as you see me do?"

"The Church is a nursery for imperfect Christians." (Maclaren)

"A languid church breeds unbelief as surely as a decaying oak breeds fungus." (Maclaren)

"When nations are to perish in their sins
'Tis in the Church the leprosy begins:
The priest whose office is with zeal sincere
To watch the fountain to preserve it clear,
Carelessly nods and sleeps upon the brink
While others poison what the flock must drink." (Cowper)

II. Aim

A. KNOWLEDGE

Stimulate thinking which leads to clear, vivid, and Biblically correct ideas about the church; develop clearly distinguished conceptions of the church as a building, the church as a local congregation, "church" as a service, church as a denomination or Synod; and church as the communion of saints, the kingdom of God, as an invisible unit extending into all churches and denominations, from this world into the next. Familiarity with related vocabulary. Memorization of pertinent texts.

B. ATTITUDE

Foster a deeply-felt concern about membership in the invisible church, gratitude for membership in it; gratitude for membership in that visible church which by the grace of God has and professes the pure Word of God and administers the sacraments as instituted; kindle a keen desire to know the history of the church, of missions, and of our own church (Synod and parish); of Lutheranism in America; awaken a desire to serve the church with the God-given talents either as a layman or as a trained worker as pastor, teacher, Sunday school teacher, lay leader; missionary, medical missionary. Foster an interest in God-pleasing Lutheran union, and appreciation of those who fought error and sought true unity.

C. HABITS, SKILLS

Train in the habit of speaking correctly, gratefully, and humbly of our own church; of speaking charitably and correctly about other churches and denominations; train in the habit of regular and fervent attendance at public worship and of willing, intelligent, sustained interest in the work and service projects of the church. Boys and girls who are willing workers. Young people who help to canvass, visit, teach, and sing.

D. ANTICIPATED OUTCOME IN TERMS OF CHRIST-CENTERED PERSONALITIES

Persons who are truly members of the invisible church, through a personal faith in and loyal attachment to Jesus; who are loyal, active, participating members of a local congregation where

THE CHURCH — Unit 22

the means of grace are in use as they were given to us and where Christian discipline is practiced; of whom God and God's people can truthfully say: They are good and faithful stewards of the manifold gifts of God.

III. Curriculum Material

A. BIBLE STUDIES

DATE USED

———————— Real Members in a Real Church. *Acts 2:41-47.*

———————— *In the Visible Church there are Real and Sham Members. *Matt. 13:47-49.*

———————— Christians — Despised by the World, Chosen by God. *1 Cor. 1:18-28.*

———————— *The Man Without a Wedding Garment. *Matt. 22:11-14.*

———————— *A Futile Attempt to Fool God. *Acts 5:1-11.*

———————— *A Praying and a Growing Church. *Acts 4:23-35.*

———————— Fruit that Abounds to the Christian's Account. *Phil. 4:16-19.*

———————— How They Loved God's Church! *1 Chron. 29:6-19.*

———————— The Church's Message: Jesus Christ Crucified. *1 Cor. 2:1-7.*

———————— "Lift Up Thy Voice with Strength!" *Is. 40:6-11.*

———————— The Church at Ephesus: Active, but Without Its First Love. *Rev. 2:1-7.*

———————— The Church at Smyrna: Poor but Rich. *Rev. 2:8-11.*

———————— The Church at Pergamos: Too Tolerant of False Doctrine. *Rev. 2:12-17.*

———————— The Church at Thyatira: Too Tolerant of Sex Sins. *Rev. 2:18-29.*

———————— The Church at Sardis: A Dying Church. *Rev. 3:1-6.*

———————— The Church at Philadelphia: A Loyal Church. *Rev. 3:7-13.*

———————— The Church at Laodicea: Lukewarm, Neither Hot nor Cold. *Rev. 3:14-22.*

———————— Fishers of Men. *Luke 5:1-11.*

———————— *The Seven Thousand Loyal Members. *1 Kings 19:8-18.*

———————— No Distinctions of Race in Christ's Church. *Gal. 3:26-29.*

———————— *The Church — An Habitation of God. *Eph. 2:13-22.*

———————— Now, Concerning the Collection. *1 Cor. 16:1-3.*

B. LUTHER'S SMALL CATECHISM
Questions 175—186.

C. MEMORY MATERIAL
1. Bible Texts

GRADE

1   (Christ) is the Head of the body, the church. *Col. 1:18.*

2   As we have many members in one body . . . so we, being many, are one body in Christ. *Rom. 12:4, 5.*

3   If ye continue in My Word, then are ye My disciples indeed; and ye shall know the truth, and the truth shall make you free. *John 8:31, 32.* (3)

They continued steadfastly in the Apostles' doctrine. *Acts 2:42.*

4   Other foundation can no man lay than that is laid, which is Jesus Christ. *1 Cor. 3:11.* (4)

Teaching them to observe all things whatsoever I have commanded you. *Matt. 28:20.* (4)

5   The kingdom of God cometh not with observation; neither shall they say, Lo, here! or, Lo, there! For, behold, the kingdom of God is within you. *Luke 17:20, 21.* (5)

Examine yourselves whether ye be in the faith; prove your own selves. *2 Cor. 13:5.* (5)

In vain they do worship Me, teaching for doctrines the commandments of men. *Matt. 15:9.*

6   If any man have not the Spirit of Christ, he is none of His. *Rom. 8:9.* (6)

Beloved, believe not every spirit, but try the spirits whether they are of God; because many false prophets are gone out into the world. *1 John 4:1.* (6)

Beware of false prophets, which come to you in sheep's clothing; but inwardly they are ravening wolves. *Matt. 7:15.* (6)

The foundation of God standeth sure, having this seal, The Lord knoweth them that are His. *2 Tim. 2:19.* (6)

7   Thou art Peter, and upon this rock I will build My church; and the gates of hell shall not prevail against it. *Matt. 16:18.* (7)

He that hath My Word, let him speak My Word faithfully. *Jer. 23:28.* (7)

Christ also loved the church and gave Himself for it that He might sanctify and cleanse it with the washing of water by the word, that He might present it to Himself a glorious church, not having spot or wrinkle or any such thing, but that it should be holy and without blemish. *Eph. 5:25-27.*

They that were scattered abroad went everywhere, preaching the Word. *Acts 8:4.*

THE CHURCH — Unit 22 175

GRADE

Ye also, as lively stones, are built up a spiritual house, an holy priesthood, to offer up spiritual sacrifices, acceptable to God by Jesus Christ. *1 Peter 2:5.*

Go ye, therefore, and teach all nations, baptizing them in the name of the Father and of the Son and of the Holy Ghost. *Matt. 28:19.*

8 Now, I beseech you, brethren, mark them which cause divisions and offenses contrary to the doctrine which ye have learned; and avoid them. *Rom. 16:17.* (8)

So hath the Lord ordained that they which preach the Gospel should live of the Gospel. *1 Cor. 9:14.*

As the rain cometh down, and the snow, from heaven, and returneth not thither, but watereth the earth and maketh it bring forth and bud that it may give seed to the sower and bread to the eater, so shall My Word be that goeth forth out of My mouth: it shall not return unto Me void, but it shall accomplish that which I please, and it shall prosper in the thing whereto I sent it. *Is. 55:10, 11.* (8)

Be ye not unequally yoked together with unbelievers. For what fellowship hath righteousness with unrighteousness? And what communion hath light with darkness? And what concord hath Christ with Belial? Or what part hath he that believeth with an infidel? And what agreement hath the temple of God with idols? For ye are the temple of the living God, as God hath said, I will dwell in them and walk in them; and I will be their God, and they shall be My people. Wherefore come out from among them, and be ye separate, saith the Lord, and touch not the unclean thing; and I will receive you and will be a Father unto you, and ye shall be My sons and daughters, saith the Lord Almighty. *2 Cor. 6:14-18.*

Ye are no more strangers and foreigners, but fellow citizens with the saints and of the household of God; and are built upon the foundation of the Apostles and Prophets, Jesus Christ Himself being the chief Cornerstone; in whom all the building, fitly framed together, groweth unto an holy temple in the Lord; in whom ye also are builded together for an habitation of God through the Spirit. *Eph. 2:19-22.*

(Endeavor) to keep the unity of the Spirit in the bond of peace. There is one body and one Spirit, even as ye are called in one hope of your calling; one Lord, one faith, one Baptism, one God and Father of all, who is above all and through all and in you all. *Eph. 4:3-6.*

If any man have not the Spirit of Christ, he is none of His. *Rom. 8:9.*

2. Luther's Small Catechism

GRADE

1–2 The Third Article. Expl. 3—8.

5–8 What the Hearers Owe to Their Pastors

3. Hymns

1–2 The Church's one foundation
    Is Jesus Christ, her Lord;
She is His new creation
    By water and the Word.
From heaven He came and sought her
    To be His holy bride;
With His own blood He bought her,
    And for her life He died.   LH 473:1

3–4 If you cannot speak like angels,
    If you cannot preach like Paul,
You can tell the love of Jesus,
    You can say He died for all.
If you cannot rouse the wicked
    With the Judgment's dread alarms,
You can lead the little children
    To the Savior's waiting arms.   LH 496:2

5–6 With might of ours can naught be done,
    Soon were our loss effected;
But for us fights the Valiant One,
    Whom God Himself elected.
Ask ye, Who is this? Jesus Christ it is,
Of Sabaoth Lord, And there's none other God;
He holds the field forever.   LH 262:2

7–8 Zion, rise, Zion, rise,
    Zion, wake, arise, and shine!
Let thy lamp be brightly burning,
    Never let thy love decline,
Forward still with hopeful yearning.
    Zion, yonder waits the heavenly prize;
    Zion, rise! Zion, rise!   LH 479:1

4. Prayers

O Lord, favorably receive the prayers of Thy church, that, being delivered from all adversity and error, it may serve Thee in safety and freedom; and grant us Thy peace in our time; through Jesus Christ, Thy Son, our Lord. Amen.

Merciful God, we beseech Thee to cast the bright beams of Thy light upon Thy Church that, being instructed by the doctrine of the blessed Apostles, it may so walk in the light of Thy truth that it may at length attain

THE CHURCH — Unit 22

to the light of everlasting life; through Jesus Christ, Thy Son, our Lord. Amen.

Collects for 5th Sunday after Trinity. Collects for the Church: *LH*, Nos. 10–24. Collects for Septuagesima Sunday. Collects for Whitsunday and Whitmonday. Collects for Church Dedication Anniversary.

D. SUMMARY OUTLINE FOR THE CHALKBOARD

The Church

1. Invisible:
   - one body
   - one head
   - one discipleship
   - holy
   - Christian
   - Wherever the Gospel is in use

2. Visible:
   - persons who use the means of grace; members of the local congregation
   - made up possibly of tares: sham members
     - and wheat: real, believing members
   - true: using the means of grace as given
   - false: mixing truth with error

3. What About You?
   - Are you a member of the invisible church?
   - Are you an active, cooperating member of a local congregation?
   - Do you avoid false churches?

IV. Instructional Methods and Materials

A. PROBLEM AND APPROACH

Is this sentence true or false: "There is no salvation outside of the church"? Explain your answer.

B. SUGGESTED TEACHING UNIT

1. Devotion
Hymn: The Church's One Foundation. *LH* 473:1.
Scripture Reading: Matt. 22:11-14.
Prayer: Collect 10, *LH*, p. 102.

2. Bible Story
Luke 5:1-11.

3. Memory Passages

John 8:31-32: If ye continue in My word.
Eph. 5:25-27: Christ also loved the church.
1 Cor. 3:11: Other foundation can no man lay.
We all confess the Holy Ghost. *LH* 252:3.
Table of Duties: To Bishops; To Hearers.
The Third Article.

4. *Luther's Small Catechism*

Questions 175—186.

5. *Liturgy*

The Proper Preface. *LH*, p. 25.
The Sanctus. *LH*, p. 26.

C. AIDS TO LEARNING

1. **Visual:** *Sanctification* — 79-104 — three filmstrips.
2. **Audio:** "Sounds from the Mission Fields — Africa and New Guinea." 79-9364 (CPH).
   "A Mighty Fortress Is Our God" — *LH* 262 — (*Album titled the same*) RCA, LM-2199; also Word, W-4017 (Stereo, WST-9003).
   "We All Believe in One True God" — *LH* 251 — (Sing unto the Lord) KFUO, HA60.
3. **Objects:** Various worship aids, such as a cross.
4. **Workbook:** * *The New Life,* Unit XXII.
   * *Building for Eternity,* Unit V.
   * *Growing in Grace,* Unit V.
   * *Growing in Christ,* Unit 22.
5. **Bulletin Board:** Pictures of various churches; clippings about church activities.
6. **Chalkboard:** Summary outline.
7. **Group Activity:** Visit your church; note the various items, symbols, etc. that are worship aids.
8. **Music:** See Audio Aids above.
9. **Art:** Pictures of various churches.
10. **Library:** S. J. Roth and W. A. Kramer, * *The Church Through the Ages.*
    F. Nohl, * *Martin Luther — Hero of Faith.*
    Inez Steen, *The March of Faith* (Augsburg).
    The World's Great Religions (Golden Press).
    W. Riess, * *Teen-Ager, Your Church Is for You.*

D. EVALUATION

Did we reach the objectives for this unit? What questions need further study?

THE CHURCH — Unit 22 179

V. Suggestions for Correlations with Other Subjects

A. READING
1. **Silent:** Acts 4:23-35.
2. **Oral:** Rev. 7:9-17; Eph. 2:13-22.
3. **Choral:** Read Acts 2 and 3 responsively.

B. ENGLISH
1. **Oral:** Report on silent reading above; report on Luther's appearance before the Diet at Worms.
2. **Written:** The story of your congregation's beginning.
3. **Vocabulary and Spelling:** church, Christian, Lutheran, catholic.
4. **Handwriting:** c — catholic, C — Catholic.

C. SOCIAL SCIENCES
1. **Home and Family Life:** Discuss — What makes home life Christian?
2. **Community and Nation:** Make a list of ways your congregation has an influence on your community.
3. **History:** Write a brief history of your congregation; trace the growth of the Christian church in the period being studied.

D. PHYSICAL SCIENCES
1. **Geography:** How has the church influenced people's lives in the area now being studied?
2. **Health:** The Christian's part in relieving suffering.
3. **General Science:** Report on the church and its contribution to the growth of scientific knowledge.

E. ARITHMETIC
What percent of growth has your congregation shown in each of the past 10 years? Compare this with the growth of your District and Synod.

F. ART
Design a church window; use colored paper, cellophane, plastic, or paints. Find examples of various forms of church architecture.

G. MUSIC
Report on the function of music in worship.

UNIT 23

THE FORGIVENESS OF SINS
(Justification)

A Pre-Reformation Week Unit

•

I. Scope and Importance

"Of all doctrines the foremost and most important is the doctrine of justification." (Walther)

"Everyone who forsakes the article of justification does not know God and is an idolater." (Luther)

"The article of justification is the only key to the Bible, without which the alarmed consciences can have no true, invariable, fixed hope." (Augsburg Confession)

"The doctrine of justification that a poor sinner is justified before God solely by grace, through faith in Christ, must be the foundation on which our church stands; the bread on which she lives and with which she feeds; the trowel with which she builds; the sword with which she wages her wars; the shield with which she protects herself; the banner under which she travels; the fortress in which she dwells; and the sun which illumines her path. If we lose this doctrine, not only we are lost, but also all our teaching and our labors are lost, and we are building Babel. But if we retain this doctrine, then we are building the house of God." (Walther)

"In my heart reigns and shall ever reign this single doctrine, faith in the Lord and Savior Jesus Christ, which is the beginning, the middle, and the end of all my spiritual and divine thoughts that I may have by day and by night." (Luther)

This basic truth is the chief and the one most distinctive doctrine of the Bible. It distinguishes the Christian religion from all others, it provides an open fountain of comfort for all penitent sinners and gives all glory to God. None dare boast and none need despair.

II. Aim

A. KNOWLEDGE

Foster thinking which leads to clear, vivid, concise, Biblical and Christ-centered ideas which answer the question: What must I do to be saved? Ferret out and destroy ideas of Pharisaic self-righteousness. Break up, freeze out, and destroy innate ideas which tend to persist that man is saved by his own good works.

B. ATTITUDE

Aim to create interest in the question: What must I do to be saved? Create felt need for God's grace and power; thoroughgoing humbleness of heart; gratitude for God's unmerited grace in Christ Jesus; faith in Jesus the Savior; gratitude to Jesus and tenacious loyalty to this basic truth.

C. HABITS, SKILLS

Train pupils in detecting elements of error as they are related to this truth; train in the skill to find Scripture sections in the Bible which speak with especial force and decisiveness on this matter; in the ability to quote pertinent Bible texts when the occasion for quoting them arises.

D. ANTICIPATED OUTCOME IN TERMS OF CHRIST-CENTERED PERSONALITIES

Boys and girls and men and women who understand, appreciate, gratefully rejoice in and loyally defend for themselves and for others this truth: Sola gratia. That makes them good Christians and good Lutherans.

III. Curriculum Material

A. BIBLE STUDIES

DATE USED

- Only God Can Forgive Sins. *Luke 5:18-26.*
- Such Power! *Matt. 9:1-8.*
- *Our Forgiving God Is Unique! *Micah 7:18-20.*
- When Jesus Wrote with His Finger on the Ground. *John 8:1-11.*
- The Church has Authority to Forgive Sins. *Matt. 18:18-20.*
- The Cost of Forgiveness: His Blood. *Eph. 1:3-7.*
- Christians Must Be Ready to Forgive Each Other. *Matt. 18:21-35.*
- *A Penitent Sinner who Went Home Justified. *Luke 18:9-14.*
- A Glorious Promise. *Is. 1:18.*
- Forgiven and Happy. *Psalm 32.*
- The Greatest Blessing: Forgiveness of Sins. *Ps. 103:1-12.*
- None Dare Boast — None Need to Despair. *Rom. 3:21-31.*
- No Wedding Garment? How Camest Thou in Hither? *Matt. 22:1-14.*
- Salvation Is by Faith (Abraham). *Rom. 4:13-18.*
- Are the Jews Different? Why? *Rom. 10:1-10.*
- Did Christ Die in Vain for You? *Gal. 2:16-21.*
- The Just Shall Live by Faith. *Gal. 3:11-15.*
- A Plea for Mercy and Forgiveness. *Psalm 51.*
- Out of the Depths! *Psalm 130.*
- With Robes Washed White in the Blood of the Lamb. *Rev. 7:9-17.*
- *Should You Not Also Forgive Others? *Matt. 18:23-35.*

B. LUTHER'S SMALL CATECHISM

Questions 187—194.

THE FORGIVENESS OF SINS — Unit 23

C. MEMORY MATERIAL
1. Bible Texts

GRADE

1. Son, be of good cheer; thy sins be forgiven thee. *Matt. 9:2.* (1)

2. In whom (Christ) we have redemption through His blood, the forgiveness of sins, according to the riches of His grace. *Eph. 1:7.*

3. (He) hath committed unto us the Word of Reconciliation. *2 Cor. 5:19.*

4. A man is justified by faith, without the deeds of the Law. *Rom. 3:28.* (4)

   Bless the Lord, O my soul, and forget not all His benefits; who forgiveth all thine iniquities; who healeth all thy diseases. *Ps. 103:2, 3.*

5. He hath made Him to be sin for us who knew no sin that we might be made the righteousness of God in Him. *2 Cor. 5:21.*

   To him that worketh not, but believeth on Him that justifieth the ungodly, his faith is counted for righteousness. *Rom. 4:5.*

6. Who shall lay anything to the charge of God's elect? It is God that justifieth. *Rom. 8:33.* (6)

   He is the Propitiation for our sins, and not for ours only, but also for the sins of the whole world. *1 John 2:2.*

   (Abram) believed in the Lord; and He counted it to him for righteousness. *Gen. 15:6.*

7. I am persuaded that neither death nor life nor angels nor principalities nor powers nor things present nor things to come nor height nor depth nor any other creature shall be able to separate us from the love of God, which is in Christ Jesus, our Lord. *Rom. 8:38, 39.* (7)

   Repentance and remission of sins should be preached in His name among all nations. *Luke 24:47.*

   I know whom I have believed and am persuaded that He is able to keep that which I have committed unto Him against that Day. *2 Tim. 1:12.*

   Unto Him that loved us and washed us from our sins in His own blood and hath made us kings and priests unto God and His Father; to Him be glory and dominion forever and ever. Amen. *Rev. 1:5, 6.*

8. There is no difference; for all have sinned and come short of the glory of God, being justified freely by His grace, through the redemption that is in Christ Jesus. *Rom. 3:22-24.* (8)

   If Thou, Lord, shouldest mark iniquities, O Lord, who shall stand? But there is forgiveness with Thee that Thou mayest be feared. *Ps. 130:3, 4.* (8)

GRADE

God was in Christ, reconciling the world unto Himself, not imputing their trespasses unto them. *2 Cor. 5:19.* (8)

To Him give all the Prophets witness that through His name whosoever believeth in Him shall receive remission of sins. *Acts 10:43.*

Neither is there salvation in any other; for there is none other name under heaven given among men whereby we must be saved. *Acts 4:12.*

Christ is become of no effect unto you whosoever of you are justified by the Law; ye are fallen from grace. For we through the Spirit wait for the hope of righteousness by faith. *Gal. 5:4, 5.*

Sirs, what must I do to be saved? And they said, Believe on the Lord Jesus Christ, and thou shalt be saved and thy house. . . . He set meat before them and rejoiced, believing in God with all his house. *Acts 16:30, 31, 34.*

2. Luther's Small Catechism

1–2 The Third Article. Expl. 3—8.

5–8 The Fifth Petition

7–8 Confession and Absolution: Office of the Keys. The Benefits of the Lord's Supper.

3. Hymns

1–2 I am trusting Thee, Lord Jesus,
    Trusting only Thee;
Trusting Thee for full salvation,
    Great and free.   LH 428:1

3–4 Rock of Ages, cleft for me,
Let me hide myself in Thee;
Let the water and the blood
From Thy riven side which flowed
Be of sin the double cure,
Cleanse me from its guilt and power.   LH 376:1

5–6 Salvation unto us has come
    By God's free grace and favor;
Good works cannot avert our doom,
    They help and save us never.
Faith looks to Jesus Christ alone,
    Who did for all the world atone;
    He is our one Redeemer.   LH 377:1

7–8 A mighty Fortress is our God,
    A trusty Shield and Weapon;
He helps us free from every need
That hath us now o'ertaken.

THE FORGIVENESS OF SINS — Unit 23

The old evil Foe Now means deadly woe;
Deep guile and great might Are his dread arms in fight;
On earth is not his equal.   LH 262:1

4. Prayers

O almighty and most merciful God, of Thy bountiful goodness keep us, we beseech Thee, from all things that may hurt us, that we, being ready, both in body and soul, may cheerfully accomplish those things that Thou wouldst have done; through Jesus Christ, Thy Son, our Lord, who liveth and reigneth with Thee and the Holy Ghost, ever one God, world without end. Amen.

Collects for 19th and 20th Sundays after Trinity. Collects for Festival of Reformation. Collects for Day of Humiliation.

D. SUMMARY OUTLINE FOR THE CHALKBOARD

Justification

God Does Forgive Sins
- a) by grace
- b) for Jesus' sake
- c) without the works of the Law
- d) through faith alone

Therefore
- a) none dare boast
- b) none need despair
- c) always and altogether everywhere: *Soli Deo Gloria!*

IV. Instructional Methods and Materials

A. PROBLEM AND APPROACH

Throughout the ages of history man has been a religious being. He has always sought the answer to a fundamental question: How can I be right with God? How can a person be right with God?

B. SUGGESTED TEACHING UNIT

1. Devotion

Hymn: Salvation Unto Us Has Come. *LH* 377.
Scripture Reading: Luke 18:9-14.
Prayer: * *Teen-Agers Pray*, p. 3.

2. Bible Story

Matt. 18:23-35.

3. *Memory Passages*

Eph. 1:7: In whom we have redemption.
Rom. 4:5: To him that worketh not.
Rom. 3:22-24: There is no difference.
Salvation unto us has come. *LH* 377:1.
The Third Article.
The Fifth Petition.
Confession and Absolution.

4. *Luther's Small Catechism*

Questions 187—194.

5. *Liturgy*

The Confession of Sins. *LH*, p. 5 or p. 15.

C. AIDS TO LEARNING

1. **Visual:** *Sanctification* — 79-104 — three filmstrips.
   Martin Luther — 79-5504 — sound filmstrip.
2. **Audio:** "Sounds from the Mission Fields — India and the Philippines" (CPH 79-9363).
   "Remember Now Thy Creator" — (Speak Four Trio) Word, W-4013. (This is a speech choir rendering of Ecclesiastes 12:1, 2, 6, 7, 13, 14)
   "Comfort Ye My People" — Handel: *The Messiah* — RCA, LD-6409.
3. **Objects:** Cross, crucifix, pagan idols and worship items.
4. **Workbook:** * *The New Life*, Unit XXIII.
   * *Learning About God*, Unit III.
   * *Growing in Faith*, Unit III.
   * *Living for God*, Unit III.
   * *Building for Eternity*, Unit III.
   * *Growing in Grace*, Unit III.
   * *Growing in Christ*, Unit 23.
5. **Bulletin Board:** Pictures and clippings about worship, both Christian and non-Christian.
6. **Chalkboard:** Summary outline.
7. **Group Activity:** Prepare a Reformation scene for dramatization.
8. **Music:** "Comfort Ye My People" from *The Messiah*.
9. **Art:** "Martin Luther" by Karoly.
10. **Library:** J. M. Weidenschilling, * *Living With Luther*.
    F. Nohl, * *Martin Luther — Hero of Faith*.
    May McNeer and L. Ward, * *Martin Luther* (Abingdon).

D. EVALUATION

Are you sure you are saved? How can you be sure?

THE FORGIVENESS OF SINS – Unit 23

V. Suggestions for Correlations with Other Subjects

A. READING
1. **Silent:** Select one or more hymns from the Reformation section, *LH* 258—269.
2. **Oral:** Gal. 2:16-21; Gal. 2:11-15.
3. **Choral:** Psalm 132.

B. ENGLISH
1. **Oral:** Report — Forgiveness of sins in the Liturgy.
2. **Written:** Write an original poem or prayer thanking God for forgiving your sins.
3. **Vocabulary and Spelling:** justification, doctrine, Reformation, Luther.
4. **Handwriting:** j — justify, J — Jesus.

C. SOCIAL SCIENCES
1. **Home and Family Life:** Panel discussion — How forgiveness shows itself in family life.
2. **Community and Nation:** Discuss — Can the government forgive, or must it apply the law?
3. **History:** How Luther became right with God.

D. PHYSICAL SCIENCES
1. **Geography:** Has the Gospel reached the area now being studied?
2. **Health:** Discuss the relationship between guilty conscience and mental illness.
3. **General Science:** How has science aided the spreading of the Gospel?

E. ARITHMETIC
What fraction of the world's people are Lutheran? Express this fraction as a percent. Show it graphically.

F. ART
Make a mural showing several important scenes from Luther's life.

G. MUSIC
Learn a Reformation hymn to be sung in the Reformation service in your church.

UNIT 24

ETERNITY

Judgment, Resurrection, Hell, Heaven

•

I. Scope and Importance

Where will you spend eternity? An important question.

Death, eternity, resurrection, judgment, hell, heaven; predestination as a source of comfort; degree of punishment and of glory: these are all of vital concern to each and every one.

"Unless men and women live for eternity, they are merely players and all their busy days are like a tale told by an idiot, full of sound and fury, signifying nothing." (Maclaren)

"All roads lead to Rome but only one road leads to heaven." (Dallmann)

"Blessed are they that are homesick, for they shall be brought to the Homeland."

"He will never go to heaven who is content to go alone."

II. Aim

A. KNOWLEDGE

Stimulate thinking and reflecting which leads to clear, vivid, and Biblical ideas about eternity and all which this term implies; twofold eternity; degrees in each; life after death. Distinguish between Christian resurrection and pagan immortality. Familiarize pupils with related vocabulary. Fix these concepts by thoroughly memorizing pertinent Scripture passages and hymn stanzas.

B. ATTITUDE

Foster a feeling of gratitude and joy that Jesus has opened wide heaven's door; joyful anticipation of heaven; create a desire to help others to find Jesus and reach heaven; create a strong desire to live a life worthy of so great a future; wean the minds and hearts away from those things which we, after all, cannot take with us, and cultivate appreciation of abiding values; set the affections upon heaven; foster a proper remembrance of sainted beloved ones.

C. HABITS, SKILLS

Train pupils to live in harmony with these truths which have or should have a deep bearing on the everyday habits of the learners; train them in the skill and habit of finding passages and chapters in the Bible which describe the joys of heaven and the terrors of judgment; train pupils in the ability to quote Scripture passages and hymn stanzas for themselves and for others as occasion or opportunity provides; the skill and habit of inviting and bringing others so that they, too, will escape the horrors of hell and enjoy the joys of heaven should be given actual practice.

D. ANTICIPATED OUTCOME IN TERMS OF CHRIST-CENTERED PERSONALITIES

Boys and girls who are heaven-conscious and who reflect this in their plans, aspirations, and in their daily living; men and women who have their conversation in heaven.

III. Curriculum Material

A. BIBLE STUDIES

DATE USED

_____ *Two Places Only in Eternity. *Luke 16:19-31.*

_____ *Are There Degrees of Punishment? (Many Stripes.) *Luke 12:47, 48.*

_____ Sowing and Reaping Bountifully. *2 Cor. 9:5-15.*

Good and Faithful vs. Slothful and Wicked Servants. *Matt. 25:14-30.*
All Flesh Is Grass. *Is. 40:6-8.*
Separating the Sheep from the Goats — Why? *Matt. 25:31-36.*
Some Mocked, Others Believed. *Acts 17:32-34.*
Lazarus Sleepeth. *John 11:1-48.*
How Foolish to Deny the Resurrection! *1 Cor. 15:35-50.*
The Resurrection of the Body a Reality. *Mark 16:1-8.*
Our Resurrection is Sure Because Christ Arose. *1 Cor. 15:12-23.*
I Go to Prepare a Place for You. *John 14:1-14.*
O Death, Where Is Thy Sting? *1 Cor. 15:51-58.*
A Glimpse at God's Throne in Heaven. *Rev. 4:1-6.*
Whence Came These? *Rev. 7:9-17.*
"God Is Not the God of the Dead, but of the Living." *Matt. 22:23-33.*
A New Heaven and a New Earth. *Rev. 21.*
A Foretaste of Heaven (Transfiguration). *Matt. 17:1-9.*
Our Election is a Source of Comfort. *Rom. 8:28-39.*
*Faithful Over One: Authority Over Ten. *Luke 19:12-27.*
"Seek Those Things Which Are Above." *Col. 3:1-4.*
"Comfort One Another with these Words." *1 Thess. 4:13-18.*
Weep Not! *Luke 7:11-17.*
The Maid is Not Dead, but Sleepeth! *Matt. 9:18-26.*

B. **LUTHER'S SMALL CATECHISM**

Questions 195—200.

C. **MEMORY MATERIAL**

1. *Bible Texts*

GRADE

1   Verily I say unto thee, Today shalt thou be with Me in Paradise. *Luke 23:43.*

2   He that shall endure unto the end, the same shall be saved. *Matt. 24:13.* (2)

3   We know that all things work together for good to them that love God, to them who are the called according to His purpose. *Rom. 8:28.*

God so loved the world that He gave His only-begotten Son, that whosoever believeth in Him should not perish, but have everlasting life. *John 3:16.*

GRADE
4   (I have) a desire to depart and to be with Christ, which is far better. *Phil. 1:23.* (4)

In Thy presence is fullness of joy; at Thy right hand there are pleasures forevermore. *Ps. 16:11.* (4)

5   The hour is coming in the which all that are in the graves shall hear His voice and shall come forth. *John 5:28, 29.* (5)

Enter ye in at the strait gate; for wide is the gate, and broad is the way, that leadeth to destruction; and many there be which go in thereat. *Matt. 7:13.* (5)

(Christ) shall change our vile body that it may be fashioned like unto His glorious body. *Phil. 3:21.*

We shall not all sleep, but we shall all be changed, in a moment, in the twinkling of an eye, at the last trump: for the trumpet shall sound, and the dead shall be raised incorruptible, and we shall be changed. *1 Cor. 15:51, 52.*

6   (They) shall come forth; they that have done good, unto the resurrection of life; and they that have done evil, unto the resurrection of damnation. *John 5:29.* (6)

Their worm shall not die, neither shall their fire be quenched; and they shall be an abhorring unto all flesh. *Is. 66:24.* (6)

I reckon that the sufferings of this present time are not worthy to be compared with the glory which shall be revealed in us. *Rom. 8:18.* (6)

Blessed are the dead which die in the Lord from henceforth: yea, saith the Spirit, that they may rest from their labors; and their works do follow them. *Rev. 14:13.* (6)

7   My sheep hear My voice, and I know them, and they follow Me; and I give unto them eternal life; and they shall never perish, neither shall any man pluck them out of My hand. *John 10:27, 28.* (6)

He that believeth on the Son hath everlasting life; and he that believeth not the Son shall not see life, but the wrath of God abideth on him. *John 3:36.* (7)

Father, I will that they also whom Thou hast given Me be with Me where I am, that they may behold My glory which Thou hast given Me. *John 17:24.* (7)

I know that my Redeemer liveth and that He shall stand at the Latter Day upon the earth; and though after my skin worms destroy this body, yet in my flesh shall I see God; whom I shall see for myself and mine eyes shall behold, and not another. *Job 19:25-27.* (7)

8   Fear not them which kill the body, but are not able to kill the soul; but rather fear Him which is able to destroy both soul and body in hell. *Matt. 10:28.*

GRADE

Beloved, now are we the sons of God, and it doth not yet appear what we shall be; but we know that, when He shall appear, we shall be like Him; for we shall see Him as He is. *1 John 3:2.*

Though after my skin worms destroy this body, yet in my flesh shall I see God; whom I shall see for myself, and mine eyes shall behold, and not another. *Job 19:26, 27.*

In hell he lift up his eyes, being in torments, and seeth Abraham afar off and Lazarus in his bosom. And he cried and said, Father Abraham, have mercy on me and send Lazarus that he may dip the tip of his finger in water and cool my tongue; for I am tormented in this flame. *Luke 16:23, 24.*

Blessed be the God and Father of our Lord Jesus Christ, who hath blessed us with all spiritual blessings in heavenly places in Christ; according as He hath chosen us in Him before the foundation of the world, that we should be holy and without blame before Him in love, having predestinated us unto the adoption of children by Jesus Christ to Himself according to the good pleasure of His will, to the praise of the glory of His grace, wherein He hath made us accepted in the beloved. *Eph. 1:3-6.*

2. *Luther's Small Catechism*

1–2 The Third Article. Expl. 3—8.

5–8 The Seventh Petition.

3. *Hymns*

1–2 All praise to Thee, who safe hast kept
And hast refreshed me while I slept.
Grant, Lord, when I from death shall wake,
I may of endless light partake.   *LH 536:3*

3–4 I fall asleep in Jesus' wounds,
There pardon for my sins abounds;
Yea, Jesus' blood and righteousness
My jewels are, my glorious dress.
In these before my God I'll stand
When I shall reach the heavenly land.   *LH 585:1*

5–6 Jerusalem, thou city fair and high,
 Would God I were in thee!
My longing heart fain, fain, to thee would fly,
It will not stay with me.
Far over vale and mountain,
 Far over field and plain,
It hastes to seek its Fountain
 And leave this world of pain.   *LH 619:1*

ETERNITY — Unit 24

GRADE
7–8 Behold a host, arrayed in white,
Like thousand snow-clad mountains bright,
  With palms they stand. Who is this band
Before the throne of light?
Lo, these are they of glorious fame
Who from the great affliction came
  And in the flood Of Jesus' blood
Are cleansed from guilt and blame.
Now gathered in the holy place,
Their voices they in worship raise,
  Their anthems swell Where God doth dwell,
Mid angels' songs of praise.   LH 656:1

4. Prayers

Lord, we pray Thee that Thy grace may always go before and follow after us, and make us continually to be given to all good works; through Jesus Christ, Thy Son, our Lord, who liveth and reigneth with Thee and the Holy Ghost, ever one God, world without end. Amen.
                    Collects for 16th Sunday after Trinity

Stir up, we beseech Thee, O Lord, the wills of Thy faithful people, that they, plenteously bringing forth the fruit of good works, may of Thee be plenteously rewarded; through Jesus Christ, Thy Son, our Lord, who liveth and reigneth with Thee and the Holy Ghost, ever one God, world without end. Amen.   Collects for 24th Sunday after Trinity

Prayers for the Sick and Dying *(LH)*.

D. SUMMARY OUTLINE FOR THE CHALKBOARD

Heaven, Hell, Eternity

All men are mortal

All men's souls are immortal

On Judgment Day
    the dead will arise
    the living will be transformed

Believers will be with Jesus in heaven

Unbelievers will be in outer darkness — weeping and gnashing teeth

Let us cling to Jesus and joyously look forward to heaven, and with His grace, make our lives heavenly now

Let us leave nothing undone to bring others to faith in Jesus.

IV. Instructional Methods and Materials

A. PROBLEM AND APPROACH

The Egyptians placed food and other necessities in the graves of their loved ones. The Greeks believed in a shadowy life after death. Christians speak of heaven. Is there life after death? What is it like? Where will you spend eternity? How can you be sure?

B. SUGGESTED TEACHING UNIT

1. Devotion
Hymn: Jerusalem, Thou City Fair and High. *LH* 610.
Scripture Reading: Rev. 7:9-17.
Prayer: ° *Teen-Agers Pray,* p. 73.

2. Bible Story
Matt. 17:1-9.

3. Memory Passages
Luke 23:43: Verily I say unto thee, Today.
Ps. 16:11: In Thy presence is fullness of joy.
John 3:36: He that believeth on the Son.
I fall asleep in Jesus' wounds. *LH* 585:1.
The Third Article.
The Seventh Petition.

4. Luther's Small Catechism
Questions 195—200.

5. Liturgy
Beati Pauperes. *LH* 668.

C. AIDS TO LEARNING
1. **Visual:** *Sanctification* — 79-104 — three filmstrips.
2. **Audio:** "I Know That My Redeemer Liveth" — Handel: *The Messiah* — RCA, LD-6409.
   "Wake, Awake, for Night Is Flying" — *LH* 609 — (The Lutheran Hour) RCA, LPM-1863, RF-6903.
   "Then Shall the Righteous Shine Forth As the Stars" — Mendelssohn: *Elijah* — Angel 3558-C.
3. **Objects:** Pictures of tombstones, funerals; cartoons relating to eternity.
4. **Workbook:** ° *The New Life,* Unit XXIV.
   ° *Growing in Faith,* Unit V.
   ° *Growing in Grace,* Unit V.
   ° *Growing in Christ,* Unit 24.
5. **Bulletin Board:** Pictures of Elijah and Jesus ascending to heaven.
6. **Chalkboard:** Summary outline.
7. **Group Activity:** Learn several songs and hymns that may be sung at a visit to a home for aged. Plan a soul-winning project such as distributing tracts, doorknob hangers, etc.
8. **Music:** Learn the hymn "I'm But a Stranger Here," *LH* 660.
9. **Art:** Prepare a poster on the theme "Heaven-centered education."
10. **Library:** Copies of several Bible story books.

D. EVALUATION
Were the objectives reached? What questions need further study?

V. Suggestions for Correlations with Other Subjects

A. READING
1. **Silent:** Read one or more hymns from the section of hymns on death, judgment, and eternal life, *LH* 585—619.
2. **Oral:** Read one of the above hymns to the class.
3. **Choral:** Psalm 96.

B. ENGLISH
1. **Oral:** Report on one of the hymns above.
2. **Written:** Write an original composition comparing your earthly home with heaven.
3. **Vocabulary and Spelling:** heaven, immortal, eternity, Enoch, Lazarus.
4. **Handwriting:** e — eternal, E — Enoch.

C. SOCIAL SCIENCES
1. **Home and Family Life:** Discuss — How the home is a training school for heaven.
2. **Community and Nation:** The Psalmist said: "Righteousness exalts a nation, but sin is a reproach to any people." What are some of the sins our nation must do away with?
3. **History:** Throughout history men have dreamed about heaven on earth — utopia. Report on some of these ideas.

D. PHYSICAL SCIENCES
1. **Nature Study:** Find touches of "heavenly" beauty in your natural environment, such as in plants, stars.
2. **Geography:** What concept of eternity did the people of the area you are studying have?
3. **Health:** Make a chart comparing life expectancy today with that of years ago.
4. **General Science:** What can space exploration tell us about heaven and eternity?

E. ARITHMETIC
Discuss the purposes for insurance. Figure rates and premiums.

F. ART
Draw or paint your impression of heaven.

G. MUSIC
The Sanctus. *LH*, p. 26.

UNIT
25

PRAYER

A Rogate Sunday Unit

•

I. Scope and Importance

Work and pray, ora et labora, is a good slogan for a Christian school.

Satan is troubled when he sees the weakest Christian on his knees.

"Prayer is David's harp before which the evil spirit flies." (Gerhard)

"To pray often is almost to conquer." (Adolphus)

"Prayer is the preface to the book of Christian living, the text of the new-life sermon, the girding on of the armor for battle, the pilgrim's preparation for his journey." (Philips)

The Christian on his knees sees more than the philosopher on his tiptoes.

"In prayer it is better to have a heart without words than to have words without the heart." (Bunyan)

Sometimes God puts men on their back to make them look up.

Pray as if all depended on God. Then work as if all depended on you.

II. Aim

A. KNOWLEDGE

Stimulate thinking about prayer which will lead to a realization of the need and privilege of prayer: We *dare* to speak to God! The kinds of prayer which are pleasing to God. Find answers to the questions: Who? To whom? Why? When? Where? How? Think of what we are praying. Mean what we say. According to the will of God. In the name of Jesus; we are unworthy — for Christ's sake. Firmly believe; if we doubt, God will not hear us.

Pray for parents, government, missions, enemies; not for the dead (Roman Catholic Mass). Pray at certain times (morning and evening). Familiarize pupils with important elements in most prayers; acquaint them with the structure of the Collect, the Litany, and the Liturgy (address, confession, plea for mercy, guidance and the power to do better, a pledge in Jesus' name), special prayers. Familiarize them with various appropriate postures in prayer, books of prayer; the hymnal as a prayer book.

B. ATTITUDE

Create felt need for divine mercy and power; deepen appreciation of the privilege of prayer; develop joy and eagerness in prayer in contrast to attitude of worldly sophisticates who scorn prayer; foster faith in the living God who can and will hear prayer in His own way and in His own time; foster resignation to the sovereign will of God.

C. HABITS, SKILLS

Train pupils in fervent, earnest, sincere, regular prayer life. Aid pupils in making their own extempore prayers as occasions for these arise, especially in sickness. Train them in having a definite reverent posture in prayer; also a definite time and place for prayer. Memorize and use classic prayers. There is room for much training in good habits in this unit.

D. ANTICIPATED OUTCOME IN TERMS OF CHRIST-CENTERED PERSONALITIES

Boys and girls of whom their parents say: Yes, they are praying boys and girls. Boys and girls who can pray extempore in connection with their problems. Young people who habitually resort to prayer before making important decisions. Adults who pray in faith and sincerity at home, in church, in the family circle, individually, and in the assembly.

III. Curriculum Material

A. BIBLE STUDIES

DATE USED

- *Let Us Kneel before the Lord our Maker. *Psalm 95.*
- Enemies Rage; Jesus Prays — All Night! *Luke 6:11, 12.*
- *O Worship the Lord; in the Beauty of Holiness. *Ps. 96.*
- *A Leper Prays with His Face on the Ground. *Luke 5:12-15.*
- *An Army Officer Prays for His Employee. *Matt. 8:5-13.*
- *A Government Official Who Prayed Regularly. *Daniel 6:10-13.*
- Prayers for a Prisoner. *Acts 12:5-11.*
- Prayers by a Prisoner. *Acts 16:25-34.*
- A Humble Prayer Richly Answered. *1 Kings 3:5-14.*
- A Confident Prayer Pleases God. *1 Chron. 5:18-20.*
- An Evil Plot Defeated by Prayer. (*2 Sam. 15:31.*) *2 Sam. 17:1-14.*
- "For This Child I Prayed." *1 Sam. 1:19-28 (11).*
- *A Thankful Heart Leads to Bended Knees. *Luke 17:11-19.*
- *A Prayer in Church Which Was Answered. *Luke 18:9-14.*
- Persistent Prayer Prevails. *Luke 11:5-13.*
- *A Good Man Prays for Bad Men. *Gen. 18:23-32.*
- God Abhors Prayers of Persons Who Live in Willful Sin. *Is. 1:11-15.*
- *A Mother Prays for Her Daughter. *Matt. 15:22-28.*
- If God Delays, Do Not Abandon, But Intensify, Prayer! *Luke 17:1-7.*
- *A Very Difficult Prayer. *Luke 23:27-34.*
- *Another Difficult Prayer. *Acts 7:54-60.*
- Christless Prayers Fail; Christian Prayers Succeed. *John 14:6-14.*
- *Jesus Teaches Us to Pray. *Luke 11:1-4.*
- Our Perfect Redeemer Intercedes for Us. *Rom. 8:33-35.*
- *Do You Know How to Pray? *Matt. 6:5-15.*

PRAYER — Unit 25 199

DATE USED

.... We Pray: "Our Father," Not: "Ave Maria."
　　　　　　　　　Eccles. 9:4-6.
.... An Earnest Prayer of an Earnest Man of God. Ps. 25.
.... David Prayed Even for That Which Had Been Promised.
　　　　　　　　　2 Sam. 7:18-29.
.... Jesus, an Example of Earnest Prayer. Matt. 26:36-46.
.... God's Own Spirit Prays With Us and For Us.
　　　　　　　　　Rom. 8:23-27.
.... *Ye Know Not What Ye Ask. Matt. 20:20-23.

B. LUTHER'S SMALL CATECHISM

Questions 201—218.

C. MEMORY MATERIAL

1. Bible Texts

GRADE

1　Pray without ceasing. 1 Thess. 5:17. (1)
　　Lord, if Thou wilt, Thou canst make me clean. Matt. 8:2.

2　Thou shalt worship the Lord, thy God, and Him only shalt thou serve. Matt. 4:10.
　　Mine hour is not yet come. John 2:4.

3　O Thou that hearest prayer, unto Thee shall all flesh come. Ps. 65:2. (3)
　　All things whatsoever ye shall ask in prayer, believing, ye shall receive. Matt. 21:22.
　　Verily, verily, I say unto you, Whatsoever ye shall ask the Father in My name, He will give it you. John 16:23. (4)

4　When ye pray, use not vain repetitions, as the heathen do; for they think that they shall be heard for their much speaking. Matt. 6:7. (4)
　　And it shall come to pass, that before they call, I will answer; and while they are yet speaking, I will hear. Is. 65:24. (4)
　　It is appointed unto men once to die, but after this the Judgment. Heb. 9:27. (4)
　　This is the confidence that we have in Him, that, if we ask anything according to His will, He heareth us. 1 John 5:14. (4)

5　Behold, what manner of love the Father hath bestowed upon us that we should be called the sons of God! 1 John 3:1. (5)
　　Lord, Thou hast heard the desire of the humble. Ps. 10:17.
　　Father, if Thou be willing, remove this cup from Me; nevertheless not My will, but Thine, be done. Luke 22:42.
　　Call upon Me in the day of trouble; I will deliver thee, and thou shalt glorify Me. Ps. 50:15.

GRADE

6   Ask, and it shall be given you; seek, and ye shall find; knock, and it shall be opened unto you. For everyone that asketh receiveth, and he that seeketh, findeth; and to him that knocketh it shall be opened. *Matt. 7:7, 8.* (6)

Pray for them which despitefully use you and persecute you. *Matt. 5:44.* (6)

What things soever ye desire, when ye pray, believe that ye receive them, and ye shall have them. *Mark 11:24.* (6)

For a small moment have I forsaken thee; but with great mercies will I gather thee. In a little wrath I hid My face from thee for a moment; but with everlasting kindness will I have mercy on thee, saith the Lord, thy Redeemer. *Is. 54:7, 8.*

For this thing I besought the Lord thrice that it might depart from me. And He said unto me, My grace is sufficient for thee; for My strength is made perfect in weakness. *2 Cor. 12:8, 9.*

7   Be careful for nothing; but in everything by prayer and supplication, with thanksgiving, let your requests be made known unto God. *Phil. 4:6.* (7)

Thou, when thou prayest, enter into thy closet; and when thou hast shut thy door, pray to thy Father, which is in secret; and thy Father, which seeth in secret, shall reward thee openly. *Matt. 6:6.* (7)

Doubtless Thou art our Father, though Abraham be ignorant of us, and Israel acknowledge us not; Thou, O Lord, art our Father, our Redeemer; Thy name is from everlasting. *Is. 63:16.* (7)

I exhort, therefore, that, first of all, supplications, prayers, intercessions, and giving of thanks be made for all men. *1 Tim. 2:1.*

I will therefore that men pray everywhere, lifting up holy hands, without wrath and doubting. *1 Tim. 2:8.*

8   Let him ask in faith, nothing wavering. For he that wavereth is like a wave of the sea driven with the wind and tossed. For let not that man think that he shall receive anything of the Lord. *James 1:6, 7.* (8)

Let the words of my mouth and the meditation of my heart be acceptable in Thy sight, O Lord, my Strength and my Redeemer. *Ps. 19:14.* (8)

If ye, then, being evil, know how to give good gifts unto your children, how much more shall your heavenly Father give the Holy Spirit to them that ask Him! *Luke 11:13.*

Ye have not received the spirit of bondage again to fear; but ye have received the Spirit of adoption, whereby we cry, Abba, Father. *Rom. 8:15.*

One God and Father of all, who is above all and through all and in you all. *Eph. 4:6.*

2. Luther's Small Catechism

GRADE

1–8 The Lord's Prayer.

3–8 The First Commandment.

4–8 The Introduction. Morning and Evening Prayers.

3. Hymns

1–2 Now the light has gone away;
Father, listen while I pray,
Asking Thee to watch and keep
And to send me quiet sleep.   *LH 653:1*

3–4 What a Friend we have in Jesus,
All our sins and griefs to bear!
What a privilege to carry
Everything to God in prayer!
Oh, what peace we often forfeit,
Oh, what needless pain we bear,
All because we do not carry
Everything to God in prayer!   *LH 457:1*

5–6 Go to dark Gethsemane,
Ye that feel the Tempter's power;
Your Redeemer's conflict see,
Watch with Him one bitter hour;
Turn not from His griefs away,
Learn of Jesus Christ to pray.   *LH 159:1*

7–8 Our Father, Thou in heaven above,
Who biddest us to dwell in love
As brethren of one family,
To cry in every need to Thee,
Teach us no thoughtless words to say,
But from our inmost heart to pray.   *LH 458:1*

4. Prayers

O God, from whom all good things do come, grant to us, Thy humble servants, that by Thy holy inspiration we may think those things that be right, and by Thy merciful guiding may perform the same; through Jesus Christ, Thy Son, our Lord, who liveth and reigneth with Thee and the Holy Ghost, ever one God, world without end. Amen.

Collects for Rogate Sunday.

D. SUMMARY OUTLINE FOR THE CHALKBOARD

Prayer

As a baptized and believing child of God you *may* and you *should pray*
   1) because your Father commands it
   2) because you and others need His help

3) to the Triune God, not to saints or idols
4) in Jesus' name, since we are unworthy
5) for good things for the body — conditionally
6) for good things for the soul — unconditionally
7) humbly, believingly, and thoughtfully, not mechanically
8) for yourself, for others, but not for the dead
9) anywhere, but particularly in church, school, and home
10) any time, but particularly before and after trouble (crises)

Lord, teach us to pray.

IV. Instructional Methods and Materials

A. PROBLEM AND APPROACH

Is there something you need or want very much? Do other persons need something? How can you supply these needs?

B. SUGGESTED TEACHING UNIT

1. *Devotion*

Hymn: Our Father, Thou in Heaven Above. *LH* 458.
Scripture Reading: Psalm 95.
Prayer: * *Teen-Agers Pray*, p. 38.

2. *Bible Story*

Mark 8:24-30.

3. *Memory Passages*

John 16:23: Verily, verily I say unto you.
Luke 22:42: Father, if Thou be willing.
Matt. 7:7-8: Ask, and it shall be given you.
Our Father, Thou in heaven above. *LH* 458:1.
The Lord's Prayer: Introduction.

4. *Luther's Small Catechism*

Questions 201—218.

5. *Liturgy*

The Litany. *LH*, p. 110.

C. AIDS TO LEARNING

1. **Visual:** *Christian Prayer* — 79-105 — filmstrip.
2. **Audio:** "Praise to the Lord" — *LH* 39 — (Let the Earth Rejoice) KFUO, HA61.
   "Bless the Lord, O My Soul" — *LH* 27 — (The Lutheran Hour) RCA, LPM-1863.

PRAYER — Unit 25

3. **Objects:** Various prayer aids, both Christian and non-Christian.
4. **Workbook:** * *The New Life,* Unit XXV.
    * *Learning About God,* Unit VI.
    * *Growing in Faith,* Unit VI.
    * *Growing in Grace,* Unit VI.
    * *Growing in Christ,* Unit 25.
5. **Bulletin Board:** Pictures and clippings about prayer, people praying.
6. **Chalkboard:** Summary outline.
7. **Group Activity:** Form a prayer circle or chain; ask each pupil to add a thought to the prayer.
8. **Music:** Jubilate Deo. *LH* 666.
9. **Art:** "Christ in Gethsemane" — Hofmann.
10. **Library:** W. A. Kramer, * *Teen-Agers Pray.*

D. EVALUATION

Have we gained a clearer understanding of the power of prayer? Are there any questions that need further study?

V. Suggestions for Correlations with Other Subjects

A. READING
1. **Silent:** 2 Sam. 7:18-29.
2. **Oral:** Psalm 100.
3. **Choral:** Psalm 95.

B. ENGLISH
1. **Oral:** Debate — Should prayer become a habit?
2. **Written:** An original theme on the topic "A Special Prayer of Mine That Was Answered."
3. **Vocabulary and Spelling:** prayer, petition, formalism, adoration.
4. **Handwriting:** p — pray, P — Paul.

C. SOCIAL SCIENCES
1. **Home and Family Life:** How does family prayer influence family behavior?
2. **Community and Nation:** Should prayers be said in public schools? in Congress? Is there such a thing as a Christian nation?
3. **History:** Cite examples of American heroes who were men of prayer.

D. PHYSICAL SCIENCES
1. **Nature Study:** Find Biblical examples of prayer changing nature's behavior.

2. **Geography:** What are the prayer habits of the people now being studied?
3. **Health:** Make a list of examples of Jesus answering the prayers of sick persons.
4. **General Science:** Report briefly on a person who is both a great scientist and a real Christian.

E. ARITHMETIC

How many times a day should a Christian pray? Discuss this in terms of the Bible words "Pray without ceasing."

F. ART

Make a poster encouraging your classmates to pray.

G. MUSIC

Learn to chant the Lord's Prayer.

UNIT
26

PRAYERS FOR THE KINGDOM
(Petitions 1, 2, 3)

A Pre-Mission Day Unit

•

I. Scope and Importance

As the Introduction of the Lord's Prayer connects closely with the First Commandment, so the First Petition connects with the Second Commandment, the Second Petition with the Third Commandment, and the Third Petition with the Fourth Commandment. The petitions may be included when these Commandments are studied.

"Observe that, in these three petitions, interests which concern God have been the object of our sincere prayers. As God's name must be hallowed and His kingdom comes without our prayers, so His will must be done and prevail although Satan and all His host arise and storm and rage against it in an attempt to utterly exterminate the Gospel." (Luther)

Here are three prayers: for the church, for true Christian faith, and for true Christian life.

The Gospel of the Kingdom is not a social Gospel but it has far-reaching social implications. Exposition.

II. Aim

A. KNOWLEDGE

Develop the meaning of these three petitions. Develop a clear understanding of pure doctrine and godly life, God's kingdom, God's will. Integrate this knowledge with ideas which they already have learned in the study of the first three Commandments and in the Unit on The Church. Foster familiarity with a related vocabulary.

Aid the children in distinguishing the true kingdom of God from the many variant conceptions of the kingdom of God which are current in our day. Millennial ideas.

B. ATTITUDE

In His model prayer Jesus evidently selected such things as are really most important in human lives. Foremost among these are Christian faith and Christian life that thus His name be hallowed, His kingdom come, and His will be done. Therefore, foster a high valuation of these three phases of being a Christian: pure doctrine, sincere faith, and a consistent godly life.

Cultivate an interest in the maintenance, extension, and social manifestation of the kingdom of God. Create a desire to be in harmony with God, to work and sacrifice for the Kingdom. Sow the seeds which may germinate into a strong desire to be a worker, a personal missionary, and perhaps even a trained, full-time worker in the Kingdom: pastor, teacher, missionary, medical missionary, deaconess, parish worker.

C. HABITS, SKILLS

Train the children in the reverent use of the name of God; train them to include mission enterprises and missionaries (home, parish, District, Synod, foreign) in their daily prayer; train in regular, proportionate, first-day-of-the-week giving for the Kingdom; give practice in using Scripture texts purposefully in the interest of soul-winning and soul-keeping. Train in the use of *D. v.* (Deo volente — if it please God).

PRAYERS FOR THE KINGDOM — Unit 26

D. ANTICIPATED OUTCOME IN TERMS OF CHRIST-CENTERED PERSONALITIES

Boys and girls, men and women who are Kingdom-conscious and who express this inner life outwardly in their active Christian living.

III. Curriculum Material

A. BIBLE STUDIES

DATE USED

....	A Great Intercessory Prayer. *John 17:1-26.*
....	Only Believers Can Truly Say, "Our Father." *Gal. 3:26-29.*
....	A Fervent Prayer for Church Members. *John 17:9-17.*
....	How Earnestly God Wants His Great Name Kept Holy! *Ezek. 36:16-36.*
....	A Prayer for Members and for Not-Yet-Members. *John 17:20-26.*
....	A Man Who Caused God's Name to Be Blasphemed. *2 Sam. 12:13, 14.*
....	°A Prayer of Earnest Soul Winners. *Acts 4:23-31.*
....	Pray for Ministers and Teachers! *Eph. 6:18-20.*
....	°When a Woman Should Have Prayed. *Gen. 3:1-9.*
....	Pray for the Spread of God's Word! *Col. 4:2-4.*
....	When a Man of Action Should Also Have Been a Man of Prayer. *Luke 22:31-34.*
....	Is This How You Pray "Thy Kingdom Come"? *Ex. 35:20—36:8.*
....	°When a Young Man Should Have Prayed: Lead Us Not Into Temptation. *Joshua 7:18-22.*
....	°God's Will may be Better than Our Own Wish and Prayer. *Gen. 50:15-21.*
....	Even a Prophet Found It Hard to Say: "Thy Will Be Done." *Deut. 3:23-28.*
....	°In the Hour of Trial. *Luke 22:54-62.*
....	°God Stands by a Staunch Man of Prayer. *Job 1.*
....	When God Answered a Prayer by Fire to Defend the Kingdom. *1 Kings 18:17-40.*
....	Beware of False Prophets! *Matt. 7:15-23.*
....	A Fervent Prayer of a Persecuted Man of God. *Psalm 143.*
....	Our Savior's Great Prayer for His Church. *John 17:1-26.*
....	Lift Up Thy Voice with Strength. *Is. 40:9-11.*

B. LUTHER'S SMALL CATECHISM
Questions 219—227.

C. MEMORY MATERIAL
1. Bible Texts

GRADE

1   This is the will of God, even your sanctification. *1 Thess. 4:3.*

2   Fear not, little flock; for it is your Father's good pleasure to give you the Kingdom. *Luke 12:32.* (2)

   He that hath My Word, let him speak My Word faithfully. *Jer. 23:28.*

3   Sanctify them through Thy truth: Thy Word is truth. *John 17:17.* (3)

   We must through much tribulation enter into the kingdom of God. *Acts 14:22.*

4   Her priests have violated My Law and have profaned Mine holy things. *Ezek. 22:26.*

   He which testifieth these things saith, Surely, I come quickly. Amen. Even so, come, Lord Jesus. *Rev. 22:20.*

5   Pray ye therefore the Lord of the harvest that He will send forth laborers into His harvest. *Matt. 9:38.* (5)

   The God of peace shall bruise Satan under your feet shortly. *Rom. 16:20.*

6   Let your light so shine before men that they may see your good works and glorify your Father which is in heaven. *Matt. 5:16.* (6)

   Brethren, pray for us that the Word of the Lord may have free course and be glorified. *2 Thess. 3:1.*

7   Love not the world, neither the things that are in the world. If any man love the world, the love of the Father is not in him. For all that is in the world, the lust of the flesh and the lust of the eyes and the pride of life, is not of the Father, but is of the world. And the world passeth away and the lust thereof; but he that doeth the will of God abideth forever. *1 John 2:15-17.* (7)

   (God) will have all men to be saved and to come unto the knowledge of the truth. *1 Tim. 2:4.*

   (Ye) are kept by the power of God through faith unto salvation. *1 Peter 1:5.*

8   Then said Jesus unto His disciples, If any man will come after Me, let him deny himself and take up his cross and follow Me. *Matt. 16:24.* (8)

PRAYERS FOR THE KINGDOM – Unit 26

GRADE

Thou that makest thy boast of the Law, through breaking the Law dishonorest thou God? For the name of God is blasphemed among the Gentiles through you. *Rom. 2:23, 24.* (8)

He said unto me, My grace is sufficient for thee; for My strength is made perfect in weakness. *2 Cor. 12:9.* (8)

I know that in me (that is, in my flesh) dwelleth no good thing. *Rom. 7:18.*

The devil, as a roaring lion, walketh about, seeking whom he may devour. *1 Peter 5:8.*

2. Luther's Small Catechism

1–2   The Lord's Prayer.

3–8   Petitions One, Two, and Three. Commandments One, Two, Three, and Four.

6–8   Table of Duties: To Pastors and Hearers.

3. Hymns

1–2
I am Jesus' little lamb,
Ever glad at heart I am;
For my Shepherd gently guides me,
Knows my need, and well provides me,
Loves me every day the same,
Even calls me by my name.   *LH 648:1*

3–4
Jesus shall reign where'er the sun
Does his successive journeys run,
His kingdom stretch from shore to shore
Till moons shall wax and wane no more.   *LH 511:1*

5–6
May we Thy precepts, Lord, fulfill
And do on earth our Father's will
  As angels do above;
Still walk in Christ, the living Way,
With all Thy children and obey
The law of Christian love.   *LH 412:1*

7–8
The will of God is always best
  And shall be done forever;
And they who trust in Him are blest,
  He will forsake them never.
He helps indeed In time of need,
  He chastens with forbearing;
They who depend On God, their Friend,
  Shall not be left despairing.   *LH 517:1*

4. Prayers

O God, who by the leading of a star didst manifest Thine only-begotten Son to the Gentiles, mercifully grant that we, who know Thee now by faith, may after this life have the fruition of Thy glorious Godhead; through the same Thy Son, Jesus Christ, our Lord, who liveth and reigneth with Thee and the Holy Ghost, ever one God, world without end. Amen.

Collects for Epiphany. Collects for Eighth Sunday after Trinity. Collects for Second Sunday after Trinity. Collects for Mission Festival.

D. SUMMARY OUTLINE FOR THE CHALKBOARD

Prayers for the Kingdom

To God and to God's People It Is Very Important, and Therefore God's People Earnestly *Desire, Pray, and Strive*

1) That God's name be hallowed
    through pure Biblical doctrine by every teacher of religion
    through Christ-centered living of every Christian
2) That God's Kingdom come
    through faithful teaching and preaching and witnessing
    through faithful hearing and learning and reading
    through humble believing and consecrated living and liberal giving
3) That God's will be done on earth as in heaven
    through breaking of the will of the devil, world, and flesh
    through a growing will and determination which is Jesus-like.

IV. Instructional Methods and Materials

A. PROBLEM AND APPROACH

Dr. Martin Marty has said that we are living in a "post-Christian era." What does that mean? Should we be disturbed because the world's population is increasing at a greater rate than the Christian church is?

B. SUGGESTED TEACHING UNIT

1. *Devotion*

Hymn: Jesus Shall Reign Where'er the Sun. *LH* 511.
Scripture Reading: John 17:1-26.
Prayer: Extempore.

2. *Bible Story*

Matt. 28:9-20.

3. *Memory Passages*

Matt. 5:16: Let your light so shine.
Matt. 9:38: Pray ye therefore the Lord of the harvest.
1 Tim. 2:4: God will have all men to be saved.
Send, O Lord, Thy Holy Spirit. *LH* 491:1
Petitions 1—3.

PRAYERS FOR THE KINGDOM — Unit 26

4. Luther's Small Catechism
Questions 219—227.

5. Liturgy
The Magnificat. *LH*, p. 43.

C. AIDS TO LEARNING

1. **Visual:** *The Lord's Prayer* — 79-106 — four filmstrips.
2. **Audio:** "We All Believe in One True God" — *LH* 251 — (Sing Unto The Lord) KFUO, HA60.
   "Lord, How Excellent Thy Name Is!" and "O Rest in the Lord" — Mendelssohn: *Elijah* — Angel 3558-C.
   "If Thou But Suffer God to Guide Thee" — *LH* 518 — (Let The Earth Rejoice) KFUO, HA61.
3. **Objects:** Various idols.
4. **Workbook:** * *The New Life,* Unit XXVI.
   * *Learning About God,* Unit VI.
   * *Growing in Faith,* Unit VI.
   * *Growing in Grace,* Unit VI.
   * *Growing in Christ,* Unit 26.
5. **Bulletin Board:** Pictures and clippings related to prayer, mission work, worship.
6. **Chalkboard:** Summary outline.
7. **Group Activity:** Plan to distribute VBS announcements and doorknob hangers.
8. **Music:** See Audio Aids above.
9. **Art:** "The Welcome Guest" — Von Uhde.
10. **Library:** Faith Forward materials.
    Rosa Young, * *Light in the Dark Belt.*
    Inez Steen, *The March of Faith* (Augsburg).

D. EVALUATION

Has your concern for spreading the Gospel deepened? What are you doing about it? How can you become an effective witness to God's love?

V. Suggestions for Correlations with Other Subjects

A. READING

1. **Silent:** Articles in * *The Lutheran Witness* and * *Spirit* related to the topic.
2. **Oral:** Acts 4:23-31.
3. **Choral:** Eph. 6:18-20.

B. ENGLISH
1. **Oral:** Panel discussion — Evangelism through our school.
2. **Written:** Report on the activities in one of our church's mission fields, such as New Guinea or Hong Kong.
3. **Vocabulary and Spelling:** kingdom, evangelism, ecumenical, unionism.
4. **Handwriting:** k — kings, K — King.

C. SOCIAL SCIENCES
1. **Home and Family Life:** Dramatize several situations calling for Christian witness.
2. **Community and Nation:** Distribute door-to-door invitations to attend church, Sunday School, or VBS.
3. **History:** Trace the history of Lutheran mission work in foreign lands.

D. PHYSICAL SCIENCES
1. **Nature Study:** Make a list of ways in which nature points to God.
2. **Geography:** Prepare a large map showing Paul's missionary journeys.
3. **Health:** Report on the work of Lutheran Medical Missions.
4. **General Science:** How does science help and hinder the missionaries work?

E. ARITHMETIC

Use growth statistics about our mission work to prepare charts and graphs. See the * *Statistical Yearbook* for information.

F. ART

Prepare posters on the theme "Thy kingdom come" and "Each one reach one."

G. MUSIC

Learn one of the hymns from the Missions section of *The Lutheran Hymnal* and sing it at a worship service. *LH* 494—512.

UNIT
27

A PRAYER FOR DAILY BREAD
(Earthly Blessings)
A Harvesttime or a Seedtime Unit

•

I. Scope and Importance

"This petition includes all that belongs to our temporal life, since only for its sake we need daily bread. Now, our life requires not only food, clothing, and other necessaries, but also concord and peace in our daily business and our dealings and intercourse of every description with the people among whom we live and move, in short, a sound regulation of all domestic and civil or political affairs. . . . It is indeed most necessary to pray for our civil authorities and government, for chiefly through them God provides for our daily bread and for our every comfort in life. For this reason it would be proper to place on the coat-of-arms of every pious prince the emblem of a loaf of bread instead of a lion or a wreath of rue, or to stamp it on the national coins, to remind princes and their subjects that we enjoy ease and protection through their office and without them we could not have the steady blessing of daily bread. Where dissension, strife, and war prevail, there our daily bread is wholly lacking or constantly reduced." (Luther)

Prayer for daily bread implies that those who pray will also *work* for what they pray for, *acknowledge* success and prosperity as coming from God, and be ready to *share* it with the needy.

This unit may be linked with the Seventh Commandment and with the First Article.

II. Aim

A. KNOWLEDGE

Stimulate observation and thinking and generalizing which leads to a clear and adequate concept of "daily bread." Aid pupils to discover the relationship among the laws of nature, God's blessing, man's effort. Familiarize with related meaningful vocabulary. Such things as relief, charity, pensions, insurance may be considered. Show how a little goes far when blessed by the Lord. Seedtime and harvest enter in. Provide guidance for a God-pleasing *vocation* in life. Vocational guidance.

B. ATTITUDE

Develop Christian attitude toward material possessions. Cultivate patience in days of poverty and distress. Stimulate desire to be self-supporting and eventually to own your own little home. Cultivate contentment when despite our best efforts we have but little to show for it. Foster willingness to share with others. Discourage worry, fretting, selfishness. Create gratitude to God for daily bread.

C. HABITS, SKILLS

Home and school should cooperate in training children to work for their bread; personal participation in gardening is desirable even in the cities; habit of table prayer should be systematically acquired.

D. ANTICIPATED OUTCOME IN TERMS OF CHRIST-CENTERED PERSONALITIES

Individuals who habitually acknowledge God as the Giver of all good gifts; are industrious and thrifty; are grateful for and contented with small blessings; are willing to share what they have.

A PRAYER FOR DAILY BREAD — Unit 27   215

III. Curriculum Material

A. BIBLE STUDIES

DATE USED

   _____ *An Unusually Successful Fishing Trip — Obedient Work Brings Success. *Luke 5:1-11.*

   _____ *God Uses Birds to Feed a Man of God. *1 Kings 17:1-7.*

   _____ The Widow Whose Bread Supply Was Always Replenished. *1 Kings 17:8-16.*

   _____ A Beautiful Confession: "God Fed Me All My Life Long." *Gen. 48:15, 16.*

   _____ *About the Farmer Who Forgot About God. *Luke 12:13-21.*

   _____ A Selfish and Dangerous Choice — for Earthly Gain. *Gen. 13:5-13.*

   _____ God is the Giver of All Good Gifts. *Psalm 136.*

   _____ A Man Who Learned that God Gives Daily Bread. *Gen. 26:12-25.*

   _____ Consider the Lilies. *Matt. 6:19-34.*

   _____ A Powerful Tonic Against Worry. *Ps. 37:3-11.*

   _____ On the Importance of Sharing Our Bread. *James 5:1-6.*

   _____ Natural Resources Are There for Man's Benefit. *Psalm 8.*

   _____ Thrifty People Shall Be Provided with Necessities. *Prov. 31:10-31.*

   _____ They Shall Be Fat and Flourishing. *Psalm 92.*

B. LUTHER'S SMALL CATECHISM

Questions 228—230.

C. MEMORY MATERIAL

1. Bible Texts

GRADE

1   It is vain for you to rise up early, to sit up late, to eat the bread of sorrows; for so He giveth His beloved sleep. *Ps. 127:2.*

2   Giving thanks always for all things unto God and the Father in the name of our Lord Jesus Christ. *Eph. 5:20.*

3   The eyes of all wait upon Thee, and Thou givest them their meat in due season. Thou openest Thine hand and satisfiest the desire of every living thing. *Ps. 145:15, 16.*

4   He maketh His sun to rise on the evil and on the good and sendeth rain on the just and on the unjust. *Matt. 5:45.* (4)

5   Having food and raiment, let us be therewith content. *1 Tim. 6:8.* (5)

GRADE

6   To do good and to communicate forget not; for with such sacrifices God is well pleased. *Heb. 13:16.*

7   Seek ye first the kingdom of God and His righteousness; and all these things shall be added unto you. Take therefore no thought for the morrow; for the morrow shall take thought for the things of itself. Sufficient unto the day is the evil thereof. *Matt. 6:33, 34.* (7)

8   If any would not work, neither should he eat. For we hear that there are some which walk among you disorderly, working not at all, but are busybodies. Now, them that are such we command and exhort by our Lord Jesus Christ that with quietness they work and eat their own bread. *2 Thess. 3:10-12.*

Two things have I required of Thee; deny me them not before I die: Remove far from me vanity and lies; give me neither poverty nor riches; feed me with food convenient for me, lest I be full and deny Thee and say, Who is the Lord? or lest I be poor and steal and take the name of my God in vain. *Prov. 30:7-9.*

2. *Luther's Small Catechism*

3–8   The Fourth Petition.

4–8   The Seventh Commandment.

5–8   The First Article.

7–8   The Ninth and Tenth Commandments.

3. *Hymns*

1–2   Praise, oh, praise, our God and King,
      Hymns of adoration sing:
      For His mercies still endure,
      Ever faithful, ever sure.   LH 570:1

3–4   God bless our native land!
      Firm may she ever stand
         Through storm and night!
      When the wild tempests rave,
      Ruler of wind and wave,
      Do Thou our country save
         By Thy great might.   LH 577:1

5–6   Come, ye thankful people, come;
      Raise the song of Harvest-home.
      All be safely gathered in
      Ere the winter storms begin:
      God, our Maker, doth provide
      For our wants to be supplied.
      Come to God's own temple, come;
      Raise the song of Harvest-home.   LH 574:1

A PRAYER FOR DAILY BREAD — Unit 27

GRADE
7–8

Feed Thy children, God most holy,
Comfort sinners poor and lowly;
O Thou Bread of Life from heaven,
Bless the food Thou here hast given!
As these gifts the body nourish,
May our souls in graces flourish
Till with saints in heavenly splendor
At Thy feast due thanks we render.   *LH* 659:1

4. Prayers

Almighty God, our heavenly Father, whose mercies are new unto us every morning, and who, though we have in no wise deserved Thy goodness, dost abundantly provide for all our wants of body and soul, give us, we pray Thee, Thy Holy Spirit, that we may heartily acknowledge Thy merciful goodness toward us, give thanks for all Thy benefits, and serve Thee in willing obedience; through Jesus Christ, Thy Son, our Lord, who liveth and reigneth with Thee and the Holy Ghost, ever one God, world without end. Amen.

Collects for Day of Special Thanksgiving. Collects for Festival of Harvest. Table Prayers.

D. SUMMARY OUTLINE FOR THE CHALKBOARD

Daily Bread

To God's people it is very important and therefore God's people earnestly *desire, pray, and strive*

a) for daily bread
  everything necessary for bodily welfare
    nourishment
    shelter against weather
    protection against enemies
b) for contentment — freedom from the feeling of want
c) for gratitude to God
d) for the habit of sharing with the less fortunate.

IV. Instructional Methods and Materials

A. PROBLEM AND APPROACH

One half of 3 billion people go to bed at night hungry. 10,000 die of starvation while America's problem is surplus! How can these problems be solved?

B. SUGGESTED TEACHING UNIT

1. Devotion

Hymn: Feed Thy Children, God Most Holy. *LH* 659.
Scripture Reading: 1 Kings 17:8-16.
Prayer: Collect 42. *LH*, p. 106.

2. *Bible Story*
   Luke 5:1-11.

3. *Memory Passages*
   Ps. 145:15: The eyes of all.
   Heb. 13:16: To do good.
   Matt. 6:33: Seek ye first the kingdom of God.
   Feed thy children, God most holy. LH 659:1.
   The Fourth Petition.
   The First Article.
   The Seventh Commandment.

4. *Luther's Small Catechism*
   Questions 228—230.

5. *Liturgy*
   The Te Deum. *LH*, p. 35.
   The Venite. *LH*, p. 33.

C. AIDS TO LEARNING

1. **Visual:** *The Lord's Prayer* — 79-106 — 4 filmstrips.
2. **Audio:** Mendelssohn: *Elijah* — Angel 3558-C.
   Pertinent Selections:
   "Help, Lord! The Harvest Now Is Over"
   "Lord, Bow Thine Ear"
   "Now Cherith's Brook" (includes: "The Barrel of Meal Shall not Waste")
   "Thanks Be to God! He Laveth the Thirsty Land"
   "Cast Thy Burden Upon the Lord"
3. **Objects:** Bread, kernels of grain, stalk of wheat.
4. **Workbook:** * *The New Life,* Unit XXVIII.
   * *Learning About God,* Unit VI.
   * *Growing in Faith,* Unit VI.
   * *Growing in Grace,* Unit VI.
   * *Growing in Christ,* Unit 27.
5. **Bulletin Board:** Pictures and clippings of grain fields, men and women at work, people hungry.
6. **Chalkboard:** Summary outline.
7. **Group Activity:** Participate in some welfare project such as CARE, Lutheran World Relief, UNESCO.
8. **Music:** Bonum Est Confiteri. *LH* 663.
9. **Art:** "Saying Grace" — Chardin.
10. **Library:** S. J. Roth and W. Kramer, * *The Church Through the Ages.*
    U. S. Government publications on conservation.
    G. Hoyer. * *I Think I'll Be* . . .

D. EVALUATION

Have we grown in our understanding and appreciation of God's blessings? Have we learned to be satisfied with what we have?

A PRAYER FOR DAILY BREAD – Unit 27   219

V. Suggestions for Correlations with Other Subjects

A. READING
1. **Silent:** 1 Kings 17:1-7; Luke 12:13-21; Luke 5:1-11.
2. **Oral:** Psalm 103; Psalm 136.
3. **Choral:** Psalm 23; Psalm 96.

B. ENGLISH
1. **Oral:** Deliver a 2-minute floor-talk on "My Part in Using Possessions Wisely," or some similar topic.
2. **Written:** An original theme on the topic: "What I Want to Be When I Grow Up."
3. **Vocabulary and Spelling:** climate, government, economics.
4. **Handwriting:** b — bread, B — Bread.

C. SOCIAL SCIENCES
1. **Home and Family Life:** Helping my family care for its possessions.
2. **Community and Nation:** Compare the U. S. standard of living with other countries. What makes ours higher?
3. **History:** Identify some of the causes for wars: economic, social.

D. PHYSICAL SCIENCES
1. **Nature Study:** Make a notebook or scrapbook on conservation.
2. **Geography:** How has machine farming made a difference in agricultural production? Relate this to the country now being studied.
3. **Health:** Is malnutrition prevalent in the U. S.? Need it be present at all?
4. **General Science:** Make a chart showing the inventions that have improved food production.

E. ARITHMETIC

Plan a budget for a family the size of your family. Try to use up-to-date information about costs, income, etc. Be sure to include God in the budget.

F. ART

Make posters about conservation of natural resources, waste in the home, etc.

G. MUSIC

Learn the Bonum Est Confiteri. *LH* 603.

UNIT
28

NECESSITIES ON OUR PILGRIMAGE TO HEAVEN

Faith, Grace, Charity, Fortitude, Deliverance from All Evil

•

I. Scope and Importance

"Be charitable and indulgent to everyone but thyself." (Joubert)

"A Christian is a person who knows no hate and harbors no enmity against anybody, who has no anger or revenge in his heart, but only love, meekness, and charity as our Lord Christ and His heavenly Father Himself." (Luther)

In these three petitions we pray for a forgiven heart, a forgiving heart, a heart which is for giving; a strong heart and a heart which enjoys the peace of God that passes all understanding.

"Everything in the Christian Church is ordered to the end that we shall daily obtain there nothing but the forgiveness of sin through the Word and signs, to comfort and encourage our consciences as long as we live here. Thus, although we have sins, the Holy Ghost does not allow them to injure us, because we are in the Christian Church, where there is nothing but continuous, uninterrupted forgiveness of sin, both in that God forgives us, and in that we forgive, bear with, and help each other." (Luther)

"Although we have obtained forgiveness and a good conscience and are wholly absolved, yet such is life that one stands today and falls tomorrow. Therefore we must ever pray that He suffer us not to relapse and to yield to trials and temptations.... When God gives us strength and power to resist temptation, even though it be not removed, that is 'leading us not into temptation.'"

"You cannot prevent the birds from flying over your head, but you can prevent them from building a nest in your hair." (Luther)

"No man knows if he ventures into the swirl of the mighty whirlpool of temptation whether or not his oar may break or his arm give out and he be sucked down to destruction. The only sensible thing is to steer clear." (Beecher)

"The devil plagues and torments us where we are most tender and weak. In Paradise he fell not upon Adam but upon Eve." (Luther)

Days of depression and days of inflation, both have their peculiar temptations.

"Americans spend $90,000,000 annually on chewing gum."

II. Aim

A. KNOWLEDGE

Stimulate thinking which leads to a thoroughgoing familiarity with the meaning and implications of these three Petitions: grace, charity, temptation, fortitude, deliverance; integrate with related vocabulary.

B. ATTITUDE

Foster humbleness of heart, penitence, gratitude for forgiveness; a charitable disposition, readiness to forgive; honesty: actually abhorring and avoiding the temptation against which protection is asked; eagerness to make a right choice; faith in the Lord thus to overcome temptation; a tempered longing for heaven and ultimate freedom from all troubles and ills.

C. HABITS, SKILLS

Foster habit and skill of finding in the Bible such sections as are of especial comfort to those who are troubled in their conscience; who strive to overcome an uncharitable disposition; who pray for boldness, courage, and fortitude; and for those who are world-weary and long for heaven. Develop ability of habitually turning away from evil influences and of looking to God for deliverance.

D. ANTICIPATED OUTCOME IN TERMS OF CHRIST-CENTERED PERSONALITIES

Boys and girls who enjoy a good conscience in Jesus, who are kindly disposed; young people who are wary and strong in character, not easily misled; adults who are mature Christians, and aged who look forward with cheerful anticipation to the day when they will be delivered from all evil and taken to heaven.

III. Curriculum Material

A. BIBLE STUDIES

DATE USED

- _____ A Long, Earnest Prayer for Forgiveness. *Psalm 51.*
- _____ A Short, Sincere Prayer for Forgiveness. *Luke 18:13.*
- _____ The Young Man Who was Ready to Forgive. *Gen. 50:15-21.*
- _____ *When Forgiven — We Should Forgive. *Matt. 18:21-35.*
- _____ Without Love, Man's Works Are in Vain. *1 Cor. 13:1-13.*
- _____ He That Loveth Not, Knoweth Not God! *1 John 4:7-21.*
- _____ As Christ Forgave You, So Also Do Ye. *Col. 3:8-15.*
- _____ Tempted, Tested, and Strengthened. *Gen. 22:1-14.*
- _____ Faith Undaunted, or Persistent Prayer. *Mark 7:25-30.*
- _____ The Devil's Harvest (Judas). *Matt. 27:3-5.*

NECESSITIES ON OUR PILGRIMAGE TO HEAVEN – Unit 28

DATE USED

- Bad Company Brings Bad Temptations. *Luke 22:54-62.*
- Do Not Run Into Temptation, but Flee It! *2 Tim. 2:19-22.*
- Fully Armed Against Temptation. *Eph. 6:10-18.*
- What to Do and What to Avoid to Escape Temptation. *1 Peter 4:1-7.*
- A Special Danger Threatening Those Who Know the Truth. *2 Peter 2:20-22.*
- Delivered by the Captain of Our Salvation. *Heb. 2:10-15.*
- A Man Who Trusted in God Despite Great Trials. *2 Cor. 11:24—12:10.*
- Danger, Despair, Deliverance. *Luke 8:22-25.*
- Delivered by Angels out of a Burning City. *Gen. 19:12-26.*
- A Man Who Waited for God's Deliverance. *Job 42:10-17.*
- A Daring Confessor Delivered from a Den. *Dan. 6:10-23.*
- Delivered from All Evil. *Luke 16:19-22.*
- A Prayer for Deliverance and God's Answer. *2 Kings 19:14-37.*
- How to Be Delivered from Evil. *Ps. 34:11-22.*
- Luther's Favorite Psalm — A Prayer of Thanksgiving. *Psalm 118.*

B. LUTHER'S SMALL CATECHISM
Questions 231—241.

C. MEMORY MATERIAL
1. Bible Texts
GRADE

1   My son, if sinners entice thee, consent thou not. *Prov. 1:10.*

2   (I have) a desire to depart and to be with Christ; which is far better. *Phil. 1:23.*

3   The Lord shall deliver me from every evil work and will preserve me unto His heavenly kingdom. *2 Tim. 4:18.*

4   Who can understand his errors? Cleanse Thou me from secret faults. *Ps. 19:12.* (4)

   Father, I have sinned against Heaven and in thy sight and am no more worthy to be called thy son. *Luke 15:21.* (4)

5   Lord, now lettest Thou Thy servant depart in peace according to Thy word; for mine eyes have seen Thy salvation. *Luke 2:29, 30.* (5)

GRADE	
	We must through much tribulation enter into the kingdom of God. *Acts 14:22.* (5)
6	My grace is sufficient for thee; for My strength is made perfect in weakness. *2 Cor. 12:9.* (6)
	Whom the Lord loveth He chasteneth, and scourgeth every son whom He receiveth. *Heb. 12:6.* (6)
	He shall deliver thee in six troubles; yea, in seven there shall no evil touch thee. *Job 5:19.* (6)
	God is faithful, who will not suffer you to be tempted above that ye are able, but will, with the temptation, also make a way to escape that ye may be able to bear it. *1 Cor. 10:13.* (6)
7	I am not worthy of the least of all the mercies and of all the truth which Thou hast showed unto Thy servant. *Gen. 32:10.*
	The publican, standing afar off, would not lift up so much as his eyes unto heaven, but smote upon his breast, saying, God be merciful to me, a sinner. *Luke 18:13.*
	Then came Peter to Him and said, Lord, how oft shall my brother sin against me and I forgive him? Till seven times? Jesus saith unto him, I say not unto thee, Until seven times; but, Until seventy times seven. *Matt. 18:21, 22.*
	The Lord is faithful, who shall stablish you and keep you from evil. *2 Thess. 3:3.*
	Take unto you the whole armor of God that ye may be able to withstand in the evil day and, having done all, to stand. *Eph. 6:13.*
8	When ye stand praying, forgive if ye have aught against any, that your Father also which is in heaven may forgive you your trespasses. But if ye do not forgive, neither will your Father which is in heaven forgive your trespasses. *Mark 11:25, 26.* (8)
	(Jesus) saith unto Philip, Whence shall we buy bread that these may eat? And this He said to prove him; for He Himself knew what He would do. *John 6:5, 6.*
	Be sober, be vigilant; because your adversary, the devil, as a roaring lion, walketh about, seeking whom he may devour; whom resist steadfast in the faith. *1 Peter 5:8, 9.*
	Demas hath forsaken me, having loved this present world. *2 Tim. 4:10.*
	Let no man say when he is tempted, I am tempted of God; for God cannot be tempted with evil, neither tempteth He any man; but every man is tempted when he is drawn away of his own lust and enticed. *James 1:13, 14.*
	Woe unto the world because of offenses! For it must needs be that offenses come; but woe to that man by whom the offense cometh! *Matt. 18:7.*

NECESSITIES ON OUR PILGRIMAGE TO HEAVEN – Unit 28

GRADE

2. Luther's Small Catechism

1–8 The Fifth, Sixth, and Seventh Petitions. Expl. 3—8. — The Sixth Commandment. Expl. 3—8.

5–8 The General Confession.

3. Hymns

1–2 Abide with me! Fast falls the eventide;
The darkness deepens; Lord, with me abide.
When other helpers fail and comforts flee,
Help of the helpless, oh, abide with me!   LH 552:1

3–4 As a mother stills her child,
Thou canst hush the ocean wild;
Boisterous waves obey Thy will
When Thou say'st to them, "Be still!"
Wondrous Sovereign of the sea,
Jesus, Savior, pilot me.   LH 649:2

5–6 In the hour of trial,
    Jesus, plead for me
Lest by base denial
    I depart from Thee.
When Thou see'st me waver,
    With a look recall
Nor for fear or favor
    Suffer me to fall.   LH 516:1

7–8 Thy way, not mine, O Lord,
    However dark it be.
Lead me by Thine own hand;
    Choose Thou the path for me.
I dare not choose my lot;
    I would not if I might.
Choose Thou for me, my God;
    So shall I walk aright.   LH 532:1

4. Prayers

Almighty God, who knowest us to be set in the midst of so many and great dangers, that by reason of the frailty of our nature we cannot always stand upright, grant to us such strength and protection as may support us in all dangers, and carry us through all temptations; through Jesus Christ, our Lord, who liveth and reigneth with Thee and the Holy Ghost, ever one God, world without end. Amen.

Collects for 4th Sunday after Epiphany.

O God, who seest that we put not our trust in anything that we do, mercifully grant that by the power of Thy Son, the Teacher of nations, we may be defended against all adversity; through the same, our Lord Jesus Christ, who liveth and reigneth with Thee and the Holy Ghost, ever one God, world without end. Amen.

Collects for Sexagesima Sunday. Collects for Jubilate Sunday; Collects for 6th and 22d Sundays after Trinity; Collects for Sunday after Christmas; Collects for 6th Sunday after Epiphany; Collects for Quinquagesima Sunday. Prayers for the Sick and Dying (*LH*).

D. SUMMARY OUTLINE FOR THE CHALKBOARD

To God's people it is very important and hence *they desire, pray, and strive*
1) for a forgiven spirit
2) for a forgiving spirit
3) for resistance to temptation
4) for fortitude and courage
5) for thoughtful consideration for the weak
6) for freedom from all evil
    a) to be spared evil
    b) to be set free from evil
    c) for patience to bear a cross
    d) for final and complete freedom from all pain, tears, evils, in heaven

"Thy way, not mine, O Lord. However dark it be!"

IV. Instructional Methods and Materials

A. PROBLEM AND APPROACH

Have you ever gone on a long trip? One that would take several days or weeks? What kind of preparations did you make? Why?

B. SUGGESTED TEACHING UNIT

1. Devotion

Hymn: In the Hour of Trial. *LH* 516.
Scripture Reading: Job 42:10-17.
Prayer: Collect for the 4th Sunday after Epiphany. *LH*, p. 60; Collect for the Sick. *LH*, p. 105.

2. Bible Story

Mark 7:25-30.

3. Memory Passages

2 Tim. 4:18: The Lord shall deliver me.
2 Cor. 12:9: My grace is sufficient.
Eph. 6:13: Take unto you the whole armor of God.
Thy way, not mine, O Lord. *LH* 532:1.
Petitions 5—7.
The First Article.

NECESSITIES ON OUR PILGRIMAGE TO HEAVEN — Unit 28

4. Luther's Small Catechism
Questions 231—241.

5. Liturgy
Nunc Dimittis. *LH*, p. 29.

C. AIDS TO LEARNING

1. **Visual:** *The Lord's Prayer* — 79-106 — four filmstrips
2. **Audio:** "If Thou Would Suffer God to Guide Thee" — *LH* 518 — (Let The Earth Rejoice) KFUO, HA61.
   "All Glory Be to God on High" — *LH* 237 — (Sing Unto The Lord) KFUO, HA60.
   Mendelssohn: *Elijah* — Angel 3558-C.
   Pertinent Selections:
   "Blessed Are the Men Who Fear Him"
   "Cast Thy Burden upon the Lord"
   "Woe unto Them Who Forsake Him!"
3. **Objects:** Mouse trap, fish hooks.
4. **Workbook:** * *The New Life*, Unit XXIX.
   * *Learning About God*, Unit VI.
   * *Growing in Faith*, Unit VI.
   * *Growing in Grace*, Unit VI.
   * *Growing in Christ*, Unit 28.
5. **Bulletin Board:** Pictures and clippings showing courage, happiness, fortitude, mercy.
6. **Chalkboard:** Summary outline.
7. **Group Activity:** Sing songs and hymns at a home for aged.
8. **Music:** See Audio Aids above.
9. **Art:** "The Lost Sheep" — Soord.
10. **Library:** *Pilgrim's Progress*.

D. EVALUATION

Have the objectives been reached? What questions or problems need further study?

V. Suggestions for Correlations with Other Subjects

A. READING

1. **Silent:** 1 Cor. 13:1-13; Gen. 19:12-26; Gen. 22:1-14.
2. **Oral:** Mark 7:25-30; 2 Tim. 2:19-22.
3. **Choral:** Psalm 51; Matt. 18:21-35.

B. ENGLISH

1. **Oral:** Dramatize one or more situations that require making apology and forgiveness.

2. **Written:** Write a letter to a friend comforting him in trouble or sickness.
3. **Vocabulary and Spelling:** forgiven, forgiving, temptation, trial, doxology.
4. **Handwriting:** t — tempt, T — Tempter.

C. SOCIAL SCIENCES

1. **Home and Family Life:** Dramatize several family situations that require forgiveness and kindness.
2. **Community and Nation:** Discuss the saying "When in Rome, do as the Romans do."
3. **History:** Discuss the history and purposes of the United Nations.

D. PHYSICAL SCIENCES

1. **Geography:** How does the country now being studied rank in medical efficiency?
2. **Health:** Discuss the benefits of hospital and medical insurance.
3. **General Science:** The physician and the pastor minister to people in need. Compare their work.

E. ARITHMETIC

Discuss social security benefits; note the rates of payment and income.

F. ART

Make a poster or mural showing God's protecting hand in men's lives.

G. MUSIC

Learn to chant the Beati Pauperes. *LH* 668.

UNIT
29

BAPTISM

What It Is

•

I. Scope and Importance

"It is of the greatest importance that we recognize Baptism in its excellent, glorious character. For it is the cause of most of our contentions and battles; the world is full of sects exclaiming that Baptism is merely an outward form and that outward forms are of no use. But whether it be an outward form or not, here stand the word and command of God, which have instituted, established, and confirmed Baptism. Whatever God institutes and commands cannot be useless; it is most precious, even if in appearance it is not worth a straw." (Luther)

"When the Word of God is taken away, the water is no different from that which the servant uses for cooking purposes; Baptism under that condition might be called bathkeeper's baptism. But when the Word of God is present according to God's ordinance, Baptism is a Sacrament and it is called Christ's Baptism. This is the first part, the nature and dignity of the Holy Sacrament of Baptism." (Luther)

"Accedat verbum ad elementum, et fit sacramentum." (The Word is added to the element and this makes a Sacrament.)

II. Aim

A. KNOWLEDGE

Beginning with *some tangible evidence* of their own Baptism such as certificate or font, lead the children to know what Baptism is, who instituted it, who is to be baptized, and how Baptism is to be administered. Familiarize with pertinent Bible sections on this matter and also with related vocabulary. Lead pupils to discover that they have two birthdays, two fathers, and that they belong to two families, and in that larger family have many brothers and sisters. Show correct use of the phrase: "Fatherhood of God and brotherhood of man." Memorize helpful memory materials.

B. ATTITUDE

Foster interest in these significant facts; develop interest in pupil's own date, place, and certificate of Baptism, also in his sponsors; the function of sponsors; create gratitude to God and the church that thus they have been adopted into the family of God's people.

C. HABITS, SKILLS

Train pupils in locating Scripture portions which relate to the various aspects of Baptism; train them also in the ability to quote memorized passages and hymns for their own comfort, defense of their faith, and to comfort others, and also allay their doubts, if and when these come.

D. ANTICIPATED OUTCOME IN TERMS OF CHRIST-CENTERED PERSONALITIES

Boys and girls, men and women, who understand the Lutheran (Scriptural) doctrine of Baptism, who are baptized, and who derive comfort, joy, and courage from Baptism.

BAPTISM — Unit 29   231

III. Curriculum Material

A. BIBLE STUDIES

DATE USED

   _____ Jesus Blesses Little Children. *Mark 10:13-16.*
   _____ Except a Man Be Born of Water and Spirit. *John 3:1-13.*
   _____ Make Disciples of All Men by Baptizing and Teaching Them. *Matt. 28:16-20.*
   _____ John Baptizes Jesus in the Jordan. *Mark 1:1-11.*
   _____ To Fulfill All Righteousness. *Matt. 3:7-17.*
   _____ By the Washing of Regeneration. *Titus 3:3-7.*
   _____ On the Baptism of Repentance for the Remission of Sins. *Luke 3:1-6.*
   _____ On Rejecting the Council of God (Baptism). *Luke 7:24-30.*
   _____ On Baptizing with Water to Manifest Jesus. *John 1:29-34.*
   _____ The Baptism of John, Whence Was It? *Matt. 21:23-27.*
   _____ The Promise of Baptismal Blessing Is Also to Your Children. *Acts 2:37-42.*
   _____ The Case of a Whole Family Being Baptized. *Acts 16:11-15.*
   _____ Despise Not One of These Little Ones. *Matt. 18:6-11.*
   _____ On the Eighth Day, in the Old Testament. *Gen. 17:9-14.*

B. LUTHER'S SMALL CATECHISM

Questions 242—252.

C. MEMORY MATERIAL

1. Bible Texts

GRADE

1. They that gladly received his word were baptized. *Acts 2:41.*

2. Go ye therefore and teach all nations, baptizing them in the name of the Father and of the Son and of the Holy Ghost. *Matt. 28:19.*

3. Arise and be baptized and wash away thy sins. *Acts 22:16.* (3)

4. Except a man be born of water and of the Spirit, he cannot enter into the kingdom of God; that which is born of the flesh is flesh. *John 3:5, 6.* (4)

5. Ye fathers, provoke not your children to wrath, but bring them up in the nurture and admonition of the Lord. *Eph. 6:4.* (5)

GRADE

All power is given unto Me in heaven and in earth. Go ye, therefore, and teach (make disciples of) all nations, baptizing them in the name of the Father and of the Son and of the Holy Ghost; teaching them to observe all things whatsoever I have commanded you. And, lo, I am with you alway, even unto the end of the world. *Matt. 28:18-20.* (5)

6   Whoso shall offend one of these little ones which believe in Me, it were better for him that a millstone were hanged about his neck and that he were drowned in the depth of the sea. *Matt. 18:6.* (6)

He shall baptize you with the Holy Ghost and with fire. *Matt. 3:11.*

7   In the mouth of two or three witnesses every word may be established. *Matt. 18:16.*

Let a man so account of us as of the ministers of Christ and stewards of the mysteries of God. *1 Cor. 4:1.*

8   When they (the Pharisees) come from the market, except they wash (baptize), they eat not. And many other things there be which they have received to hold, as the washing (baptizing) of cups and pots, brazen vessels, and of tables. *Mark 7:4.*

They brought young children to Him that He should touch them; and His disciples rebuked those that brought them. But when Jesus saw it, He was much displeased and said unto them, Suffer the little children to come unto Me and forbid them not; for of such is the kingdom of God. Verily I say unto you, Whosoever shall not receive the kingdom of God as a little child, he shall not enter therein. *Mark 10:13-15.*

2. *Luther's Small Catechism*

1–8   The Nature of Baptism.

3. *Hymns*

1–2   I was made a Christian
      When my name was given,
    One of God's dear children,
      And an heir of heaven.
    In the name of Christian
      I will glory now,
    Evermore remember
      My baptismal vow.   CH 215:1

3–4   The Savior kindly calls
      Our children to His breast;
    He folds them in His gracious arms,
      Himself declares them blest.   LH 302:1

BAPTISM – Unit 29   233

GRADE
5-6   Baptized into Thy name most holy,
         O Father, Son, and Holy Ghost,
      I claim a place, though weak and lowly,
         Among Thy seed, Thy chosen host.
      Buried with Christ and dead to sin,
      Thy Spirit now shall live within.   LH 298:1

7-8   He that believes and is baptized
         Shall see the Lord's salvation;
      Baptized into the death of Christ,
         He is a new creation.
      Through Christ's redemption he shall stand
      Among the glorious heavenly band
         Of every tribe and nation.   LH 301:1

4. Prayers

Almighty God, who hast given us Thine only-begotten Son to take our nature upon Him, grant that we, being regenerate and made Thy children by adoption and grace, may daily be renewed by Thy Holy Spirit; through the same Jesus Christ, Thy Son, our Lord. Amen.

O God, who, through the grace of Thy Holy Spirit, dost pour the gifts of charity into the hearts of Thy faithful people, grant unto Thy servants health both of mind and body that they may love Thee with their whole strength and with their whole heart perform those things which are pleasing unto Thee; through Jesus Christ, Thy Son, our Lord. Amen.

Prayers found in Forms for Baptism I, II, and Adult and for Confirmation. General Collects – *LH*, pp. 108, 109, Nos. 58–74.

D. SUMMARY OUTLINE FOR THE CHALKBOARD

Baptism
   What?
         A means of grace — water and the Word — to offer, give, and seal the forgiveness of sins.
   Who?
         ordained it
         should baptize
         should be baptized
   How?
         by immersion
         by pouring
         by sprinkling
   When?
         in infancy
         as adults
   Why?
         God wants it
         sinners need it.

IV. Instructional Methods and Materials

A. PROBLEM AND APPROACH

"You must be born again," said Jesus to Nicodemus. What did Jesus mean by that? Nicodemus wondered. Can you explain the saying?

B. SUGGESTED TEACHING UNIT

1. **Devotion**

    Hymn: Baptized Into Thy Name Most Holy. *LH* 298.
    Scripture Reading: Acts 16:11-15.
    Prayer: * *Teen-Agers Pray*, p. 75.

2. **Bible Story**

    Acts 2:37-42.

3. **Memory Passages**

    John 3:5-6: Except a man be born.
    Matt. 28:18-20: All power is given unto Me.
    Acts 22:16: Arise and be baptized.
    Baptized into Thy name most holy. *LH* 298:1.
    The Nature of Baptism.
    The Blessings of Baptism.

4. **Luther's Small Catechism**

    Questions 242—252.

5. **Liturgy**

    The Morning Suffrages. *LH*, p. 115.

C. AIDS TO LEARNING

1. **Visual:** *Holy Baptism* — 79-108 — filmstrip.
2. **Objects:** Baptismal certificates; font, shell.
3. **Workbook:** * *The New Life*, Unit XXIX.
    * *Learning About God*, Unit VIII.
    * *Growing in Grace*, Unit VIII.
    * *Growing in Christ*, Unit 29.
4. **Bulletin Board:** Pictures of a baptism, font, sponsors.
5. **Chalkboard:** Summary outline.
6. **Group Activity:** Observe a baptism.
7. **Art:** "Baptism of Christ."

D. EVALUATION

Do you have a clearer understanding of Baptism and its power in your life?

BAPTISM — Unit 29 235

V. Suggestions for Correlations with Other Subjects

A. READING
1. **Silent:** Baptism, Luther's Large Catechism; 1 John 4:4-11; *LH* hymns 298—303.
2. **Oral:** Eph. 4:20-30; 1 Peter 3:18-22.
3. **Choral:** Psalm 51.

B. ENGLISH
1. **Oral:** Report on one of the silent readings above.
2. **Written:** Write a short theme on the topic "What My Baptism Means to Me."
3. **Vocabulary and Spelling:** disciple, regeneration, certificate, baptize.
4. **Handwriting:** b — blessing, B — Baptism.

C. SOCIAL SCIENCES
1. **Home and Family Life:** Write a short paragraph on the topic "How Baptism Affects Family Life."
2. **Community and Nation:** Discuss the topic "Does Baptism Affect My Life as a Citizen?"
3. **History:** Persons in history whose influence was determined by Christian faith. What does the church say about integration?

D. PHYSICAL SCIENCES
1. **Geography:** Christ sends His disciples into all the world to preach the Gospel and baptize. To what extent has this task been accomplished in the world? In the area now being studied?
2. **Health:** Compare physical cleansing needed daily to the spiritual cleansing in Baptism.
3. **General Science:** Faith and science both change a person's way of living. How?

E. ARITHMETIC
Prepare problems about the ratio of baptized to unbaptized in your school, Sunday school, parish.

F. ART
Make symbols for the Holy Spirit, Baptism.

G. MUSIC
Memorize one of the Baptism hymns (*LH* 298—303); sing it in a worship service.

UNIT
30

BAPTISM
(Its Blessings and Implications)

An Introductory Unit or Pre-Confirmation Week Unit

•

I. Scope and Importance

"Every Christian has enough in Baptism to study and practice all his life. For he must always *remember* to heed and believe firmly what Baptism promised and brings him, victory over the devil and death, forgiveness of sins, God's grace and the complete Christ and the Holy Spirit with His gifts." (Luther)

"A Christian's life is but a daily baptism, which once entered upon requires us incessantly to fulfill its conditions. Without ceasing we must purge out what is of the old Adam, so that what belongs to the new may come forth. What is the old Adam? Inherited from Adam, he is passionate, hateful, envious, unchaste, miserly, lazy, conceited, and, last but not least, unbelieving; thoroughly corrupt, he offers no lodgment to what is good. Now, when we enter Christ's kingdom, such corruption should daily decrease and we should become more gentle, more patient, more meek and ever tread away more and more from unbelief, avarice, hatred, envy, and vainglory." (Luther)

BAPTISM — Unit 30

"Children who forget their baptismal vow are doing what Noah's raven did: the raven forgot the ark when he found a carcass." (Caspari)

"The three handfuls of water that were poured over my head in Holy Baptism are worth more to me than the crown I am wearing." (Louis the Pious of France).

II. Aim

A. KNOWLEDGE

Stimulate observing and thinking which leads to clear, vivid, and correct Biblical ideas about the blessings and the implications of Baptism. The blessings, the power, and the significance of Baptism are to be made intelligible to the learners with the aid of Bible stories and passages; also with illustrations. Familiarize pupils with memory texts and with a related vocabulary. Learn the baptismal vow with the Confirmation vow. Familiarize with long and short Baptism forms.

B. ATTITUDE

Foster gratitude for God's unmerited blessing conveyed in Baptism. Kindle a fervent desire increasingly to live up to the implications of Baptism; foster the desire to grow and walk in newness of life.

C. HABITS, SKILLS

Train in using the Bible to defend baptism, including infant baptism; develop skill in quoting Scripture passages which are pertinent to this unit; being born in the image of Jesus (God), children should be trained to be like Jesus and to follow in His footsteps.

D. ANTICIPATED OUTCOME IN TERMS OF CHRIST-CENTERED PERSONALITIES

Boys and girls who are aware of and who live out the implications of Baptism; twice-born young people who are increasingly weaned away from the ways of the world; adults who draw comfort and guidance from their baptism; live the new life; in whom the new man dominates the old.

III. Curriculum Material

A. BIBLE STUDIES

DATE USED

---------------- Shall We Who Are Baptized Continue in Sin? *Rom. 6:1-12.*
---------------- He Went on His Way Rejoicing. *Acts 8:26-40.*
---------------- Baptism for the Remission of Sins. *Acts 22:10-16.*
---------------- When You Remove the Cause, You Remove the Effect (Sin, Death). *1 Cor. 15:53-58.*
---------------- Baptism Doth Also Now Save Us. *1 Peter 3:18-22.*
---------------- Little Children, Ye Are of God. *1 John 4:4-11.*
---------------- Let No One Reject the Counsel of God. *Luke 7:29, 30.*
---------------- Baptized? Cleansed? Be Fruitful in Every Good Work. *Col. 1:9-14.*
---------------- You Are Washed? Do You Strive to Keep Clean? *1 Cor. 6:9-11.*
---------------- Baptized Believers Shall Be Saved. *Mark 16:14-16.*
---------------- Put on the New Man — Are You Up to Expectation? *Eph. 4:20-30.*
---------------- Christ Liveth in Me — Does He? *Gal. 2:16-21.*
---------------- Cleansed by the Grace and Power of God. *Luke 17:11-19.*
---------------- I Follow After — Do YOU? *Phil. 3:12-14.*

B. LUTHER'S SMALL CATECHISM

Questions 253—266.

C. MEMORY MATERIAL

1. Bible Texts

GRADE

1 He that believeth and is baptized shall be saved. *Mark 16:16.* (1)

2 Baptism doth also now save us. *1 Peter 3:21.*

3 Ye are all the children of God by faith in Christ Jesus. For as many of you as have been baptized into Christ have put on Christ. *Gal. 3:26, 27.* (3)

4 If any man be in Christ, he is a new creature. *2 Cor. 5:17.*

5 Repent and be baptized, every one of you, in the name of Jesus Christ for the remission of sins. *Acts 2:38.*

6 They that are Christ's have crucified the flesh with the affections and lusts. *Gal. 5:24.*

7 But ye are washed, but ye are sanctified, but ye are justified in

BAPTISM — Unit 30   239

GRADE

the name of the Lord Jesus and by the Spirit of our God. *1 Cor. 6:11.*

Put off concerning the former conversation the old man, which is corrupt according to the deceitful lusts. *Eph. 4:22.*

8   Put on the new man, which after God is created in righteousness and true holiness. *Eph. 4:24.*

Christ also loved the church and gave Himself for it that He might sanctify and cleanse it with the washing of water by the word. *Eph. 5:25, 26.*

2. Luther's Small Catechism

1–8   Blessings of Baptism.

3–8   Power of Baptism and Significance of Baptizing with Water.

3. Hymns

1–2   Who so happy as I am
Even now the Shepherd's lamb?
And when my short life is ended,
By His angel host attended,
He shall fold me to His breast,
There within His arms to rest.   LH 648:3

3–4   Hear us, dear Father, when we pray
For needed help from day to day
That as Thy children we may live,
Whom Thou in Baptism didst receive.   LH 288:3

5–6   Thine forever, God of Love!
Hear us from Thy throne above;
Thine forever may we be
Here and in eternity!   LH 338:1

7–8   If God Himself be for me,
    I may a host defy;
For when I pray, before me
    My foes, confounded, fly.
If Christ, my Head and Master,
    Befriend me from above,
What foe or what disaster
    Can drive me from His love?   LH 528:1

4. Prayers

Keep, we beseech Thee, O Lord, Thy church with Thy perpetual mercy; and because the frailty of man without Thee cannot but fall, keep us ever by Thy help from all things hurtful, and lead us to all things profitable to our salvation; through Jesus Christ, Thy Son, our Lord, who who liveth and reigneth with Thee and the Holy Ghost, ever one God, world without end. Amen.

Collects for Fourteenth Sunday after Trinity.

Lord of all power and might, who art the Author and Giver of all good things, graft in our hearts the love of Thy name, increase in us true religion, nourish us with all goodness, and of Thy great mercy keep us in the same; through Jesus Christ, Thy Son, our Lord, who liveth and reigneth with Thee and the Holy Ghost, ever one God, world without end. Amen.

Collects for Sixth Sunday after Trinity.

D. SUMMARY OUTLINE FOR THE CHALKBOARD

Blessings and Implications of My Baptism

1. *I believe* that in my Baptism
   a) God washed away my sins
   b) God in His sovereign power and grace delivered me from death and the devil
   c) God gave me eternal life — heaven
2. *I Should Therefore Earnestly Pray and Strive*
   a) to drown my old Adam
   b) to let the new man have his way in my life and daily live a *new life*
   "Buried with Christ and dead to sin,
   Thy Spirit now shall live within!"

IV. Instructional Methods and Materials

A. PROBLEM AND APPROACH

Do you have any brothers or sisters? How many? Did you know that you have millions of brothers and sisters? Read Mark 3:31-35.

B. SUGGESTED TEACHING UNIT

1. **Devotion**

   Hymn: Lord, Help Us Ever to Retain. *LH* 288.
   Scripture Reading: 1 John 4:4-11.
   Prayer: * *Teen-Agers Pray,* p. 75.

2. **Bible Story**

   Acts 8:26-40.

3. **Memory Passages**

   1 Peter 3:21: Baptism doth also.
   Gal. 3:26: Ye are all the children of God.
   1 Cor. 6:11: But ye are washed.
   Thine forever, God of Love. *LH* 338:1.
   The Power of Baptism.
   The Significance of Baptism.

BAPTISM — Unit 30   241

   4. **Luther's Small Catechism**
   Questions 253—266.

   5. **Liturgy**
   The Offertory. *LH,* p. 12.
   The Gloria Patri. *LH,* p. 6.

C. **AIDS TO LEARNING**
   1. **Visual:** *Holy Baptism* — 79-108 — filmstrip.
   2. **Audio:** "Salvation Unto Us Has Come" — *LH* 377 — (Let the Earth Rejoice) KFUO, HA61.
   "Beautiful Savior" — *LH* 657 — (The Lutheran Hour) RCA, LPM-1863; also Word, W-4017 (Stereo WST-9003).
   3. **Objects:** Water, baptismal certificate.
   4. **Workbook:** * *The New Life,* Unit XXX.
   * *Learning About God,* Unit VIII.
   * *Growing in Grace,* Unit VIII.
   * *Growing in Christ,* Unit 30.
   5. **Bulletin Board:** Pictures of Biblical and modern baptisms; clippings from * *The Lutheran Witness,* * *Spirit.*
   6. **Chalkboard:** Summary outline.
   7. **Group Activity:** Invite a missionary to tell of his experiences in baptizing in the mission field.
   8. **Music:** See Audio Aids above.
   9. **Art:** "Christ Blessing Little Children" — Plockhorst; study symbolism on a baptismal certificate.
   10. **Library:** A. De Vries, * *The Children's Bible.*

D. **EVALUATION**
   Have you gained a wider viewpoint about your relationship to others? Do you understand better Baptism's power in your daily life?

V. Suggestions for Correlations with Other Subjects

A. **READING**
   1. **Silent:** "Children of God in the Forest," from * *Treasury of Christian Literature,* p. 410.
   2. **Oral:** Gal. 2:16-21; Phil. 3:12-14.
   3. **Choral:** "There Still Is Room!" from * *Treasury of Christian Literature,* p. 281.

B. **ENGLISH**
   1. **Oral:** Report on a recent "This Is the Life" program.

2. **Written:** Write a letter to your baptismal sponsors, thanking them for their concern for you.
3. **Vocabulary and Spelling:** disciple, sanctified, reverent, righteousness, regeneration, conversion.
4. **Handwriting:** b — blessing, B — Baptism.

C. SOCIAL SCIENCES

1. **Home and Family Life:** Is it evident in your classroom that your classmates are baptized? What can be done to make it more evident?
2. **Community and Nation:** What can your class, as a group of Christians, do to influence life in your neighborhood or community?
3. **History:** Report on the beginning of the Sunday school or vacation Bible school movement.

D. PHYSICAL SCIENCES

1. **Geography:** What is the dominant religion in the area now being studied? What progress has Christianity made?
2. **Health:** Can a good understanding of Baptism's power help mental health?

E. ARITHMETIC

Compare baptism statistics of 13 years ago with the confirmation statastics of this year. Can you account for the difference?

F. ART

Make symbols for the Holy Spirit.

G. MUSIC

Learn the Nunc Dimittis. *LH*, p. 29.

UNIT
31

THE OFFICE OF THE KEYS AND CONFESSION

•

I. Scope and Importance

The importance of confessing sin, the church's power to remit and to retain sins, a good conscience, church discipline, the status and role of the minister as spokesman for God and for the congregation — these are the topics that enter into this unit.

The three hardest words to pronounce in the English language: I was mistaken.

Confess that you were wrong yesterday; it will show that you are wiser today.

Frederick the Great wrote to the Senate: "I have just lost a great battle, and it was entirely my own fault." Goldsmith says: "This confession displayed more greatness than all his victories." (Spurgeon)

A French officer whose ship had been taken by Nelson was brought on board Nelson's vessel. He walked up to the great Admiral and extended his hand. "No," said Nelson, "your sword first, please." So it is with the forgiveness of the Gospel. Many people would take Christ's hand and say He is a noble character. But that is not the step in the right order. First admit your guilt. Then Christ will take your hand.

The prodigal son, David, the publican, the Ninevites, all indicate just how important confession is and what a great privilege and power is inherent in the Office of the Keys.

What a great movement toward peaceful and amiable relations between husbands and wives, parents and children, brothers and sisters, pastor and teacher, parish and parish workers, races and nations, if all should learn the difficult art of humble confession of guilt and charitable remission of guilt!

To be at peace with God, to enjoy peace within, and to be at peace with fellowmen — what priceless possessions!

Abuse and proper use of The Office of the Keys.

II. Aim

A. KNOWLEDGE

Stimulate discriminating thinking which leads to clear, vivid, and correct ideas about confession, the power of the church to absolve, the status and role of the pastor, church discipline, excommunication. Matthew 18. Familiarize with and make meaningful a wide related vocabulary.

B. ATTITUDE

Kindle the desire for peace with God and peace with all fellow men; encourage willingness to confess faults to God and to others; to accept in true faith the absolution; likewise willingness to forgive; shake hands and make up; create a group sentiment that is deeply grieved at wrong and that makes its influence felt to bring the individual member of the group into line with the true aristocracy of the group; cultivate a high regard for the ministry, and work toward willingness to use the intermediary services of the pastor or teacher in case of a serious quarrel; make confession of sin and fault very important for the sake of peace with God, peace within the conscience and with those with whom we live from day to day.

THE OFFICE OF THE KEYS AND CONFESSION — Unit 31

C. HABITS, SKILLS

Train children in confessing their faults to their parents, their pastor, their teacher, and to one another; train them to show a high regard and respect for called ministers of Christ; show the children how to ask for pardon and how to make up after a quarrel.

D. ANTICIPATED OUTCOME IN TERMS OF CHRIST-CENTERED PERSONALITIES

Boys and girls, men and women who are forgiven and forgiving and who are for giving liberally to maintain the ministry of the Word; who are living epistles to be read by others, and who have the reputation that they are willing to make up and to live at peace with all men; who are nevertheless effective, disciplining members of the local congregation.

III. Curriculum Material

A. BIBLE STUDIES

DATE USED

- *Whosoever Sins Ye Remit. *John 20:19-23.*
- *I Will Arise and Go to My Father. *Luke 15:11-23.*
- *I Water My Couch with My Tears. *Ps. 6.*
- *When I Kept Silence, My Bones Waxed Old. *Ps. 32.*
- *Whiter than Snow. *Ps. 51.*
- *Out of the Depths. *Ps. 130.*
- He Wept Bitterly. *Matt. 26:69-75.*
- *The Prodigal Son. *Luke 15:11-24.*
- *Matthew Eighteen! *Matt. 18:15-20.*
- *Christ Gave Pastors — for the Perfecting of the Saints. *Eph. 4:11-16.*
- He that Humbleth Himself. *Luke 18:9-14.*
- Swallowed Up with Overmuch Sorrow. *2 Cor. 2:4-10.*

B. LUTHER'S SMALL CATECHISM

Questions 267–295.

C. MEMORY MATERIAL

1. Bible Texts

GRADE

1   Believe on the Lord Jesus Christ, and thou shalt be saved. *Acts 16:31.* (1)

GRADE

        Son, be of good cheer; thy sins be forgiven thee. *Matt. 9:2.*

2   He said unto them, Go ye into all the world, and preach the Gospel to every creature. *Mark 16:15.*

        I will give unto thee the keys of the kingdom of heaven. *Matt. 16:19.*

3   Whosoever sins ye remit, they are remitted unto them. *John 20:23.*

        Verily I say unto you, Whatsoever ye shall bind on earth shall be bound in heaven. *Matt. 18:18.*

4   Confess your faults one to another. *James 5:16.* (4)

        Repent ye, therefore, and be converted, that your sins may be blotted out. *Acts 3:19.*

5   He that covereth his sins shall not prosper; but whoso confesseth and forsaketh them shall have mercy. *Prov. 28:13.* (5)

        Bring forth, therefore, fruits meet for repentance. *Matt. 3:8.*

        Put away from among yourselves that wicked person. *1 Cor. 5:13.*

6   David said unto Nathan, I have sinned against the Lord. And Nathan said unto David, The Lord also hath put away thy sin; thou shalt not die. *2 Sam. 12:13.*

        Whatsoever thou shalt bind on earth shall be bound in heaven; and whatsoever thou shalt loose on earth shall be loosed in heaven. *Matt. 16:19.*

        Let a man so account of us as of the ministers of Christ and stewards of the mysteries of God. *1 Cor. 4:1.*

        The Word preached did not profit them, not being mixed with faith in them that heard it. *Heb. 4:2.*

7   Verily I say unto you, Whatsoever ye shall bind on earth shall be bound in heaven; and whatsoever ye shall loose on earth shall be loosed in heaven. *Matt. 18:18.* (7)

        The sacrifices of God are a broken spirit; a broken and a contrite heart, O God, Thou wilt not despise. *Ps. 51:17.* (7)

        If we say that we have no sin, we deceive ourselves, and the truth is not in us. If we confess our sins, He is faithful and just to forgive us our sins and to cleanse us from all unrighteousness. *1 John 1:8, 9.* (7)

        (Christ) breathed on them and saith unto them, Receive ye the Holy Ghost: Whosoever sins ye remit, they are remitted unto them; and whosoever sins ye retain, they are retained. *John 20:22, 23.*

        If I forgave anything, to whom I forgave it, for your sakes forgave I it in the person of Christ. *2 Cor. 2:10.*

8   Ye are a chosen generation, a royal priesthood, an holy nation, a peculiar people; that ye should show forth the praises of Him

THE OFFICE OF THE KEYS AND CONFESSION — Unit 31

GRADE

who hath called you out of darkness into His marvelous light. *1 Peter 2:9.*

If thou bring thy gift to the altar and there rememberest that thy brother hath aught against thee, leave there thy gift before the altar and go thy way; first be reconciled to thy brother and then come and offer thy gift. *Matt. 5:23, 24.*

Jesus came and spake unto them, saying, All power is given unto Me in heaven and in earth. Go ye therefore and teach all nations, baptizing them in the name of the Father and of the Son and of the Holy Ghost; teaching them to observe all things whatsoever I have commanded you. And, lo, I am with you alway, even unto the end of the world. *Matt. 28:18-20.*

If he shall neglect to hear them, tell it unto the church; but if he neglect to hear the church, let him be unto thee as an heathen man and a publican. Verily I say unto you, Whatsoever ye shall bind on earth shall be bound in heaven; and whatsoever ye shall loose on earth shall be loosed in heaven. . . . For where two or three are gathered together in My name, there am I in the midst of them. *Matt. 18:17, 18, 20.* (The local congregation). (8)

2. Luther's Small Catechism

6–8 The General Confession.

3–8 The Office of the Keys. The Confession and Absolution.

6–8 The Office of the Ministry.

3. Hymns

1–2 Jesus, Savior, wash away
All that has been wrong today;
Help me every day to be
Good and gentle, more like Thee.   LH 653:2

3–4 With broken heart and contrite sigh,
A trembling sinner, Lord, I cry.
Thy pardoning grace is rich and free,
O God, be merciful to me.   LH 323:1

5–6 How beauteous are their feet
   Who stand on Zion's hill;
Who bring salvation on their tongues
   And words of peace reveal!   LH 487:1

7–8 Jesus sinners doth receive;
   Oh, may all this saying ponder
Who in sin's delusions live
   And from God and heaven wander!
Here is hope for all who grieve:
Jesus sinners doth receive.   LH 324:1

4. Prayers

O Lord Jesus Christ, the Son of the living God, we thank Thee that Thou hast bestowed upon all true believers the power to absolve one another from their sins in Thy name, and to this end hast in particular established the ministry of reconciliation; and we beseech Thee, give us grace, that we may not from pride and self-righteousness despise Thy comforting ordinance, but, recognizing therein Thy love to us, may use it for the comfort and salvation of our souls, and by sincere amendment of our lives continually thank Thee, who livest and reignest with the Father and the Holy Ghost, ever one God, world without end. Amen.

Collects for Quasimodogeniti Sunday. First Sunday after Easter.

D. SUMMARY OUTLINE FOR THE CHALKBOARD

The Office of the Keys (Power and Duty of the Church)

1. *To the church* — believers — the local congregation
2. *Christ gave spiritual power*
   - to administer the means of grace, ordinarily through a called minister
   - to preach and teach
   - to baptize
   - to absolve the penitent
   - to commune
   - to discipline and refuse Communion to the impenitent (Matt. 18)

Christian!

Consider your station — in the mirror of the Law, of the Life of Jesus, of the Sermon on the Mount.

Confess your faults — frankly and humbly
- to God
- to one another
- to the pastor, and

forgive one another. *Today! Now!* For Jesus' sake!

IV. Instructional Methods and Materials

A. PROBLEM AND APPROACH

Read the portion of the Communion Liturgy called "The Confession of Sins." *LH*, pp. 15-16. In pronouncing The Absolution, the pastor says: "I forgive you all your sins." Does he have this authority? Doesn't God alone have such power?

THE OFFICE OF THE KEYS AND CONFESSION – Unit 31

B. SUGGESTED TEACHING UNIT

1. Devotion

Hymn: With Broken Heart and Contrite Sigh. *LH* 323.
Scripture Reading: John 20:19-23.
Prayer: The General Confession. *LH*, p. 16.

2. Bible Story

Luke 15:11-24.

3. Memory Passages

James 5:16: Confess your faults.
1 John 1:8-9: If we say that we have no sin.
Matt. 18:17-20: If he shall neglect to hear them.
Jesus sinners doth receive. *LH* 324:1.
Confession.

4. Luther's Small Catechism

Questions 267—295.

5. Liturgy

The Confession of Sins. *LH*, pp. 15—16.
The Litany. *LH*, p. 110.

C. AIDS TO LEARNING

1. **Visual:** *Office of the Keys and Confession* — 79-109 — filmstrip.
2. **Audio:** "He Shall Feed His Flock" and "O Thou That Tellest Good Tidings to Zion" — Handel: *The Messiah* — RCA LD-6409.
   "O Come, Everyone That Thirsteth" and "Hear Ye, Israel" — Mendelssohn: *Elijah* — Angel 3558-C.
3. **Objects:** Keys, locks.
4. **Workbook:** * *The New Life*, Unit XXXI.
   * *Growing in Grace*, Unit IX.
   * *Growing in Christ*, Unit 31.
5. **Bulletin Board:** Biblical pictures related to forgiveness; persons praying; instances of social ostracism.
6. **Chalkboard:** Summary outline.
7. **Group Activity:** Prepare an assembly program to emphasize the importance of friendliness and forgiveness at school.
8. **Music:** The De Profundis. *LH* 664.
9. **Art:** "Christ, the Consoler" — Plockhorst.

D. EVALUATION

Are there questions that need further study? Have we become more forgiving at home and school?

V. Suggestions for Correlations with Other Subjects

A. READING
1. **Silent:** Luke 22:14-20; Ex. 12:3-17.
2. **Oral:** Mark 14:10-26.
3. **Choral:** O Lord, We Praise Thee. *LH* 313.

B. ENGLISH
1. **Oral:** Report on silent reading above.
2. **Written:** "A Confession I Had To Make."
3. **Vocabulary and Spelling:** confession, absolution, excommunicate, counselor, discipline.
4. **Handwriting:** c — confess, C — Christ.

C. SOCIAL SCIENCES
1. **Home and Family Life:** Discuss avoiding ill feelings in the family circle.
2. **Community and Nation:** Practicing confession and forgiveness in neighborhood problems.
3. **History:** Keeping the powers of church and state separate.

D. PHYSICAL SCIENCES
1. **Nature Study:** Does nature (natural law) forgive?
2. **Health:** An old saying states that "confession is good for the soul." Is it also good for the body? How?
3. **General Science:**

E. ARITHMETIC

Keep a record of the number of times you needed to say "I'm sorry" in one day. Figure how many times you would need to say it in a month, year.

F. ART

Make a poster encouraging forgiveness; make a series of cartoons illustrating some ordinary happening in which confession and forgiveness are needed.

G. MUSIC

Learn the De Profundis. *LH* 664.

UNIT
32

THE SACRAMENT OF THE ALTAR

History and Nature

•

I. Scope and Importance

"Analogous to the Ten Commandments, the Lord's Prayer, and the Creed, which remain unimpaired in their essence and authority, irrespective of man's disposition to obey, to pray, and to believe, this most precious Sacrament remains unimpaired both in essence and quality regardless of man's worthiness when he uses it. What! Do you think God is so influenced by our faith and conduct as to permit these to affect His ordinances? All temporal things remain as God created and ordained them, regardless of how we treat them. This must always be maintained. This argument cannot be used too zealously; for it is a thorough refutation of all the fustian of the sectarians, who, contrary to the Word of God, view the Sacraments as human performance." (LLC)

"In the Lord's Supper there is an earthly material, bread and wine, and a celestial material, the body and blood of Christ. The doctrine of transubstantiation identifies these; that of consubstantiation or impanation confuses and mingles them; the symbolic doctrine separates them; the Lutheran doctrine of the real presence unites them." (Voigt, *Biblical Dogmatics*)

Those who have communed humbly and believingly may, refreshed and strengthened in spirit, say with Simeon, "Lord, now lettest Thou Thy servant depart in peace according to Thy Word, for mine eyes have seen Thy Salvation: which Thou hast prepared before the face of all people, a Light to lighten the Gentiles and the Glory of Thy people Israel." Glory be to the Father and to the Son and to the Holy Ghost; as it was in the beginning, is now, and ever shall be, world without end. Amen.

II. Aim

A. KNOWLEDGE

Stimulate observation and thinking which will lead to clear, vivid, Biblical ideas about the origin and nature of the Sacrament. Familiarize pupils with a meaningful related vocabulary.

B. ATTITUDE

Create a reverent, serious interest in the Sacrament of the Altar; create a felt need for participation in Holy Communion and a desire to commune as soon and as frequently as possible.

C. HABITS, SKILLS

Overt behavior: Train in reverently observing what is said and done when Communion is celebrated, including the Confessional service.

D. ANTICIPATED OUTCOME IN TERMS OF CHRIST-CENTERED PERSONALITIES

Boys and girls who are reverently interested in the Sacrament of the Altar. Young people and adults who humbly, believingly, reverently, and frequently appear at the Lord's Table and who derive the comfort, refreshment, guidance, and strength for a holier life which God intended they should have.

THE SACRAMENT OF THE ALTAR — Unit 32

III. Curriculum Material

A. BIBLE STUDIES

DATE USED

_____ *The Feast of the Unleavened Bread. *Matt. 26:17-30.*

_____ *Celebrating the Passover. *Mark 14:10-26.*

_____ *This Do in Remembrance of Me. *Luke 22:14-20.*

_____ *Ye Do Show the Lord's Death. *1 Cor. 11:23-34.*

_____ All Things Are Ready. *Matt. 22:1-10.*

_____ Ebenezer: Hitherto Hath the Lord Helped Us. *1 Sam. 7:3-12.*

_____ This Is Done Because of That Which the Lord Did. *Ex. 13:3-10.*

_____ When I See the Blood, I will Pass over You. *Ex. 12:3-17.*

B. LUTHER'S SMALL CATECHISM

Questions 296—312.

C. MEMORY MATERIAL

1. Bible Texts

GRADE

1. When He had given thanks, He brake it. *1 Cor. 11:24.*

2. They continued steadfastly in the Apostles' doctrine and fellowship, and in breaking of bread, and in prayers. *Acts 2:42.*

3. This is My blood of the new testament. *Mark 14:24.*

4. The Word of the Lord is right; and all His works are done in truth. *Ps. 33:4.* (4)

5. Come unto Me, all ye that labor and are heavy laden, and I will give you rest. *Matt. 11:28.* (5)

6. Whosoever shall eat this bread and drink this cup of the Lord unworthily shall be guilty of the body and blood of the Lord. *1 Cor. 11:27.* (6)

   Ye cannot be partakers of the Lord's Table and of the table of devils. *1 Cor. 10:21.* (6)

   Though it be but a man's covenant, yet if it be confirmed, no man disannulleth or addeth thereto. *Gal. 3:15.*

7. By one offering He hath perfected forever them that are sanctified. . . . Now, where remission of these (sins) is, there is no more offering for sin. *Heb. 10:14, 18.* (7)

   As often as ye eat this bread and drink this cup, ye do show the Lord's death till He come. Wherefore whosoever shall eat this bread and drink this cup of the Lord unworthily shall be guilty of the body and blood of the Lord. But let a man examine

GRADE

himself, and so let him eat of that bread and drink of that cup. *1 Cor. 11:26-28.* (7)

When ye come together, therefore, into one place, this is not to eat the Lord's Supper. *1 Cor. 11:20.*

This do ye, as oft as ye drink it, in remembrance of Me. For as often as ye eat this bread and drink this cup, ye do show the Lord's death till He come. *1 Cor. 11:25, 26.*

8   The cup of blessing which we bless, is it not the communion of the blood of Christ? The bread which we break, is it not the communion of the body of Christ? *1 Cor. 10:16.* (8)

For we, being many, are one bread and one body; for we are all partakers of that one bread. *1 Cor. 10:17.*

They all drank of it. *Mark 14:23.*

Unto Him that is able to do exceeding abundantly above all that we ask or think, according to the power that worketh in us, unto Him be glory in the church. *Eph. 3:20, 21.*

2. *Luther's Small Catechism*

1–8   What is the Lord's Supper?

4–8   Where is this written?

5–8   Christian Questions.

3. *Hymns*

1–2	The death of Jesus Christ, our Lord, We celebrate with one accord; It is our comfort in distress, Our heart's sweet joy and happiness.	*LH 163:1*
3–4	The guest that comes with true intent To turn to God and to repent, To live for Christ, to die to sin, Will thus a holy life begin.	*LH 163:7*
5–6	An awe-full mystery is here To challenge faith and waken fear: The Savior comes as food divine, Concealed in earthly bread and wine.	*LH 304:1*
7–8	Chief of sinners though I be, Jesus shed His blood for me; Died that I might live on high, Lived that I might never die. As the branch is to the vine, I am His, and He is mine.	*LH 342:1*

THE SACRAMENT OF THE ALTAR — Unit 32

4. Prayers

Almighty and everlasting Father, the God of all grace, who forgivest the sins of the penitent, we beseech Thee, create in us new and contrite hearts, that, deploring our transgressions and acknowledging our wretchedness, we may obtain perfect remission, through Jesus Christ, our Lord. Amen.

O Lord Jesus Christ, who alone art able to make us meet for a salutary eating and drinking of Thy true body and blood in the Holy Supper, we pray Thee, enable us to partake worthily of Thy holy Sacrament. Grant us knowledge of our sins, that we may be truly penitent; grant us knowledge of Thy grace, that by faith we may draw nigh unto Thee; and work in our hearts a sincere resolve to serve Thee in holiness and pureness of living. Have mercy upon us for Thy name's sake. Amen.

Prayers for Confessional Service. Collects for Maundy Thursday.

D. SUMMARY OUTLINE FOR THE CHALKBOARD

The Sacrament of the Altar

1. Names: Holy Communion, Lord's Table, Eucharist
2. Nature: The Word and the elements:
   bread and wine; body and blood
   Real sacramental presence:
   No transubstantiation
   No mere symbolic representation
3. By whom? Christ, the God-man
4. For whom? Penitent believers
5. For what purpose?
   For a stronger faith
   in the forgiveness of sins, a godlier life
   a closer union with God and with God's people
6. How often? Often
   An awe-full mystery is here
   To challenge faith and waken fear!

IV. Instructional Methods and Materials

A. PROBLEM AND APPROACH

Have you attended a Communion service? What happened? What did it all mean? Why do people go to "Communion"?

B. SUGGESTED TEACHING UNIT

1. Devotion

Hymn: The Death of Jesus Christ, Our Lord. *LH* 163.
Scripture Reading: Matt. 26:17-30.
Prayer: For Grace to Love and Serve God. *LH*, p. 107.

2. Bible Story

Luke 22:14-20.

3. Memory Passages

Matt. 11:28: Come unto Me.
Heb. 10:14-18: By one offering He hath perfected.
1 Cor. 11:25-26: This do ye, as oft as ye drink it.
The death of Jesus Christ, our Lord. *LH* 163:1.
What is The Lord's Supper?
The Benefits of the Lord's Supper.

4. Luther's Small Catechism

Questions 296—312.

5. Liturgy

The Order of the Holy Communion. *LH*, p. 15.

C. AIDS TO LEARNING

1. **Visual:** *The Lord's Supper* — 79-107 — filmstrip.
2. **Audio:** "Alas, My God, My Sins Are Great" — *LH* 317 — (A Mighty Fortress) Word, W-4017 (Stereo WST-9003).
3. **Objects:** Bread and wine, chalice, flagon, paten.
4. **Workbook:** * *The New Life*, Unit XXXII.
    * *Living for God*, Unit VIII.
    * *Growing in Grace*, Unit X.
    * *Growing in Christ*, Unit 32.
5. **Bulletin Board:** The Last Supper; pictures of contemporary communion scenes; related articles.
6. **Chalkboard:** Summary outline.
7. **Group Activity:** Ask the pastor to explain the symbolism and purposes of the communion vessels and their use in the service.
8. **Music:** See Audio Aids above.
9. **Art:** "The Last Supper" — Da Vinci.
10. **Library:** E. Kurth, * *Catechetical Helps*.
    R. A. Zimmer and Others, * *Catechism of Christian Worship*.

D. EVALUATION

Has the Lord's Supper become more meaningful to you? Are there questions still to be answered?

THE SACRAMENT OF THE ALTAR — Unit 32　　　　　　　　257

V. Suggestions for Correlations with Other Subjects

A. READING
1. **Silent:** Matt. 22:1-10; Ex. 12:3-17.
2. **Oral:** Psalm 32; Psalm 23.
3. **Choral:** Psalm 51.

B. ENGLISH
1. **Oral:** Report on silent readings above.
2. **Written:** An original theme on the topic "How I Feel About Taking the Lord's Supper the First Time."
3. **Vocabulary and Spelling:** sacramental, union, communion, fellowship.
4. **Handwriting:** s — sacred, S — Sacrament.

C. SOCIAL SCIENCES
1. **Home and Family Life:** Does receiving the Lord's Supper as a family strengthen family ties? How?
2. **Community and Nation:** What is the church's future in secular America?
3. **History:** The church as a major factor in history: the Crusades, the knights of the Holy Grail.

D. PHYSICAL SCIENCES
1. **Geography:** Make a map of the Holy Week events, or of the routes of the Crusaders.
2. **General Science:** Science, the gift of a gracious God.

E. ARITHMETIC
Use Communion attendance statistics to develop problems in ratios, percentage, charts, and graphs.

F. ART
Make symbols for the Lord's Supper; illustrate a scene from the Last Supper.

G. MUSIC
Practice singing the Communion liturgy.

UNIT 33

THE SACRAMENT OF THE ALTAR

Blessings, Power, Salutary Use, Implications

•

I. Scope and Importance

"He who does not highly value this Sacrament shows thereby that he has no sin, no flesh, no devil, no world, no death, no danger, no hell; that is to say, he does not believe that such evils exist although he may be deeply immersed in them, and completely belong to the devil. On the other hand, he needs no grace, no life, no Paradise, no heaven, no Christ, no God, no good thing. For if he believed that he was involved in such evils and that he was in need of such blessings, he could not refrain from receiving the Sacrament, wherein aid is afforded against such evils and again such blessings are bestowed." (Luther)

"If a person does not seek nor desire the Lord's Supper at least some four times a year, it is to be feared that he despises the Sacrament and is not a Christian." (Luther)

"The early Christians called the Lord's Supper the viaticum of dying Christians." (Walther)

"Christ wishes to establish the most intimate union between Himself and us in the Holy Supper. That is why He chose, as the bearers of His body and blood, the visible elements of bread and wine; for nothing becomes so closely united to us in our natural life as food and drink." (Gerhard)

"At the close of a Communion service Samuel Morse, the inventor of the telegraph and a very devout Christian, said: "Oh, this is something better than standing before princes." (Dallmann)

Communing at the Lord's table is a confession of spiritual unity with those who commune with us at the same table. But it is also a means through which God creates and fosters that unity of faith and strengthens the ties that unite us into one.

II. Aim

A. KNOWLEDGE

Stimulate observation and thinking which leads to clear, vivid, and Biblical ideas about the purpose, the blessing, the power, the proper preparation and salutary use, and the anticipated results of Communion; define: close Communion; open Communion; excommunication. Familiarize with related meaningful vocabulary.

B. ATTITUDE

Create a humble and earnest desire to commune as soon as possible and thereafter as frequently as possible; gratitude for the privilege of communing.

C. HABITS, SKILLS

Overt behavior: Train in reverent behavior during celebration of Communion; lead up to the habit of humble, frequent, fervent, and joyous participation in Communion.

D. ANTICIPATED OUTCOME IN TERMS OF CHRIST-CENTERED PERSONALITIES

Young people and adults who are the kind of Christians that God wants them to be: Humble and yet cheerful, buoyant, mature, at peace within, with God, with others. Strong in spirit; living the truly victorious life.

III. Curriculum Material

A. BIBLE STUDIES

DATE USED

....	Let a Man Examine Himself. *1 Cor. 11:27-34.*
....	Friend, How Camest Thou in Hither? *Matt. 22:11-14.*
....	Making Clean the Inside of the Cup. *Matt. 23:25-28.*
....	If Ye Forgive Not Every One (70 times 7). *Matt. 18:21-35.*
....	Mine Eyes Have Seen Thy Salvation. *Luke 2:25-32.*
....	We Love Him Because He First Loved Us. *1 John 4:13-21.*
....	To Obtain Strength for a Holier Life. *1 John 5:1-5.*
....	Why Halt Ye Between Two Opinions: A Day of Decision. (Confirmation.) *1 Kings 18:17-39.*
....	Faithful Unto Death (Stephen). *Acts 7:54-60.*

B. LUTHER'S SMALL CATECHISM

Questions 313—331.

C. MEMORY MATERIAL

1. Bible Texts

GRADE

1. They continued steadfastly in the Apostles' doctrine and fellowship, and in breaking of bread, and in prayers. *Acts 2:42.*

2. Him that cometh to Me I will in no wise cast out. *John 6:37.* (2)

3. Lord, I believe; help Thou mine unbelief. *Mark 9:24.*

4. Be thou faithful unto death, and I will give thee a crown of life. *Rev. 2:10.* (4)

5. If thou bring thy gift to the altar and there rememberest that thy brother hath aught against thee, leave there thy gift before the altar and go thy way; first be reconciled to thy brother, and then come and offer thy gift. *Matt. 5:23, 24.*

6. Hold that fast which thou hast, that no man take thy crown. *Rev. 3:11.* (6)

   He that eateth and drinketh unworthily, eateth and drinketh damnation to himself, not discerning the Lord's body. *1 Cor. 11:29.*

7. He died for all, that they which live should not henceforth live

THE SACRAMENT OF THE ALTAR — Unit 33

GRADE

unto themselves, but unto Him which died for them and rose again. If any man be in Christ, he is a new creature. *2 Cor. 5:15, 17.* (7)

I beseech you, brethren, mark them which cause divisions and offenses contrary to the doctrine which ye have learned; and avoid them. *Rom. 16:17.*

8   A bruised reed shall He not break, and the smoking flax shall He not quench. *Is. 42:3.* (8)

Let a man examine himself, and so let him eat of that bread and drink of that cup. *1 Cor. 11:28.* (8)

2. Luther's Small Catechism

4–8   Benefits, Power, and Salutary Use.

6–8   Christian Questions.

7–8   Vow of Confirmands.

3. Hymns

1–2   Our trembling hearts cleave to Thy Word;
All Thou hast said Thou dost afford,
All that Thou art we here receive,
And all we are to Thee we give.   *LH 314:3*

3–4   One bread, one cup, one body, we,
United by our life in Thee,
Thy love proclaim till Thou shalt come
To bring Thy scattered loved ones home.   *LH 314:4*

5–6   Let me be Thine forever,
    Thou faithful God and Lord;
Let me forsake Thee never
    Nor wander from Thy Word.
Lord, do not let me waver,
    But give me steadfastness,
And for such grace forever
    Thy holy name I'll bless.   *LH 334:1*

7–8   Soul, adorn thyself with gladness,
Leave behind all gloom and sadness;
Come into the daylight's splendor,
There with joy thy praises render
Unto Him whose grace unbounded
Hath this wondrous Supper founded.
High o'er all the heavens He reigneth,
Yet to dwell with thee He deigneth.   *LH 305:1*

4. Prayers

O Lord God, heavenly Father, who hast given Thine only Son to die for our sins and to rise again for our justification, quicken us, we beseech

Thee, by Thy Holy Spirit, unto newness of life that through the power of His resurrection we may dwell with Christ forever; through the same Jesus Christ, Thy Son, our Lord. Amen.

Collects for Maundy Thursday. Prayers for Confessional Service. General Collects (*LH*, p. 102, Nos. 1—9).

D. SUMMARY OUTLINE FOR THE CHALKBOARD

In Holy Communion
1) God strengthens my faith in forgiveness
2) God helps me
    a) to confess my Savior
    b) to live a more Christ-like life
    c) to remain loyally united with God's people

With God's help *I will commune*
1) humbly
2) believingly
3) frequently
4) joyously

IV. Instructional Methods and Materials

A. PROBLEM AND APPROACH

Why is loyalty an important characteristic of a good soldier; of a good citizen?

B. SUGGESTED TEACHING UNIT

1. **Devotion**

    Hymn: Let Me Be Thine Forever. *LH* 334:1.
    Scripture Reading: 1 Kings 18:17-39.
    Prayer: * *Teen-Agers Pray*, p. 13.

2. **Bible Story**

    Acts 7:54-60.

3. **Memory Passages**

    Acts 2:42: They continued steadfastly.
    Rev. 2:10: Be thou faithful.
    2 Cor. 5:15-17: He died for all.
    The Power of the Lord's Supper.
    Salutary Use of the Lord's Supper.

4. **Luther's Small Catechism**

    Questions 313—331.

THE SACRAMENT OF THE ALTAR — Unit 33   263

5. **Liturgy**
   The Rite of Confirmation.

C. AIDS TO LEARNING

1. **Visual:** *The Lord's Supper* — 79-107 — filmstrip.
   The Order of Holy Communion — 79-650 — filmstrip.
2. **Audio:** "He That Shall Endure to the End" — Mendelssohn: *Elijah* — Angel 3558-C.
   "Nunc Dimittis" — (Sing Unto the Lord) KFUO, HA60.
3. **Objects:** Communion wafer, wine, chalice, flagon, paten; confirmation certificate.
4. **Workbook:** ° *The New Life,* Unit XXXII.
   ° *Living for God,* Unit VIII.
   ° *Growing in Grace,* Unit X.
   ° *Growing in Christ,* Unit 33.
5. **Bulletin Board:** Pictures and clippings of persons distinguished for loyalty; pictures of Passover and Communion scenes.
6. **Chalkboard:** Summary outline.
7. **Group Activity:** A class gift to the church or school.
8. **Music:** Hymns 332—338 in ° *The Lutheran Hymnal.*
9. **Art:** "The Last Supper" — Da Vinci.

D. EVALUATION

Have you gained a clearer understanding of the Lord's Supper and its blessings? What questions do you still have in mind?

V. Suggestions for Correlations with Other Subjects

A. READING

1. **Silent:** Rev. 2—3.
2. **Oral:** Psalm 1.
3. **Choral:** Rev. 7:9-17.

B. ENGLISH

1. **Oral:** Report on silent reading above; dramatize one or more situations in which Christian witness is called for.
2. **Written:** Write a letter to your sponsors inviting them to attend your confirmation service.
3. **Vocabulary and Spelling:** communion, fellowship, stewardship, koinonia.
4. **Handwriting:** g — good, G — God.

C. SOCIAL SCIENCES

1. **Home and Family Life:** How does Christian home life influence the community?
2. **Community and Nation:** Where does the Christian's first loyalty lie? What does this mean for his country?
3. **History:** Report on great religious Americans; Is the Christian life identical with the American way of life?

D. PHYSICAL SCIENCES

1. **Nature Study:** Compare families in nature to God's family.
2. **Geography:** Does God observe political boundaries; In what sense can we speak of "one world"?
3. **General Science:** Discuss — Can a scientist be true to God and to science?

E. ARITHMETIC

Compare membership statistics: young to old members, baptized to confirmed, voting to communicants. Develop problems involving fractions, ratios, percentage, graphs.

F. ART

Study the painting "Washing Disciples' Feet" by Brown.

G. MUSIC

Learn one of the Confirmation Hymns. *LH* 332—338.

BIBLIOGRAPHY

Barr, A. S., W. H. Burton, and L. J. Brueckner. *Supervision: Principles and Practices in the Improvement of Instruction.* New York: D. Appleton-Century, 1938.

Beck, William F. *The Christ of the Gospels.* St. Louis: Concordia Publishing House, 1959.

Bode, B. H. *How We Learn.* Boston: D. C. Heath & Co., 1940.

Boettcher, Henry J. *Activities in Religious Education.* Minneapolis: University of Minnesota Library, 1949.

Boettcher, Henry J. *Learning and Living.* St. Louis: Concordia Publishing House, 1945.

Boettcher, Henry J. *The New Life.* St. Louis: Concordia Publishing House, 1946.

Brameld, Theodore. *Ends and Means in Education: A Mid-Century Appraisal.* New York: Harpers, 1950.

Brueckner, L. J. *The Changing Elementary School.* New York: Inor Publishing Co., 1939.

Brueckner, L. J., anl E. O. Melby. *Diagnostic and Remedial Teaching.* Boston: Houghton Mifflin Co., 1931.

Dewey, John. *Experience and Education.* New York: Macmillan, 1938.

Demiashkevich, M. J. *The Activity School (in Europe).* New York: Little and Ives, 1926.

Forrell, George W. *Faith Active in Love.* New York: The American Press, 1954.

Gifted Student, The. Washington, D. C.: U. S. Department of Health, Education and Welfare, Office of Education, 1963.

Gilbert, W. Kent. *The Age Group Objectives of Christian Education.* Lutheran Boards of Parish Education, Board for Parish Education of Each Synodical Group, 1958.

Harap, Henry, et al. *The Changing Curriculum.* Tenth Yearbook, Department of Supervisors. N. E. A.

Havighurst, Robert. *Human Development and Education.* New York: Longmans, Green, 1953.

Hawkes, H. E., E. F. Linquist, and C. R. Mann. *The Construction and Use of Achievement Tests.* Boston: Houghton Mifflin Co., 1936.

Hoban, C. H., C. H. Hoban, Jr., and S. B. Zisman. *Visualizing the Curriculum.* New York: The Cordon Co., 1937.

Horn, Ernest. *Methods of Instruction in the Social Studies.* New York: Scribner's, 1937.

Jersild, H. T., et al. *Children's Interests and What They Suggest for Education.* New York: Bureau of Publications, Teachers College, Columbia University, 1949.

Jones, A. J., E. D. Grizzell, and W. J. Grinstead. *Principles of Unit Construction.* New York: McGraw-Hill Book Co., Inc., 1939.

Judd, C. H. "How Shall the Enriched Curriculum Be Made Systematic?" *Elementary School Journal,* May 1937.

Kilpatrick, W. H. "A Reconstructed Theory of the Education Process." *Teachers College Record,* March 1931.

Koehler, Edward W. A. *A Christian Pedagogy.* St. Louis: Concordia Publishing House, 1930.

Kramer, William A. *Teen-Agers Pray.* St. Louis: Concordia Publishing House, 1955.

Kramer, William A. *Units in Religion for Lutheran Schools.* St. Louis: Concordia Publishing House, 1955.

Kramer, William A., and S. J. Roth. *The Church Through the Ages.* Saint Louis: Concordia Publishing House, 1949.

Krause, Victor. *Lutheran Elementary Schools in Action.* St. Louis: Concordia Publishing House, 1963.

Krey, A. C. *A Regional Program for the Social Studies.* New York: Macmillan, 1938.

Kurth, E. *Catechetical Helps.* Brooklyn 6, N. Y., 79 George St.: The Studio Press. St. Louis: Concordia Publishing House *(Revised Edition).*

Lee, J. M., and D. M. Lee. *The Child and His Curriculum.* New York: D. Appleton-Century Co., 1940.

Luther, Martin. *The Large Catechism.* Minneapolis: Augsburg Publishing House, 1935.

Luther, Martin. *The Small Catechism, A Contemporary Translation.* Saint Louis: Concordia Publishing House, 1963.

Lynd, Robert S. *Knowledge for What?* Princeton, N. J.: Princeton University Press, 1939.

Marty, Martin E. *The Hidden Discipline.* St. Louis: Concordia Publishing House, 1962.

Maus, Cynthia Pearl. *Christ and the Fine Arts.* New York: Harpers, 1938.

McKown, H. C., and A. B. Roberts. *Audio-Visual Aids to Instruction.* New York: McGraw-Hill Book Co., 1940.

Miller, Arthur L. *Tests and Measurements in Lutheran Education.* River Forest, Ill.: L. E. A. Yearbook, 1957.

Morrison, Henry C. *The Curriculum of the Common School.* Chicago: University of Chicago Press, 1940.

Morrison, J. C. "Trends in Elucational Method." *Educational Method,* XIII, 129—137.

National Council of Teachers of English. *An Experience Curriculum in English.* Monograph No. 4. New York: D. Appleton-Century, 1935.

National Society for the Study of Education. "The Activity Movement." *33d Yearbook,* Part Two, chaps. 2, 8, 9, 10. Bloomington, Ill.: Public School Publishing Co.

Norton, John, and Margaret Norton. *Foundations of Curriculum Building.* Boston: Ginn and Company, 1936.

Phillips, J. B. *The New Testament in Modern English.* New York: Macmillan Company, 1958.

Strommen, Merton P. *Profiles of Church Youth.* St. Louis: Concordia Publishing House, 1963.

Unit Planning and Teaching in Elementary Social Studies. Washington, D. C.: U. S. Department of Health, Education and Welfare, Office of Education, 1963.

Wesley, Edgar B. *Teaching the Social Studies.* Boston: D. C. Heath & Co., 1937.

Wrightstone, J. W., et al. "Measuring Social Performance Factors in Activity and Control Schools in New York City." *Teachers College Record,* XL, 423—432.

www.ingramcontent.com/pod-product-compliance
Lightning Source LLC
Chambersburg PA
CBHW030335240426
43661CB00052B/1643